POLICE AND
CRIME COMMISSIONERS

The transformation of police accountability

Bryn Caless and Jane Owens

GW00455161

P

First published in Great Britain in 2016 by

Policy Press
University of Bristol
1-9 Old Park Hill
Bristol
BS2 8BB
UK
+44 (0)117 954 5940
pp-info@bristol.ac.uk
www.policypress.co.uk

North America office:
Policy Press
c/o The University of Chicago Press
1427 East 60th Street
Chicago, IL 60637, USA
t: +1 773 702 7700
f: +1 773 702 9756
sales@press.uchicago.edu
www.press.uchicago.edu

British Library Cataloguing in Publication Data
A catalogue record for this book is available from the British Library

Library of Congress Cataloging-in-Publication Data
A catalog record for this book has been requested

ISBN 978-1-4473-2069-2 hardcover
ISBN 978-1-4473-2070-8 paperback
ISBN 978-1-4473-2073-9 ePub
ISBN 978-1-4473-2074-6 Mobi

Cover design by Hayes Design
Front cover image: www.alamy.com
Printed and bound in Great Britain by CMP, Poole
Policy Press uses environmentally responsible print partners

Bryn Caless would like to dedicate this book to
Daphne Caless, née Mayall, 1938–2015,
who sadly died during its making

Jane Owens would like to dedicate
this book to Gareth Owens
and to all young people starting out on their careers

Contents

List of tables and figures

Tables

Figures

Glossary of terms

Policing has a plethora of terms and abbreviations which are familiar only to the insider (and the poor academic who has to study them); the PCC has added a few more. The following is a selection of these terms explained.

ACPO
The Association of Chief Police Officers, now defunct. It acted as the spokesperson for the police at a national level and dealt with government departments and committees such as the Home Affairs Select Committee. ACPO was replaced in April 2015 by the National Police Chiefs' Council (NPCC).

APCC
The Association of Police and Crime Commissioners acts as a national level spokesperson for the Commissioners, organises an annual conference and maintains a website on PCC and policing issues

Chief Constable, Deputy Chief Constable, Assistant Chief Constable
These are *chief police officer* ranks (London is different) that hold strategic command of police forces in the UK.

Assistant Chief Constables
(ACC) usually hold specific portfolios for areas such as Territorial Policing (local and community), Serious and Organised Crime and Support Services. Terms vary from force to force.

Deputy Chief Constables
(DCC) stand in for the Chief, and often hold remits for force disciplinary and professional standards.

Chief Constables
(CC) are the heads of police forces. They are appointed (and can be dismissed) by the PCC; and their term of service, like most of their subordinate chief officers, is a renewable five-year contract.

College of Policing
The College of Policing was officially launched in February 2013 to replace the National Policing Improvement Agency (NPIA). The

College regards itself as 'the professional body for policing' and states that it will 'provide maximum support to help the service implement [...] standards' (College of Policing, 2015). It has largely supplanted the ACPO function and has begun to develop a role in the formulation of strategic policing. It has made encouraging noises about commissioning research too.

CSP
Community Safety Partnership(s). Under the 1998 Crime & Disorder Act, local authorities-led crime reduction and disorder partnerships which included the police, fire and rescue, primary healthcare and the police authority, with other public service participation as needed. PCCs have since replaced the police authorities and much of the current PCC partnership-building and, while not intending to undermine CSPs, will eventually make them redundant

European Working Time Directive
This gives EU workers the right to a break of at least 11 hours in any 24; controls excessive work at night; and provides a right to work no more than 48 hours per week. It was first established in the early 1990s and updated in 2003 (see 2003/88/EC; and the UK government's www.gov.uk/maximum-weekly-working-hours/overview). Given the excessive hours worked by PCCs, including into late evening, the Directive is merely advisory; see Chapter Seven.

HASC
Home Affairs Select Committee; a powerful cross-party committee of the House of Commons chaired by Keith Vaz MP, it enquires into domestic matters and has a reputation for robust questioning.

HMIC
Her Majesty's Inspectorate of Constabulary; the inspection system for policing composed of Home Secretary appointments drawn from the civil service, the police and other organisations. The current Chief Inspector, Sir Thomas Winsor, was formerly a railway lawyer and is the first non-police officer since the nineteenth century to be appointed to the post.

HO
Home Office, the department of state responsible for the police, the UK Border Agency, the Security Service (MI5), and, astonishingly, British Summer Time.

HS
The Home Secretary, the Cabinet-rank senior politician who heads up the Home Office, since 2010 it has been the Rt. Hon. Theresa May MP.

IPCC
Independent Police Complaints Commission; a national body charged with investigation of complaints against the police, deaths in the custody of the police, and serious misconduct. Since 2013, IPCC has the remit to investigate complaints of *criminal* behaviour by PCCs, but has no other 'watchdog' function for commissioners.

MOPAC
In London, the Mayor's Office for Policing and Crime, headed by the Deputy Mayor who is the de facto Police and Crime Commissioner.

NPCC
The National Police Chiefs' Council that, in April 2015, replaced ACPO; it is intended to be a national voice for strategic policing but many of ACPO's functions in this respect have passed to the national College of Policing.

OPCC
The Office of the Police and Crime Commissioner: the staff that support the work of each PCC. Numbers vary, but statutorily must include a Chief Executive Officer (CEO) and a separate Finance Director. Some PCCs have deputies, others do not. There is usually a small administration team drawn normally from police headquarters staff, and retained specialists such as media advisers and diarists.

Police authorities (PAs)
Police authorities existed from 1964 until 2012. They were composed of (up to 9) elected councillors appointed to the authority and (up to 8) appointees, making 17 authority members in most police forces. Usually part time and unsalaried, their role was to hold the police to account and oversee the police budget. In practice, PAs were often ineffectual and some were manipulated by unscrupulous chief officers (Caless, 2011), and were criticised by HMIC and the Home Office because they were unchallenging and 'invisible'. Few members of the public even knew the PA existed, let alone who its members were. They were replaced in November 2012 by Police and Crime Commissioners, but some PA members went on to become members of the PCP.

PCC
Police and Crime Commissioner; an elected role in each of the 41 police forces outside London (MOPAC performs a similar role in London), serving four-year terms, with the primary role of holding the Chief Constable to 'democratic account'.

PCP
Police and Crime Panel; this is a group of mixed elected councillors and appointees whose task is to advise commissioners and act as a counter-balance to them. The panels have largely been found wanting because PCCs can ignore their advice or bypass their attempted restraints. The role of the PCP is under active review (see 'recall').

Police and Crime Plan
The PCC is required to produce a Police and Crime Plan, and revisit it yearly, in which both to articulate the strategic aims of local policing and to chart progress against targets and aspirations.

'recall'
A process devised by the Home Office to enable challenge of and delay to proposals made by PCCs and, in ways similar to 'de-selection' of MPs, give the PCP some powers to hold a PCC to account. It should be noted that PCP powers have not yet been tested in the courts where PCCs are expected to argue that, as elected representatives, they cannot be held to account by appointees (*vox constituit*, as opposed to *vox populi*; see below). A person is elected by the will of the people: commonly this is regarded as trumping any appointed role.

'vox pop'
The phrase in full is *Vox populi, vox dei* (Latin: *the voice of the people is the voice of the gods*), but the phrase as currently used means opinion sampling from a random number of people, for example in a street.

Acknowledgements

We proffer sincere and grateful thanks to all those Police and Crime Commissioners who gave up their time to talk to us frankly about the issues they face, and to the chief police officers who did the same, and to both sides who gave us private perspectives on how they think the other performs. We thank all those staff members of the PCCs' Offices who spoke privately to us, and to the PAs of chief police officers who did the same. We are particularly grateful to Nick Alston, CBE, Chair of the Association of Police and Crime Commissioners and his (APCCs and PCC Essex) staff for including us in the APCCs' Partnership Summit conference at Harrogate, North Yorkshire, on 17 and 18 November 2014, and for allowing us access to many of the PCCs and chief police officers attending. We wish to thank additionally:

Former Chief Constable Jim Barker-McCardle QPM, for conversations and lunches in which we learned much about strategic thinking in the police.

Former Assistant Chief Constable Gary Beautridge for many conversations about police accountability and his insights into police command. Zoe Bellingham, HM Inspectorate of Constabulary for an on-the-record interview on 24 April 2014. Jess Garland and Chris Smith of the Electoral Reform Society for permission to reproduce their 2013 psephology table. John Graham and Gavin Hales of The Police Foundation for their invitation in February 2015 to consider police leadership and the PCCs in a roundtable discussion, as well as for their profound knowledge about policing and their analytic skills in understanding it. Dr Graham Hooper, colleague and Senior Lecturer in Criminal Justice Studies at Canterbury Christ Church University, who gave us interesting insights from his personal experience into the ways PCCs function. Barry Spruce; late of Kent Police and now in the Health Ministry, long-time writing colleague, for his thoughts and suggestions on the original proposal.

Our colleague Dr Steve Tong, Director of Policing Studies, Canterbury Christ Church University, who looked through most of the draft chapters and made valuable and constructive comments for which we are grateful. Bryn Caless thanks Maddy and Astrid for listening, the rest of the family for their tolerant forbearance and of course Clarey, the sine qua non. Jane Owens thanks Tom (there are no words that can truly acknowledge or do justice to the value I place on your unending support and love for me). Both authors thank their colleagues at Canterbury Christ Church University for their support, interest and belief in this project from the beginning.

Introduction

When the authors attended the Annual APCC Conference in Harrogate in November 2014, a delegate took Bryn Caless aside in a queue for coffee and told him that:

> 'It's far too early to be studying PCCs; your research is premature. You should wait at least ten years before analysing things like this.'

There was no guarantee then (or now) that Police and Crime Commissioners (PCCs) would still be around in 2024, let alone either of the authors. Waiting ten years before undertaking research is a utopian prescription that bears very little resemblance to the real world, and none at all to the pragmatic level that the authors occupy. So we soldiered on regardless of the dire warnings of 'prematurity'; progressively studying the nature of governance of the police; interviewing confidentially both PCCs and members of their chief police officer teams; and accumulating the 'rich detail' of our empirical research, the outcomes of which we present in this modest volume. And we discovered something interesting on the way: many police officers and PCCs have found common cause and have learned to work together quite well, despite doomsayers (plenty of whom are to be found in the pages that follow) who thought that introducing PCCs was the apocalyptic end of the policing world as we knew it. The doomsayers may have had a point four years or so earlier. When PCCs arrived at police headquarters all over England and Wales after the November 2012 elections, police forces generally, and the chief officer teams in particular, were largely hostile to, or at least wary of, these elected cuckoos that had been foisted on them, ousting the old comfortable Police Authority from the nest and demanding instead to be heard, fed and obeyed. Understandably, police forces did not welcome with open arms these insistent newcomers. For their part, the PCCs anticipated hostility or resistance, and most already knew, or thought they knew, what was wrong with policing and what they needed to do to put it right. There was some tightly-controlled aggression on their part too, especially when they encountered surly opposition or even mendacity from their police teams.

For a while, the two sides circled each other, hackles raised, prepared to be affronted, quick to take offence. There were a number of well-publicised and angry departures by serving Chief Constables, and one or two protracted wrangles about who could stay and who should go. In the event, the PCCs flexed their 'hire and fire' muscles and the rest of the police took stock, some mutinously muttering from a distance the while. Time passed; PCCs produced their local Police and Crime Plans and the police discovered, with varying degrees of astonishment, that many PCCs proved quite adept at positive publicity, courting the media, resolutely engaging with the public, holding Chief Constables to account in open forum and relaying to the police, often in blunt language, what people thought of the way they were policed. Nothing quite like this had happened before. At the same time there were other portents: external and cooperative partnerships were pursued both locally and nationally, the rest of the criminal justice system sat up, looked at PCCs and took somnolent note, the media slowly changed from general hostility to eager seekers after 'copy'; while that cherished symbol of chief officerdom, the limited company known as ACPO, withered slowly on the vine because PCCs withheld 'top-sliced' force funding, following a critical report that they had themselves commissioned on this previously unchallenged "old boys' club" (as one of them described it).

Many of the chief police officer teams watched all this activity and bustle with some bemusement and a little alarm: these newcomers seemed prepared to use their wide ranging powers freely and vigorously. It eventually became clear to all police officers that executive and strategic power had tangibly moved from their chief officer teams across to the PCCs. This did not impinge (much) on police 'operational independence', but it did mean a reorientation of local priorities towards neighbourhood and community policing, and it proved harder than the police expected to interest PCCs in serious, organised and major crimes; in fact in anything at all apart from neighbourhood policing and funding. Into this interesting realignment of powers, priorities and principles, intruded severe budget cuts: forces had their central allocations of funds reduced, resources immediately became harder to manage, savings were demanded and staff had to be shed. Some PCCs pushed very hard for an increase in local funding (the 'precept') to compensate for national funding cuts and the police realised that, in fact, both sides were facing the same problems and both were searching for solutions. At the same time in the larger political world, a campaign was being run during the Scottish independence referendum, called 'Better Together', which espoused the virtues of a United Kingdom. That phrase began to have some local resonance in police forces, because common purpose with PCCs began to emerge in a number of ways, not least a kind of joint struggle: police and

PCC were indeed 'better together' to mitigate as much as possible the effects of the deep financial austerity imposed by central government.

Chief police officers began to change their views, at least privately: instead of opposition and obstruction, there emerged cooperative enterprise; rather than hostility, some police chiefs began to voice unqualified admiration of their PCCs. PCCs for their part started to talk approvingly about police adaptability and chief officers having a newly-businesslike approach to local policing. It did not mean for one moment that everything in the garden was lovely: pockets of angry criticism persisted, some police briefed against the new system, some PCCs commissioned HMIC to investigate process abuses, a few PCCs courted unfortunate headlines and hostile media coverage, a number of forces persisted in active antipathy to their PCCs and PCCs themselves, in the media and in print, openly criticised police failures. Such a state of affairs, though somewhat modified, continues to this day; what our researches have shown, and as we explore in greater detail in the pages that follow, in the majority of cases the chief police teams and the PCCs are 'better together' than opposed. Each side has made some accommodation of the other, the alignment of aims is now more coherent, the old police authorities are neither mourned nor missed, and attention is turning – at least for those PCCs seeking re-election – to what might characterise a second term in the PCC office. Some newspapers can still default to damning the 'quality' or 'mediocrity' of PCCs, but the media's subjective prejudice, often trying to pass itself off as critical commentary (see later), sounds increasingly strained and unconvincing.[1] Whether one approves of PCCs wielding 'democratic oversight' or not, whether one thinks that they are a necessary corrective to maverick police actions or not, whether or not one shares some newspapers' unfailing hostility to the role, and whether or not it is premature to make an assessment of the impact of PCCs – these are exciting times in policing.

---

[1]   *The Times*, that august newspaper of record, commented ponderously on 5 June 2015 that 'police and crime commissioners [...] were a byword for mediocrity' compared with Members of Parliament (leading article, 'Paying for Parliament', p. 29), which is a bit rich. This shallow judgement is not remotely supported by what we have seen of the role over three years, where the 'quality' of PCCs actually compares very favourably with that of MPs. The latter were mired in scandals over their expenses less than a decade ago, but *The Times* seems to have a selective memory as well as a penchant for generalising from the particular.

Organisation of our findings

We discuss in the note on our methodology below, how we undertook our research from 2013 to 2015, its problems and its unexpected pleasures. Throughout the chapters that follow, we also try to relate the current academic literature to what is happening in the police, and we seek illustrative commentary and analysis where it helps us understand the processes of change. But let us be clear about one thing at the very outset: whether or not PCCs survive beyond 2020, and whether or not the original concept undergoes transformation and change, this has been the profoundest change in our police system in England and Wales for a generation or more. Indeed, *for the very first time in policing history, a person elected by the people and representing their views and concerns has formal oversight of policing, with wide ranging powers vested in statute.* It could be argued (and is, by some PCCs) that they have now outgrown their original rather vague and indeterminate remit, and that the future may entail a larger sphere of activity and a bigger local stage on which to exercise their oversight. But that is not to gainsay the seismic shock that their original arrival caused in policing. It is our aim in this book carefully to explore in sequence how the earthquake occurred, how the first elections proceeded, what relations were like between PCCs and the police at first (and what they are like now), how well or not PCCs handle the media and how they engage the public, how they strive to communicate what they do, how partnerships have been developed or discarded at local and national levels, how the PCCs have moderated their ambitions within the restraints of tight budgeting, and what they look forward to in their possible second terms. All this is done anonymously: none of the people who spoke to us is identified by name or force and what they say is not attributable. You will not be able to play the time-honoured game of 'spot the source'[2] because we have deliberately edited our interviewees' responses to avoid giving their identities away, and in some instances, where interviewees agree on a point of view, we have conflated answers to typify that response. There are perfectly sound academic precedents for doing this, and we are firmly in a tradition of qualitative research that seeks the 'rich detail' of primary actors' anonymous responses to contemporary issues.[3]

We believe strongly that our interlocutors, both PCCs and chief police officers, would not have been as honest and open with us, had they been identified publicly with what they said. The interviewees

---

[2]   Whether PCC or chief police officer.

[3]   For example, Reiner (1991); or, more generally, Duffy (2014).

are often funny, often provocative, often piercingly critical; they are also occasionally anxious, sometimes downcast or at a loss, vulnerable and lonely at times, and now and then utterly fixated on what they think they have to do to get the job done. Nearly every one of those we interviewed spoke openly about how they felt in response to the ten common questions we asked each of them. One or two followed a rather constrained line of interaction with us, and their somewhat over-guarded responses will be seen for what they are in the pages that follow.

A note on the research methodology

There were many reasons for writing this book: the context of the role of PCC; the fact that this is the most significant change to have taken place in police governance in 50 years and the very first time the 'overseer' of the police has been elected specifically to perform that function; the national press interest in the PCCs' successes and failures; contested political issues surrounding the role, and the efficacy of individual governance as against group oversight. Even before the election of the 41 PCCs in England and Wales took place in November 2012, the role attracted considerable adverse media comment accompanied by unyielding and deep-seated resistance from ACPO and some political parties. Within months of the PCCs' appointment we saw the resignation and retirement of many sitting Chief Constables (such as Colin Port from Avon and Somerset) and a variety of faux pas by Commissioners (such as that in Lincolnshire). This seemed to us to be a fertile place to explore the tensions of oversight, and from the outset we determined that we would talk in confidence both to PCCs and to representatives of their chief officer teams, so that we could get a perspective on claims and opinions from each side. We also considered that we should explore national aspects to the new role, its seemingly inevitable politicisation, the intense media interest in the role and why that interest tended in the early months so often to the negative.

Data collection

In order to achieve these lofty aims we decided that we would need to have a triangulation[4] of evidence: the information available to the researcher in the published public and academic domain, compared with the commentaries by the PCC and the relevant chief police officer. From this, we developed sets of questions which we believed covered the qualitative ground of our enquiry.[5] The principal issues that we identified form the chapter structure of this book. We considered the option of sending a written questionnaire to all PCCs and chief police officers, but we thought that the reservations associated with such an approach would stop us from achieving rich data.[6] We chose the confidential interview as our main source of data collection with PCCs and Chief Constables for a number of reasons: first, because the 'live' interviewer can respond to what is said, explore an issue and also, on occasion, challenge the speaker. We also felt that this was a research mode that enabled us to clarify language, perceptions and values. Our intention was to interview representative numbers of PCCs and chief police officers together with interested parties (ACPO, APCC, HMIC, Home Office). In the event, ACPO faded away during the research phase and it was not appropriate to seek the opinions of its successor organisation[7]; the APCC has anyway published its views comprehensively and the Home Office, for gnomic reasons of its own, declined to engage with us. We might have foreseen some of this, but research into police governance and strategic issues in policing is fraught with sometimes unheralded change (the disappearance of the Policing Pledge in 2010 for example, or the introduction of PCSOs in 2002), and we have no pretensions to forecast the future.

---

[4] Triangulation is a powerful tool to strengthen the qualitative research design. It allows the researcher to be more confident of their results due to the increased reliability and validity (Holtzhausen, 2001).

[5] Both sets of questions are reproduced in the Appendix.

[6] Written questionnaires have strengths – they are easy to use, available in quantity and simple to administer. However, we ruled out the 'ubiquitous sent questionnaire' from this research because of the likelihood of poor response rates from busy people; the apparent impersonality of the questionnaire method; the probability that respondents would ignore some questions; the unsuitability of questionnaires to explore complex issues and, unlike the normal 'blanket' approach for questionnaires, we had a very specific target audience (www.evalued.bcu.ac.uk/tutorial/4a.htm)

[7] The National Police Chiefs' Council, formed in April 2015, so far speaks only on police issues.

We established two interview schedules[8] with specific questions that would be asked respectively of each PCC and chief police officer. The questions were mostly 'open', designed to ensure that interviewees' own words were captured. Questions to PCCs were directed at gathering information regarding their relationship with their significant partners and issues as noted above. Questions to chief police officers were mostly concerned to seek information regarding their opinion of the PCC role, the performance of their own individual PCC and how well (qualitatively) they themselves work with their PCC. Although the interview plan would be structured,[9] we expected that it would in fact become somewhat semi-structured[10] as we had anticipated (correctly) that supplementary questions would arise. The interview schedules were both piloted on a select group of colleagues and (former) police officers and adjusted accordingly to ensure efficient evidence gathering.

Data-gathering and interviewing

We interviewed *20 chief police officers* and *23 PCCs*, which is representative of each occupation by some margin: slightly fewer than half of police chiefs, whom we wanted to talk to as a counterbalance to the PCC (of a nominal total of 41; 20 = 49%); and just more than half of those available in the case of the PCCs (total: 41; 23 = 56%). These totals are more impressive than perhaps they seem at first sight. Chief police officers and PCCs are each guarded by efficient and occasionally formidable gatekeepers. In turn, this can lead to difficulty in obtaining access that thwarted some of our endeavours throughout the whole research period. In one or two cases, we never got past the gatekeeper, and, because time was pressing, we had no leisure to devise other routes.[11] However, there were many things that made our task easier. Initially we gained access to some chief police officers and PCCs as a consequence of our own contact list and through introductions from other known significant contacts. We also developed a 'snowball'

---

[8] An 'interview schedule' is a set of prepared questions designed to ensure that each interviewee is asked the same question (Mcleod, 2014).

[9] 'Structured interviews' are easy to replicate as a fixed set of questions are used – this means it is easy to test for reliability. This also means that the findings can be considered to be representative (http://ukdataservice.ac.uk/teaching-resources/interview/structured.aspx).

[10] A 'semi-structured interview' is open-ended and flexible, allowing new ideas to be discussed during the interview as a result of what is said (http://ukdataservice.ac.uk/teaching-resources/interview/semi-structured.aspx).

[11] Though we saw more PCCs than police officers.

research approach, in which we asked the present interlocutor to allow us to approach others in his or her name. This worked comparatively well with PCCs, though in the early stages of research in late 2013, they only really knew a handful of colleagues. This improved later and in 2015 this was the most successful technique of all. The 'snowball' technique worked well from the outset with chief police officers who, often unprompted, suggested that we used their names to approach other police officers. We found that both chief police officers and PCCs discussed our research and they sometimes recommended to their colleagues that the latter took part. This was particularly the case after an interview was concluded. As a consequence some chiefs and a few PCCs contacted us directly and agreed to be involved. We also approached PCCs and police forces directly by phone and indirectly through email and hard-copy correspondence. Some ignored our requests completely (there is a limit to how many times you can badger a PCC, apparently), and others refused to take part, as of course, is their right. On the whole, PCCs were more amenable to approaches than were chief police officers; the latter were notably reluctant to speak without specific guarantees of anonymity. PCCs were entirely comfortable with telephone or Skype interviews; chief police officers were demonstrably less comfortable with either, and many preferred direct personal contact away from force headquarters or police premises. Some Skype sessions took place in the evenings and at weekends, when Commissioners' diaries were less fraught and many police chiefs were off duty.

We were grateful to be invited in November 2014 to the Association of Police and Crime Commissioners' Summit in Harrogate, where we were able to mix with and 'pitch' PCCs and chief police officers, renew acquaintances and be introduced to new ones, as well as record some direct conversations, comments and debates.

Interviewing

Personal (that is, face-to-face) interviews were mostly conducted at the police force offices of the interviewee; however, on occasion it proved useful to meet in London as a halfway house, given the geographical spread of Commissioners and their police forces. Interviews took from an hour to 90 minutes to complete[12] and were transcribed by

---

[12] A rare couple took three and a half hours and included lunch...

the interviewer using contemporaneous notes.[13] In hindsight it might have been more useful for the researcher to have been accompanied by a separate note-taker, as this recording method slowed down the interview process and made one or two interviewees less animated and free speaking. We considered approaching Chief Constables who had left policing within a year of the PCCs' arrival, but decided that we would be better placed talking to those still in the role.

Confidentiality

We entirely appreciated the sensitive nature of our study and acknowledged that some of our questions would be regarded as provocative and (by nervous individuals) as inflammatory. We expected reservations and concerns from our interviewees in respect of disclosing what they told us. We guaranteed complete confidentiality to anyone who spoke to us because we knew from experience[14] that this would elicit more truthful, honest and full responses. We undertook confidential storage of the information from interviews by allocating each interviewee a number and by storing the data in password-protected and encrypted accounts in the university's secure internal sites. We made each interviewee aware of the following statement:

> Replies will not be attributable to you by name and all information relating to your identity will be removed. Your replies to questions, if used in subsequent publications, are guaranteed anonymity and will be assigned a random 'interviewee number'.

We have adhered to this undertaking faithfully, and *the identity of our interlocutors is known only to themselves and to the two authors.* That is how it will stay and all those who spoke to us can have the completest confidence in our fierce guardianship of who they are. In the pages that follow, verbatim quotations from our interviewees[15] are displayed, followed by an interviewee number. Interviewee numbers for PCCs

---

[13] Contemporaneous notes are a record made at the time or written up very shortly thereafter.

[14] Bryn Caless used the method in his *Policing at the Top* in 2011, and in his joint research with Steve Tong in *Leading Policing Across Europe* in 2015.

[15] As noted earlier, some identical views have been conflated under one number, for convenience and further obfuscation.

are in the range from *Interviewee 51 to 74*; those for chief police officers are in the range *CO1 to CO20.*

The value of this research

More than anything else, we think that the replies from PCCs and chief officers to our questions shine light into places that are normally hidden from us as citizens, even though it is in our name that policing is 'done'. Our interviews open up for examination, relationships within policing that have had tensions and difficulties as well as triumphs and successes, and we give a unique perspective on the interior strategic world of policing that has not been seen before. The commentaries, from both sides of the action, reveal more than we would otherwise know of the dynamics of power and the accommodation of strategic aims. PCCs have been bedding into the job and learning about policing, while the police have been accustoming themselves to something much more dynamic and proactive in their oversight than they were used to. Some of the off-the-cuff comments and jokes that result may seem insensitive or harsh, but they must be seen in the context of contemporaneous commentary on situations that were apt to change from week to week, and certainly from month to month. We think it is a fascinating journey inside policing, and we hope that you think so too.

ONE

Governance: the Police and Crime Commissioner and police accountability in context

The politicians of the centre right in England and Wales were in no doubt: police chief constables had to be made more accountable. The lead was given nationally in 2005 by Michael Gove MP, then Shadow Housing Spokesman, when he declared in *The Times* that:

> The level of democratic accountability to which the police are subject in Britain today is woeful. (Gove, 2005)

A prominent Conservative theorist,[1] who had headed the Policy Exchange think-tank and who had been formerly a *Times* columnist, Gove led the charge in 2005 against 'failing chief constables', because:

> There is no adequate mechanism in Britain for holding a failing chief constable satisfactorily to account. [...] Making chief constables directly accountable to a single individual elected to oversee their efforts would not be welcomed by all. Real accountability never is. But our weakest chief constables [...] desperately need someone to put the fear of God into them. (Gove, 2005)

Three years later, writing in *The Scotsman*, Gove asserted that:

> [T]he public deserve [sic] a say in deciding what the police's priorities should be. Whether it is directly electing the people who serve on police authorities and boards, or making the police chief in a given area directly accountable

---

[1] Nick Herbert, who became the Policing Minister in 2010, took over the lead in 2007 when he incorporated the notion of the 'police commissioner' into a Conservative policy paper. The Policy Exchange, according to a House of Commons Research Note by Pat Strickland in 2013, had '... advocated the introduction of directly elected police commissioners at least since 2003', citing publication of a paper by Barry Loveday and Anna Reid (2003).

to the elected mayor, the methods can be debated but the direction of travel is clear – towards greater democracy. (Gove, 2008)

This notion of 'direct accountability' actually derives from elected commissioners of police in the United States, and Gove is here in line with a fine tradition of importing American policing methods into the UK.[2] It followed with rather remorseless logic that his suggestion of a person who could 'put the fear of God' into chief constables in 2005 should become a 'directly elected individual' in 2008, and find its way into the Conservative Party manifesto as 'a directly elected Police and Crime Commissioner', two years later.[3] By the time the Conservative Party had formed the majority in a coalition government with the Liberal Democrats in 2010, the suggestion of an elected person to hold the police directly to account had become policy and was a key part of the Queen's Speech.[4] The Home Secretary in the new administration was the Rt. Hon. Theresa May MP, and her Police Reform and Social Responsibility Act of 2011 enshrined the principle of directly elected Police and Crime Commissioners for each

---

[2] Remember 'zero-tolerance policing'? Other importations from the US which did not last the distance included 'problem-oriented policing' (POP) and COMPSTAT, which held the police accountable for performance at district command level (Basic Command Unit or BCU). POP mutated and expanded into Signal Crime Theory, see Innes (2014).

[3] The text of the 2010 manifesto read as follows: '**Police:** Voters will be able to elect police commissioners who will hold chief constables to account for the performance of their forces. [...] Commissioners would be responsible for "setting the budget and the strategy for local police forces", while the police retain "operational independence"'. A summary of the 2010 manifesto is available at www.telegraph. co.uk/news/election-2010/7165000/conservative-manifesto.html. It is worth remembering that the notion of elected democratic accountability for the police was first raised by the Labour Party, through David Blunkett, the then-Home Secretary, in 2003.

[4] Noted in Caless (2011, pp. 141–2).

police force in England and Wales other than London.[5] A year later, in November 2012, elections were held and 41 Police and Crime Commissioners were given a mandate – of a rather qualified kind, given the percentage turnout (Crawford, 2012) – to act in the name of the people in overseeing the police.

This at least is the bald outline of events in the last ten or so years, but in criminological terms and more directly in terms of understanding policing, we need to examine the proposition of democratic governance in greater detail. Specifically, we need to ask why there is a need for oversight of the police and to look at the theoretical constructs of that governance as well as entering the debate about the need to hold a balance between, on the one hand, the police being required to justify what they do in our name and, on the other, not fettering the police so tightly that they can neither be operationally effective nor exercise discretion in whether or not to bring charges against an individual. Additionally, there is a second debate to be had about the balance between police operational independence and independent scrutiny of what they do.

We should also consider to what precisely the public is being asked to acquiesce in the election of Police and Crime Commissioners: the

---

[5]   The Metropolitan Police is answerable to The Mayor's Office for Policing and Crime (MOPAC) while the City of London Police, a much smaller force, is overseen by City of London Police Authority, part of the Lord Mayor's Office. These roles in essence are more European than American. In October 2008, the incoming (Conservative) Mayor of London, Boris Johnson, discarded the incumbent Commissioner of the Metropolitan Police, Sir Ian Blair, by stating that the latter did not have the Mayor's confidence (see, for example, www.telegraph. co.uk/news/newstopics/ianblair/3124924/Met-police-chief-Sir-Ian-Blair-forced-out-by-mayor-Boris-Johnson.html). Sir Ian (later Lord Blair) was the only one surprised by this decision, which in turn appears to have bolstered the Conservatives' determination to obtain elected representatives of the people in all other English and Welsh police forces. Gove noted that 'When he was effectively dismissed Sir Ian objected that his departure might pave the way for a New York-style approach to appointing police chiefs.' (Gove, 2008). Sir Ian's prescience was justified: the role of Mayor in London is now designated additionally as the 'Police and Crime Commissioner' for the capital – in practice the Deputy Mayor does this on behalf of the Mayor – but the title seems honorific in the absence of specific elections to such a post. The assumption appears to be that the role of PCC comes integrally with the office of elected Mayor; witness what is proposed for Manchester in 2017 and for other mayoralties of large conurbations. The plan for Manchester may be seen in 'Greater Manchester Agreement, Devolution to the GMCA and transition to a directly-elected mayor', by HM Treasury and GMCA, November 2014, available at: www.gov.uk/government/uploads/system/uploads/attachment_data/file/369858/Greater_Manchester_Agreement_i.pdf.

principal difference from what has gone before appears to be that those who now call the police to account are *elected*. Does that make any practical difference? Are there still variations and individual 'tweaks' in how police accountability is applied across the 41 Police and Crime Commissioners (PCC) jurisdictions and do they matter? In other words, is there more to the election of PCCs than simply replacing 17 or so 'well-meaning people' (Gove, 2005) with one focused, full-time, salaried representative?[6]

In *The Republic*, Plato suggests that a guardian class be created, whose whole job and purpose is to protect the people. He then typically poses a question that calls such a proposal into doubt. Who would guard these guardians?[7] In other words, what mechanisms or oversight would ensure that the liberty of the many was not compromised by unchallenged power in the hands of the few? Plato did not conceive of the possibility of state officials abusing their powers; we are rather more familiar with the concept in the 21st century.[8] Yet, curbs on the power of officials and politicians alike in democracies are familiar to us, both because there have been so many instances of the systematic abuse of power[9] and because we are aware that we surrender to the

---

[6] Lord Stevens in his 'Independent Police Commission' (2013) opined that the PCC should be replaced with an 'elected Board' serving more or less the same function.

[7] The question is commonly posed in Latin as *Quis custodiet ipsos custodes?* (Who guards the guards?) because it is most often attributed to the Latin writer Juvenal in his *Satires*, No. 6, though some scholars believe the line to have been a later interpolation. Plato, had he used the phrase exactly rather than referentially through Glaucon (a character who discusses with Socrates the possibility of perfecting the state), would have posed the question in Greek (Ποιος θα παρακολουθήσουν τους φύλακες); see The Republic, translated by Desmond Lee, Penguin, 2003. Two of the best discussions of what is meant in contemporary society by the phrase are, respectively, in Leonid Hurwicz's Nobel Prize for Economics acceptance speech in 1998, available at www.econ.umn.edu/workingpapers/hurwicz_guardians.pdf; and in T. Besley and J. Robinson (2010) 'Quis Custodiet Ipsos Custodes? Civilian Control over the Military', *Journal of the European Economic Association*, Vol. 8, pp. 655–63.

[8] For example, one of the less edifying features of evidence presented to the Enquiry under the chairmanship of Lord Leveson into the *News of the World*'s phone-hacking was the frequency with which Metropolitan Police officers passed information to journalists for money. If police discretion and independence of action are so profoundly corrupted, the question *Who polices the police?* takes on a bitter contemporary edge. For a newspaper take (*Guardian*), see www.theguardian.com/media/2012/nov/28/leveson-inquiry-report-essential-guide; for more dispassionate academic commentary, see Keeble and Mair (2012).

[9] By politicians as well as others in public office: we should not forget the 'cash for questions' scandals in John Major's government of 1995 or the regular abuse of MPs' expense claims in 2008–10.

state some parts of our freedom in exchange for our security, however much of a moveable feast that security can be.[10] For some, the arrival of Police and Crime Commissioners evoked a welcome that verged on the ecstatic:

> Directly-elected Police & Crime Commissioners (PCCs) are the boldest reform of policing since the 1960s. In May 2012 there will be 41 new political beasts in England and Wales with large, direct mandates. They look set to transform policing and public debate about crime. (Gibbs, 2010)

Aside from getting the election date wrong (it was November, not May), and predicting a 'large direct mandate [...]',[11] and erroneously supposing that 'successful PCCs will have mandates from up to several million electors each', Blair Gibbs (2010) was right to suppose that the election of PCCs would provoke 'public debate about crime'. He went on to assert in his laudatory essay that 'governance of policing is rightly, and by its nature, political', which excuses the political platforms upon which the majority of PCC 'beasts' stood as candidates.[12] Stuart Lister and Michael Rowe applied a corrective to that over-optimistic view in 2013, in an astringent article that questioned, among other things, whether it was appropriate that PCCs should be so closely aligned with mainstream politics (Lister and Rowe, 2013). We must make some (sceptical) allowance for Blair Gibbs though; he is himself a partisan observer – 'head of crime and justice' at the right wing *Policy Exchange* – and he actually echoes the careful mantra used by

---

[10] As debated by Jean-Jacques Rousseau in *The Social Contract*, (*Du contrat social ou Principes du droit politique*; 1762), Book 1, Chapters 1–5; see also Williams, D. (2014) *Rousseau's 'Social Contract': An Introduction*. Cambridge: Cambridge University Press. The notion of surrendering freedoms in exchange for security was queried in the USA by Benjamin Franklin who growled 'Those who surrender freedom for security will not have, nor do they deserve, either one.' (Reply to the Governor, November 11, 1755; see *The Papers of Benjamin Franklin*, edited by L. Labaree (1963) Yale University Press, Vol. 6, p. 242).

[11] In fact a less than convincing 14.7% overall (Crawford, 2012; Strickland, 2013); see also Chapter Two of this study.

[12] Though some stood successfully, if occasionally misleadingly, as 'Independents'. A psephological map (from the LGA) is given in Chapter Two and shows a band of independent PCCs stretching in a curve from Kent to North Wales. Some commentators believed that the politically 'Independent' PCC will vanish at the elections in 2016 and then the mainstream political parties would dominate the PCC profile (Lister and Rowe, 2013).

Conservatives whenever the inadequacy of police authorities vis-à-vis the PCC is invoked. Gibbs calls them 'weak and invisible', noting that they cost £65 million a year and fail adequately 'to hold chief constables to account'. When the Home Secretary wrote the foreword to a recent (2014) collection of essays by PCCs about their roles, she commented on 'the failings of the invisible, unelected, and unaccountable police authorities', and remarked that only '7 per cent of the public knew that police authorities even existed'.[13] She elaborated on this in a speech to the Association of Police and Crime Commissioners' Partnership Summit on 18 November 2014,[14] when she asserted that:

> Police authorities were *invisible committees of unknown appointees* that had no contact with the public, whose members were installed and not elected, and who lacked the mandate to provide the leadership necessary to get things done. (May, 2014a; our italics)[15]

A PCC pointed out in more detail differences between the police authority role and his own:

> 'I can manage the change more directly than the old invisible police authority [PA] could ever have done, and what is more, I am experienced in public office in a way that PA members generally were not, plus of course I spend a huge amount of time listening to what the public thinks. None of them is backward in coming forward to tell me what they feel, and this is consultation on a continuing big

---

[13] See the 2014 http://thinkblueline.uk/wp-content/uploads/2014/09/Think-Blue-Line_FINAL.pdf. A note of caution is needed here since all the PCCs who wrote essays for this collection are Conservatives, and they are all, of course, in favour of the PCC role, and claim to be doing it well, though retaining an article by Mark Reckless MP (who subsequently defected to UKiP) might be regarded as unfortunate. Reckless lost his seat at Rochester and Strood for UKiP in May 2015.

[14] Both authors were present but she would not talk to us.

[15] Not surprisingly, this acid description is also applied by some less-than-enchanted PCCs to the Police and Crime Panels that are supposed to monitor what the Commissioners do. We look at this in more detail in Chapter Six; it is sufficient here to note that the Police Authority, the 'invisible committee of unknown appointees', may have reappeared in an equally invisible Police and Crime Panel that also lacks 'the mandate ... to get things done' (May, 2014a).

scale which PA members only dreamed of.' (Interviewee 64)[16]

The same PCC went on to say that a further and exponential difference from the previous police authority system is that he is "full time, salaried and consultative" which means that he can devote considerable amounts of attention to seeing his ideas implemented and can monitor progress on his reforms on practically a daily basis, whereas the police authority met less frequently and had other concerns in their 'day jobs'. In that sense the PCC is able to hold the police more promptly to account, can have more frequent dialogue with chief officers and also can be responsive to public concerns more readily than was the case before 2012.

However, none of this means that the Police and Crime Commissioner post is without its critics. In an (anonymous) leading article in *The Times* on 1 December 2014, entitled 'Spent Force', it was claimed that:

> An experiment in directly electing police chiefs has proved a fiasco.
>
> [...] A well-intentioned attempt to decentralise decision-making and make police forces accountable has failed. (*The Times*, 1 December 2014, p. 32)

We should not expect from ephemeral journalism the same evidential rigour as is required in dispassionate academic commentary, but this *Times* leader was particularly notable for the highly emotional content of its commentary (which referred to PCCs as 'mediocrities' of 'generally poor quality'[17]), and for the absence of evidence to support any of its criticism of the role. That however, is incidental to a more serious charge, which was that the article damned PCCs on the basis that in 2013–14, the Independent Police Complaints Commission had investigated (or at least had considered) 41 complaints against 23 PCCs. This newspaper attack on the PCC role patently confuses accusation with proof, and, just as arrest is not of itself evidence of guilt, the *process* cannot meaningfully be considered identical with *outcome*. This is not to excuse PCCs from the seriousness of some of the complaints against them, but to try to give the statistic the objective context that *The*

---

[16] PCCs are interviewees numbered from 51–74; chief police officer interviewees are numbered from CO1–CO20.

[17] In June 2015, *The Times* again called PCCs 'a byword for mediocrity' (see Introduction).

Times signally fails to provide. Actually, all but six of the complaints were referred back to forces as being below the Independent Police Complaints Commission's (IPCC) threshold,[18] and only four of the six remained unresolved at the time that the leading article was written. Thus, for *The Times'* crime reporter Fiona Hamilton to claim elsewhere in the same edition of the newspaper that 'more than half' of PCCs had been investigated by 'the policing watchdog' is simply misleading; while headlining 'more than 40 complaints' is just about technically correct but is scarcely objective commentary (Hamilton, 2014).

Predictably, this waspish and one-sided attack on the PCC role drew responses from others, one of whom, Lord Wasserman, asserted that PCCs had:

> ... introduced a more holistic approach to crime prevention, achieved better value for money, encouraged more innovation in the way local policing is delivered and forged closer links between police forces and their communities. (Letters to the Editor, *The Times*, 3 December 2014)

Another, a serving PCC, noted that:

> In my two years in office, crime has fallen, financial prudence has been maintained and praised, and our plans to re-engineer policing have been lauded by Her Majesty's Inspector of Constabulary. (Sir Clive Loader, PCC Leicestershire & Rutland, Letters to the Editor, *The Times*, 4 December 2014, p. 35)

One correspondent was less impressed, observing that:

> The many qualities [Lord Wasserman] ascribed to the majority of PCCs should perhaps be supported by examples.

adding:

> In my experience, I fail to recognise any of them (Dr C. L. Murray, Letters, *The Times*, 4 December 2014)

The point of airing this controversy is not to give undue credence to a typical newspaper correspondence storm-in-a-teacup, but to note that

---

[18] Currently, to investigate complaints of criminality only against PCCs.

the role of Police and Crime Commissioner, and its effectiveness in holding the police to account, continues to be contentious and debated, as well as a central manifesto difference between the major parties.[19] While Sir Clive Loader's response above may be interpreted both as defensive special pleading and as aggrieved self-justification (crime has also 'fallen' where he is *not* the PCC), the reaction of other PCCs to *The Times*' criticism has been dismissively robust, one remarking to us that "It can't be all bad if Murdoch doesn't like me!"[20] The centrality of the PCC role, controversial or not, continues to be that of holding the police to account on behalf of the public. That is not all that matters, of course. In the chapters that follow, we look in detail at the role of the PCC, the relationships and partnerships that the postholder must cultivate and the quality of the relationship that he or she has with the media and the public, as well as examining criticisms of the role itself and broader questions about the politicisation of the police; all of which are illuminated by the comments and views of those whom we interviewed. Before turning the spotlight on the PCC *per se*, we need to examine more closely the 'governance' concept and what is entailed in 'the accountability of the police', aiming off for any journalistic excesses on the way.

---

[19] Labour declared that it would abolish PCCs on return to power, replacing the role with 'an elected Board', based on Lord (John) Stevens' *Report* of November 2013 (see Note 6). Although the *Report* claims in its subtitle to be 'An independent inquiry focusing on the future of policing in England and Wales', it was actually commissioned by the Labour Party and written by a former police officer, see the full *Report* at: http://independentpolicecommission.org.uk/. Jack Dromey MP, Shadow Minister of State for Policing and Justice, claimed in a speech at the Association of Police and Crime Commissioners' Partnership Summit in Harrogate on 18 November 2014 that the Stevens' *Report* was 'to all intents a Royal Commission on the Police'. [Given that the evidence to Lord Stevens was not given under legal compulsion; the *Report* was not given a Parliamentary all-party remit or terms-of-reference at the outset, and Lord Stevens (a former Commissioner of the Metropolitan Police) cannot for a moment be considered a neutral Chair, this claim simply doesn't add up.] In the event, the Labour Party lost so heavily at the May 2015 general election that its intentions to abolish PCCs are now academic until at least 2020.

[20] Rupert Murdoch, the controversial global media figure, owns *The Times* and was embroiled in the phone-hacking scandal that closed his *News of the World* in 2012. See Note 8 and, for example, Watson and Hickman (2012) and Keeble and Mair (2012).

Governance and accountability

The notion, in the UK at least, that the police should be directly accountable to the people derives in part from the so-called *Peel's Principles* written in about 1829,[21] among which is the assertion that the police should:

> [...] maintain at all times a relationship with the public that gives reality to the historic tradition that the *police are the public and the public are the police*, the police being only members of the public who are paid to give full time attention to duties which are incumbent on every citizen in the interests of community welfare and existence. (Home Office, 2012; our italics)

Even as long ago as 1829, invoking the 'tradition' of a symbiotic relationship between the citizen and those charged with maintaining public security and lawfulness, was resonant. However, the history of policing up to the formation of Peel's 'New Police for the Metropolis' in 1829, had been largely a matter of localism in dealing with crime and criminality and subordination of the parish constable to the magistracy (Stone, 1983; Emsley, 2009). Widespread public disorder – typically short-lived rioting or demonstration in cities – was usually contained by the military (often in the form of county yeomanry or militia)[22] sometimes in response to magistrates reading 'the Riot Act'.[23] The police were not routinely deployed to control crowds until the mid-1840s and the rise of Chartism (Swift, 2007). The *Principles*, then, appear to be the first formal articulations of a relationship between

---

[21] Actually, there is no evidence that Sir Robert Peel himself wrote the Principles that bear his name. On its website, the Home Office notes that they were 'likely devised by the first Commissioners of Police of the Metropolis (Charles Rowan and Richard Mayne)'. There are nine 'Peelian Principles' in all, which were issued to the first constables of the 'New Police of the Metropolis' as 'General Instructions' in 1829; see Home Office (2012).

[22] Some of whom were responsible in 1819 for the 'Peterloo Massacre' when mounted yeomanry charged a peaceable crowd listening to the orator Henry Hunt; see Poole (2006).

[23] The Riot Act dates from 1714, and the part read aloud by magistrates is: 'Our Sovereign Lord the King chargeth and commandeth all persons, being assembled, immediately to disperse themselves, and peaceably to depart to their habitations, or to their lawful business, upon the pains contained in the Act made in the first year of King George, for preventing tumults and riotous assemblies. God Save the King!' (see Garnham, 2006)

police and the policed, or the people and their 'guardians'. It is worth noting that, in the Home Office at least, the *Principles* have become elevated to a British 'philosophy of policing':

> Essentially, as explained by the notable police historian Charles Reith in his 'New Study of Police History' in 1956, [the 'Peelian Principles' constituted] a philosophy of policing 'unique in history and throughout the world because it derived not from fear but almost exclusively from public co-operation with the police, induced by them designedly by behaviour which secures and maintains for them the approval, respect and affection of the public'. (Home Office, 2012)

To obtain 'the approval, respect and affection of the public' may continue to be an ideal sought by those in policing and in politics through better engagement with communities and greater local responsiveness to the rule of law, but an objective observer would be forced to conclude, regretfully, that this largely remains elusive. One PCC explained the ethical dimension of accountability in these terms:

> '[...] accountability is wider and deeper than just meeting targets or aspirations in a Crime and Policing Plan. It's about the ethical conduct of the police, it's concerned with standards of behaviour in a public office and it is to do with the interaction of the police with the public.' (Interviewee 64)

Police 'behaviour' has not always been such as to 'secure and maintain' the public's approval; indeed, the continued insistence on accountability in policing is, at least in part, directly related to abuses of the trust presumed to exist between the people and the police. The catalogue of such abuses is long,[24] but examples in the last 25 years include: the

---

[24] And not, by any means, confined to Britain: in Europe, in addition to the Dutroux paedophile scandal that rocked Belgium in 2004, there were 'calls for greater scrutiny of the police following the actions of the Special Unit for Police Affairs of the Norwegian Police in 2007 (four officers were responsible for more than half of the complaints against the Unit); the casual killing of a student by Greek Police in 2008 and the riots in cities in Greece that followed, the Romanian police corruption scandal of 2010 in which criminal files were purposely destroyed and instances of police brutality in Macedonia in 2011 which provoked widespread demonstrations' (Caless and Tong, 2015, Chapter Three).

Hillsborough football stadium disaster of 1989; the Stephen Lawrence murder investigation in 1993 and the subsequent McPherson Inquiry 1999; the fatal shooting of Jean-Charles de Menezes in 2005; the death of Ian Tomlinson at the G20 demonstrations in 2009; the phone-hacking scandal of 2011–12; and 'Plebgate' also in 2012.[25] Corrupt practice may not be endemic in the police, but it is systemic (Punch, 2009), while ineptitude and misjudgement are commonplace (Fielding, 1984). In combination, all three (ineptitude, misjudgement and corrupt practice) produce the unflattering list briefly outlined above, and have together and separately led to recurrent calls for more oversight of the police, for police operational decision-making to be opened up to scrutiny and for increased transparency in the exercise of police discretion (Brown, 1981; Feilzer and Hood 2004). What ought to be a relatively straightforward matter of trust, where honest officers police honest citizens, has become complex, fraught, a matter of mutual suspicion and shot through with presumptions of chicanery and power politics on both sides (Prenzler and Ronken, 2001). The arguments for increased accountability and the requirements for police officers to justify their actions are built on the back of persistent police failures to be trustworthy and a nagging suspicion on the part of politicians, citizens and the media that the police deliberately refuse transparency. The police for their part seem to meet most suggestions for reform with a defensive and aggrieved posture, resisting change from 'outsiders' who do not understand policing (Metcalfe and Dick, 2000; Stott et al, 2007).

The wider context

On a broader, even global, scale, the United Nations believes that accountability in policing and governance of what the police do is integral to the proper working of a democracy:

---

[25] This was the occasion in September 2012, when the then Conservative Chief Whip Andrew Mitchell MP was not permitted to wheel his bicycle through the main gate of Downing Street and was told by police to use the side gate instead. Mitchell lost his temper and was accused of calling the duty PC, Toby Rowland, a ' f***ing pleb'. Although he strenuously denied saying it, Mitchell was subsequently found to have done so (court judgement 27 November 2014); other police officers lied, embroidered their accounts or used what happened to gain political capital. The whole matter was unedifying to say the least, and few emerged from the episode and its aftermath with any credit or reputation.

> Accountability [...] aims to prevent the police from misusing
> their powers, to prevent political authorities from misusing
> their control over the police, and most importantly,
> to enhance public confidence and (re-)establish police
> legitimacy. (Osse and Dossett, 2011, p. 8)

What the UN is arguing is that the nation state's monopoly of force[26] must entail acting justifiably and in the public interest. If there is no democratic legitimacy in public policing, the public will not be confident that they are being protected and that their rights are respected. One of the important points in the brief citation given above is that of political control over the policing function. The UN notes that 'political authorities' must be prevented or inhibited from abuse of their control of the monopoly of force. There are plenty of world examples of repressive political regimes that have used their police forces to stifle political dissent, ensure public compliance and punish offenders.[27] Against this, the UN declares that governance of the police must be so balanced and counter-weighted that no single political party can use the police to impose itself unchallenged on the populace. The temptation to over-ride formal police independence of the political machine is always somewhere in the background of governance,[28] and in Europe, this subordination is sometimes characterised by the phrase much used by politicians to the police: 'we steer, you row'.[29] And you can see why: there are too many historical precedents for citizens in democracies to trust either police or politicians without a system of checks and balances, and, unlike autocracies, democracies offer at least the semblance of choice.

At a conference on European police accountability in 2001, the veteran Dutch academic Cyrille Fijnaut noted that oversight of what constituted 'policing' became complicated when one considered its range and variety across the European Union, where the permutations already existing within single member states were multiplied at least ten times. There was therefore no meaningful sense in which we could talk about 'the police' and by that term embrace every detail of every

---

[26] We omit discussion of the use of force by military organisations in this context.

[27] Ranging from the Gestapo and the KGB through to the *Tontons Macoutes* in Haiti and Chinese police action against dissidents. There are more repressive regimes than democracies.

[28] It is now widely accepted that the government's use of the police to 'break' the Miners' Strike in UK in 1984 was a political act; see MacIntyre (2014).

[29] Punch (2007), p. 40.

manifestation of public policing in Europe. Fijnaut and his fellow contributors (Fijnaut, 2002) agreed that more research is needed on the nature of police accountability, particularly at the 'transnational' level, but this remains, more than a decade later, an area which is still under-researched and not as well understood as it should be, nor is the larger societal or organisational structure examined in any detail by contemporary commentators or analysts.[30] The addition to the European Union since 2002 of 13 more member countries, bringing with them at least two more permutations on the policing structure, has complicated further an already-multiplex scene. The dilemma that confronts the commentator in making sense of these various versions and components of 'policing' is that such a broad front creates a 'fuzzy layer' where meanings become imprecise and where consensus becomes difficult. That has not prevented the UN from opining that the democratic accountability of the police is, by its nature, a good thing, and that political governance of the police has to be exercised responsibly and with sufficient checks and balances in play to prevent abuse or exploitation of the police for political ends.

Contemplating the 'democratic policing model' chosen by the emergent post-Soviet states in the Baltic and Central Europe from 1991 onwards, Gorazd Meško remarked what accountability means, or should mean, to citizens who had shaken off decades of Russian domination:

> The police can be trusted, but not unconditionally and external accountability is crucial. In a democratic society, the police have a duty to explain themselves when challenged or asked about their conduct. *They have to accept the reality that others will judge their performance and have a right to do so.* Accountability and civilian supervision should not only function to discipline the police after misconduct on their part; but also serve to guard against the normalisation of small-scale abuses [...] within the police role. (Meško, 2007, p. 30, fn 14; our italics)

There is resonance in Meško's words for any democratic nation state, but the important point for us in England and Wales is that the police themselves accept that oversight of what they do, and demands of them to justify their actions, are integral within the job. If, as the police claim, they want to be considered as a profession, then acceptance of,

---

[30] A couple of exceptions are: Caless and Tong (2015), and Hoogewoning et al (2015).

and adherence to, ethical standards and the adoption of a 'contract' with the public about what it means to be policed, are prerequisites. Scrutiny will come with the territory.

The UN describes this scrutiny as 'a conglomerate of processes', ranging from internal inspection regimes, through national executive, legislative and judicial processes, to international bodies such as the European Committee for the Prevention of Torture. This is a multi-layered business; the police, while largely accepting of the principle of accountability, occasionally jib at the necessity of explaining themselves in so comprehensive a way to so many, so often. It is important for them to acknowledge, therefore, that much of the widespread political insistence that someone 'guards the guards' derives in the first place from public dismay about police malpractice and deviant behaviour. By that token, we should be wary of those who try to reduce police accountability from highly complex processes to bland and simplistic common denominators. That should also extend to the 'aggrieved defensive' default posture adopted by some strategic police leaders when challenged (Waters and Brown, 2000). We know that this is not simply a British problem, but knowing the universality of the need to hold the police to account does not mean that foolproof methods are easily come by.

The media are often more comprehensively intrusive than formal governance processes, at the same time as being less responsible than those charged officially with oversight of the police. The quest for a story, scoop or 'copy' can lead to excessive abuse of the investigative journalist's role and can be carelessly destructive of others, as was exemplified in the 'phone-hacking' scandal in the UK in 2012. There is a mutuality between police and media: one avid to present a positive image of themselves and to put 'spin' on their activities; the other omnivorous of police information on everything from investigating serial killers to passing on 'insider' titbits about celebrities (Reiner, 2003; Mawby, 2010). That tension can be dynamic and creative, but it can also be bitterly destructive and venal. So too, there can be an inherent tendency in the media to trivialise, over-simplify and report the superficial rather than the complex reality (such as the painstaking accumulation of evidence, or ambiguities about guilt; see Cushion, 2012). While the more responsible media play a 'guardianship' role about policing, it would perhaps be as unwise to trust oversight of the police to journalists as it would be entirely to trust politicians. What do 'the people' think?

'Vox pop'[31]

A research exercise into people's opinions was carried out in England and Wales by Ipsos Mori in 2010 at the behest of the then Association of Police Authorities, to ascertain what people felt and thought about governance of the police. (The subtext, of course, was whether there was any widespread popular support for the notion of the Police and Crime Commissioner, which the incoming coalition government evidently preferred to the existing police authorities, as we have already observed.) The Ipsos Mori exercise was not a conventional quantitative survey by mass questionnaire, but a focused *qualitative* study of people's views of police governance in four police regions, each chosen to represent a mix of urban and rural policing and economic variation.[32] The research, as Ipsos Mori itself points out, is not 'statistically representative'; that is, the conclusions 'are indicative and not generalisable to the wider population'. Rather, they are 'exploratory and discursive' (Ipsos Mori, 2010, p. 2).[33] Nonetheless, some of the general findings make interesting reading in the context of this discussion about governance and oversight of the police. There is a 'general desire' on the part of the public for 'greater visibility in police accountability' and:

> this translated into a strong preference for a visible and named figurehead [...] in each area. Participants thought that this figurehead should not only provide an element of visibility, but should also be a symbol of transparency and independence. (Ipsos Mori, 2010, p. 2)

The research indicated that participants wanted clear and unambiguous independence for the figurehead, and considered that the role could not be done by 'someone with an obvious political allegiance.' At the same time, a strong opinion about accountability was that the police could not be allowed to be self-regulating. Only a minority of participants wanted one individual who would be solely responsible for holding

---

[31] Opinion sampling from a random number of people, see Glossary.

[32] The four regions were Sussex, West Midlands, South Wales and Cumbria and the 'workshops' took place in these areas in August 2010 (Ipsos Mori, 2010, p. 7).

[33] Ipsos Mori went on: 'Qualitative research is not by its nature designed to be statistically representative. It is intended to be illustrative, providing detailed and insightful levels of in-depth understanding around a research topic' (2010, p. 7). This is a viewpoint with which we thoroughly concur, since it informs our approach too.

the police to account. Most considered that a panel was preferable which would work alongside the figurehead in 'both an advisory and scrutiny role' (Ipsos Mori, 2010, p. 3). This desire for visibility and transparency did not necessarily entail 'support for greater democratic involvement'. Indeed, participants were not only sceptical of any government devolving responsibility for police accountability but also questioned the 'knowledge base on which an electorate would [...] decide who should take responsibility' (Ipsos Mori, 2010).We cannot take these observations and comments as more than simply indicative of general public opinion, but a number of the points raised in this context of governance of the police bear closer examination. The preference for someone independent in the role of police scrutineer is of interest, particularly since the elections of the PCCs in 2012 were overtly political. We deal with the psephology of the elections in more detail in Chapter Two; it will be enough here to note that formal 'independence' was adopted by 12 of the 41 elected PCCs, together with 16 Conservative and 13 Labour Party affiliates. Whether that will be repeated at the elections in 2016 and 2020 is a moot point, but the preference for *non*-political affiliation was emphatic on the part of those surveyed. The 'near universal consensus' for political independence appeared to be driven by the belief that elected figureheads would lead invariably to decisions being governed by political motives (rather than a needs-based pragmatism) and the supposition that promises might be made that might not then materialise when the candidate was elected. Ipsos Mori remarked about this response that it was driven 'by a latent cynicism towards the political process and politicians more generally' (Ipsos Mori, 2010, p. 17).

The second general conclusion to be examined is the agreement by participants that the police should not be self-regulating. They felt that 'forces could not be trusted to do this in an objective and trustworthy manner' (Ipsos Mori, 2010, p. 10). In a separate survey carried out in 2013, Ipsos Mori researched the 'trustworthiness of the professions', and found that 89% of those surveyed trusted doctors, 82% trusted judges, 65% trusted the police, but only 21% trusted journalists and merely 18% trusted politicians (Ipsos Mori, 2013).[34] Of course these

---

[34] This is an annual survey, conducted by Ipsos Mori since 1983. The categories that 'rank' above the police include the clergy, scientists and TV newsreaders; while those below include civil servants, trades unionists and government officials. The rating for the police has risen from an average of 60% in the 1980s, and policing is still among the most trusted of 'professions'. The contrary picture is that 72% believed that journalists did not tell the truth and 77% thought that politicians did not tell the truth. That compares with 28% who did not think the police told the truth and 9% who believed doctors were untruthful.

data are impressionistic and survey a different cross-section of the population from those in the 2010 police accountability survey, but they indicate that most people rather guardedly trust the police. People feel that the police should nonetheless be subjected to oversight and governance by an independent person or body, who was actively 'visible [... and] publically [sic] accountable for the decisions made in relation to policing' (Ipsos Mori, 2010, p. 11).

A final point to be made is that few of those questioned wanted or expected the 'figurehead' to act alone. The strong supposition was that the activities of the 'figurehead' would be modulated through, and to an extent overseen by, 'a panel' either of experts or of elected councillors. This seems to be another example of the desire to balance power and accountability. It is perhaps unfortunate that Police and Crime Panels have to date proved less effective than hoped in modifying the actions of a PCC or in calling him or her to account.[35] While this particular view was asserted in the early years of the PCC role, it echoes what a number of commissioners have since told us: that the Police and Crime Panel seems to be largely ineffectual and largely irrelevant to what the Commissioner does or decides. This came to a head in mid-2014 when there were calls for Shaun Wright, the PCC of South Yorkshire, to resign when he was identified as the councillor responsible for children's' services in Rotherham in a report about the sexual abuse of children in the town. There was no suggestion in the vociferous calls for him to go that he could not do his job as an elected PCC, rather that it was inappropriate for him to exercise oversight of the police when both he and the police were criticised for failure to act.[36] This may help to explain the decision by the Home Secretary to build in some mechanism of 'recall' into the remit of the Police and Crime Panel so that it can then question, amend and modify what the PCC

---

[35] See the final part of Chapter Six.

[36] See, for example, the BBC report of 16 September 2014, titled 'PCC Shaun Wright resigns over Rotherham child abuse scandal', available at www.bbc.co.uk/news/uk-england-29220535. This is not the place to go into detail about the Jay Report published in August 2014 and Wright's refusal at first to resign. Its importance for this discussion is only that the incident pointed out how difficult it is to remove a sitting PCC. It was probably media pressure that led to Wright's decision: he had earlier resisted calls to resign from the Prime Minister, the Labour Party and from his own Deputy PCC.

is doing (May, 2014a[37]). This looks dangerously like a veto over the PCC, which in turn raises constitutional issues about the legality of a non-elected body frustrating the activities of an elected person.[38] *Vox populi*, the voice of the people, might be over-ridden by *vox constituit*, the voice of the appointed. This might in turn create ambiguities of control and authority in the relationship between the PCC and the panel. Others have called for a legal ombudsman or judge, to whom such issues of contention could be referred,[39] but it is still difficult to see how someone elected to a post can be subject to non-legislative rulings that are not derived from a popular mandate.Interviewee 51 goes to the heart of the dilemma when asserting that "The PCC cannot be held to account by people who are not elected. Only the people can do that." The crux of the issue is surely that when the PCC notion was first conceived, no one believed that there would ever be a reason other than a criminal act to remove a PCC who had been duly elected. The contingent point is that none of the existing accountability or investigatory mechanisms works. The IPCC can intervene only when a PCC has been accused of a criminal act; HMIC has no *locus* to investigate the actions of a PCC and, individually and collectively, Police and Crime Panels lack the mandate to suspend a PCC. In other words, the PCC role is inviolate other than by election at four-yearly intervals. We return to this later, in Chapter Six, when we consider the remit and powers of the Police and Crime Commissioner in the context of his or her own accountability. The debate has continued in the wake of Shaun Wright's resignation and, in the half dozen or so serious complaints against PCCs elsewhere, seems likely to induce some sort of (retrospective?) legislation or procedure to call serious PCC failings to account. Thus '*quis custodiet ...?*' continues as a moral and constitutional conundrum. One thing is sure: the 'invisible' police authorities were never this exciting. Interviewee 53 may have the last word for the moment:

---

[37] May was blunt in her condemnation, saying: 'There is a very good reason Shaun Wright is not sat here among us today. It is because he — as the publicly visible police and crime commissioner in South Yorkshire — was held to account by the people who elected him. The failure by the police, Rotherham council and other agencies in Rotherham, to confront appalling child sexual exploitation, is inexcusable and exposes a complete dereliction of duty.' (May, 2014a). In reality, Wright was not 'unseated' by the electorate; he resigned because of intense pressure from the media and those around him. May is being disingenuous.

[38] The technical term for this is acting *ultra vires* (outside or beyond one's legal remit).

[39] The proposal was informally discussed at the APCC Partnership Summit in Harrogate on 17 November 2014.

'As the elected representative of the people I am unassailable except by them or if I break the law.'

This brings us fairly neatly to examining how PCCs themselves conceive of their governance role of the police and their views on police accountability.

"There was something not quite right in policing"

'I had realised, sort of instinctively, that there was something not quite right in policing – all the scandals and complaints, the dissatisfaction people had with outcomes and the poor press profile – so doing something about that, remedying it if you like, had lots of appeal.' (Interviewee 54)

Interviewee 54's comment flags up to us the often unspecified unease with the way policing is conducted, and suggests that the police can be less than whole-hearted about embracing genuine reform. Too often, it seems, the "something not quite right" has to do with a superficiality in the police response to calls for greater accountability. Most of the PCCs to whom we spoke were agreed that the police needed 'reform', but varied in what that entailed. The common thread was, as Interviewee 54 tries to indicate, a sense that there was "something not quite right" about policing. The difficulty arises in articulating more exactly what that 'something' is. Views ranged from the police needing an infusion of 'fresh blood' from outside, to fill the top command jobs with people more versed in answering their critics (or more experienced in responding to calls for greater transparency), through to a need to ensure that the police understood that the balance of power had shifted very tangibly from the police themselves to the office of the Police and Crime Commissioner. Several PCCs noted an initial reluctance on the part of the chief officer teams to recognise that the fundamental shift had been from May's 'invisible' police authority, to a full-time elected individual who was going to have an impact on policing in a very tangible way.[40]

A rather testy exchange between one of the authors and a PCC (Interviewee 56) developed from an attempt to understand how this impact was going to work:

'...I was also very excited by the role: it represents the biggest reform to policing in this country since 1830.'

---

[40]   This is explored further in Chapter Three.

[*Interviewer:* Really? You think creating the PCC post is on a par with Peel's creation of the Metropolitan Police?]

'Well, not precisely since you push me, but it is a very profound and game-changing development. We have not begun to see the full effects of a people's representative in charge of policing yet.'

[*Interviewer:* Is that what you conceive yourself to be? In charge of policing?]

'In charge of the delivery, certainly.'

[Interviewer: Forgive me, but I understand the job to be primarily about accountability and that your function on behalf of the public that elected you is to hold the chief constable to account]

'Why, so I do'

[*Interviewer:* Where does the 'in charge of the delivery of policing' come from?]

'I think you are being very pedantic; what I mean is that I am responsible to the public for the delivery of policing that they want. Inevitably that means that I pay close attention to the conduct of policing, the priorities of policing and the results of policing in my country'

[*Interviewer:* you said 'country']

'I meant 'county'. This has not begun well, has it? Please do not harass me.'

[*Interviewer:* That is not my intention, but I want to know what you mean]

(Interviewee 56)[41]

---

[41] This sounds more bad-tempered than it was and there were actually some smiles during the exchange.

In several ways this extract raises important points of principle and that is why it has been given here verbatim. PCCs are not inviolate: they could and should be challenged by their interlocutors, especially when their 'sound bites' are probed and found to be rather woolly and exaggerated. Second, it is important to understand precisely how the PCC would translate these ideas and aspirations into the realities of action and what effect those actions might have. Third, the PCC is evidently irritated by rather persistent questioning about the importance of the new role and the relevance of police accountability to it, despite the centrality of that relationship and the need to understand its mechanics. Occasionally, PCCs seemed to get excited about a wholesale reform of the police (headed of course by themselves) when what is really at issue is how the governance of the police will go forward and how precisely the chief constable will be called to account by the PCC. The role may be "very profound and game-changing", as Interviewee 56 claims, but that should not mean that we the public are not privy to the means as well as to the intent. There was certainly ill-disguised astonishment at being challenged by a presumptuous interviewer, and while the exchange was taking place, the mask slipped momentarily to show the ardent and politically ambitious person beneath the PCC's characteristically bland public face.

Another PCC commented on his motivation to stand for office:

> 'I became a PCC because I was appalled by the way that the police had become separated from the public they were supposed to serve. The police answered to occasional national politicians and to themselves – not to the people. [...] the police authority was utterly futile: it did not hold the police force to account and merely okayed what the chief constable wanted. The chief did what he liked: he paid lip service to the authority and to the public, but you didn't have to be a genius to see that really he didn't care what they thought.' (Interviewee 58)

There is greater precision in this response, focused as it is upon the nature of accountability and the consequences of changing from the collective, if diffuse, responsibility exercised by the old police authority to the sharper power play of the elected individual Commissioner. Needless to say, the chief constable of this particular force parted company with the incoming PCC in short order, as was implicit in the description of the disappearance of the chief constable's 'okaying' mechanism. The point, though, is a similar one: real power has passed from the police to the PCC and this means that the chief constable and others now have to justify what they do, and account for the consequences of decisions they make and actions they take, to a single elected person who is watching them narrowly and persistently. In some forces, this call to accountability had happened in the time of police authorities, but such occasions were rare, HMIC said (McLaughlin, 2005). Now, of course, the salaried PCC is able to focus full time on policing and is able to track changes and the implementation of decisions on a daily basis. That was never possible with the more widely spread responsibilities and part time or occasional nature of the police authority.

Another PCC was in no doubt what the changes really meant and how accountability was increasingly a fact of police life:

> 'Among other things, including an insistence on community policing and engagement with the public, I have reoriented [sic] the police in this county to accountability. The chief officer team knows that they are answerable to me and that I will insist that they do what the public wants, and not what they think the public ought to have. There's a step change in process, and it's not surprising as a result that the crime has gone down.' (Interviewee 59)

It is not at all certain that the changes in accountability that this PCC has implemented have of themselves caused the drop in crime rates (these were falling anyway and may have done so irrespectively of the actions of the newly elected 'figurehead'; see Farrell, 2013). What is interesting here, however, is the direct correlation made by the PCC between his appointment and improvements in police responsiveness. The mindset of believing that they alone know what is right for the public is slow to change in the police – often because crime investigation is also slow to recognise new parameters – but change in function is what the PCC claims credit for.[42] Notably, serious and organised crime investigation seldom appears in the PCCs' spectrum of action. One wonders what priority is made for matters other than "community policing and engagement with

---

[42] Not always plausibly, see Sir Clive Loader's claims cited earlier.

the public", amid the "step change in process" and 'reorienting' of the police.

Additionally, this PCC believed that it was not simply holding to account that had changed, it was the thoroughness of engagement with the public. The PCC was streets ahead in such consultation:

> '[T]his is the point: the police cannot gainsay my consultations with the public. They can't say "Oh it's different in this town from that town" because I will have been to both and know what is going on as well as and often better than they do. The fact that I am tightly linked with communities and I represent the voice of the public are my greatest strengths and the fact that they are not connected in this way is the police's biggest weakness.' (Interviewee 52)

Not all the claims of impact and making a difference by PCCs can be quantified in this way. For most PCCs, the general remit encompasses something like this:

> 'I control the police budget; I hire and fire the chief constable; I am the voice of the people in the echoing corridors of police headquarters; I prepare and sanction the Policing Plan and I am the visible presence that ensures that the police are and will remain accountable.' (Interviewee 62)

What are described here are tangible processes, predicated on an agreed Policing Plan and paid for from a (shrinking) police budget, all of which are modulated through the person of the PCC. What this proposes is that systemic activities are 'personalised' through an individual, who is visible, present and persistent as a representative of the people. While this PCC can declare that all that happens is through and because of him, some more reflective commissioners had strong reservations about the quality of those at the top in policing and, consequently, worried about the leadership of an organisation in crisis:

> 'I thought that when I first came to this role that the chief officers (and many of the ranks just below them) were paralysed by ineptitude. They didn't know where they were going or how to get there. Very poor leadership was an issue, as was not having a clear sense of strategy; and everything seemed compounded by the awful 'inwardness' of policing, by which I mean that the police are self-regarding and

measured only against the yardstick of themselves and their peers inside the police.' (Interviewee 52)

It is not enough to have the systems in place to call the police to account, however assiduous the PCC may be. The suggestion is rather that the police themselves compound the problem of insufficient accountability by not being good leaders and by the internalisation of problems. This latter characteristic was memorably defined by another PCC as the tendency in the police "to mark their own homework" (Interviewee 64) and therefore not to be subject to external referents. Not surprisingly, the PCCs believe that they can supply this deficiency, and that:

> '[f]or the first time in our history, the police are held personally and collectively to account for what they do, and have to justify their actions, to someone acting on behalf of the people.' (Interviewee 51)

There may be a sense of aggrandisement underlying this assertion but there is no doubt that Interviewee 51 believes, along with many other PCCs, that holding the police to account is the central tenet of the Commissioner role. One or two PCCs did not fit this mould, and one in particular took delight in questioning what he was doing and why:

> 'I have to say that I'm not actually 100% convinced about the need for this role just yet. Don't get me wrong: I think that there is a need to hold the police to account, and the mandate for that needs to be democratic, locally chosen and locally accountable. I just need to be persuaded that you can vest all that power in a single individual and still represent everyone. From the experience of the last two years I don't think it's possible to do or have it all.' (Interviewee 65)

It cannot be wrong for the guardians to call into question the nature of their guardianship like this, and such reflectiveness may encourage us to believe that the role of PCC is not one for the power-hungry despite some bizarre reportage in the first few years. It is timely now to look in greater depth at the character and personality of those who have been elected as PCCs, to look at their motivations and ambitions in the role and to examine the psephology of the election in November 2012.

TWO

The psephology of the November 2012 election: motive, means and opportunity

'The Home Office ran the elections and did it badly because they were not experienced enough to know what to do and left all the organisation far too late, so people didn't know what was going on, and didn't really understand what the issues were. It was a typical British cock-up.' (Interviewee 51)

The election: obstacles and hurdles

The citation from a disaffected PCC with which this chapter begins is typical of the reaction of many Police and Crime Commissioners to the events and problems that beset candidates in the run up to the PCC election in November 2012 and in its aftermath. Many were unhappy with the speed and what they saw as the ill-preparedness of the election process, begun only months before, and some independents jibbed at the idea of having to compete as amateurs against sophisticated party political machines. The same PCC commented on the general impression that matters were rushed unnecessarily, just so that political parties could "get their preferences in", at a time of austerity in public expenditure:

'The PCC elections were going to cost a fortune at a time of great economic danger, and it was clear that the political parties had all judged this to be an opportunity to get their preferences in this position of considerable local power. So it was about cost, but also about timing too. The coalition government should have taken longer to consider what was involved and to have planned it more carefully: there was no real reason why the election of PCCs could not have waited until May 2013, but no, they had to run it as soon as feasible.

That was part of the weakness I saw, and so that's when I decided to stand.' (Interviewee 51)

Part of the problem about timings of the election was related to the government's wish to push through with the PCC elections because it had been a manifesto commitment,[1] but also because a substantial period could elapse before the next general election, by which time, they hoped, the PCCs would be 'embedded' in local policing. There were misjudgements about the amount of publicity the elections required to impact on public consciousness, and an assumption that announcing the *fact* of the elections would be enough to involve the electorate. There did not seem to the coalition to be enough time available both for the necessary legislation to be passed and for the preparatory processes to be completed by May 2012 to coincide with the usual local elections held annually at that time. The next feasible date was November 2012. Jenny Watson, Chair of the Electoral Commission, commented after the event on all these shortcomings, and proposed that:

> there are [...] lessons to be learnt from the PCC elections about the way elections are run, and specifically what needs to be done if there are plans to introduce more new elections or to create new elected public positions. [...] *The overriding lesson is that the Government cannot assume holding an election is enough on its own to inspire participation.* People have to know what they are voting for, and understand what different candidates might offer, in order to participate. And to make sure that voters can play their part easily, *those responsible for running the polls must have clarity far enough in advance of election day to allow for proper planning.* The legislation for Police and Crime Commissioner elections failed to deliver on both these points. (Electoral Commission, 2013; our italics)

To be fair, the Home Office was feeling its way with these proposals, since the concept of an elected individual to have governance of a police force was entirely new for England and Wales. But that should not be an excuse for failing to put in place adequate and comprehensive processes

---

[1] Adam White argues cogently that the 'privatisation' window at this time was open for such a short period in police forces because the government had become concerned that some aspiring PCCs campaigned on an anti-privatisation agenda and this could gather momentum (White, 2014b).

in time for the election itself, since the Home Office had had more than two years to do so from the time the coalition government came to power in May 2010. 'Clarity far enough in advance of election day' was not evident and there was insufficient thought given to informing voters and publicising the event. Candidate PCCs complained that they were not able to do a 'leaflet drop' to households as is common practice in general and local elections, and this prevented a wider 'sensibilization' of the electorate. Jenny Watson noted with some asperity that:

> the decision to limit public support to candidates in getting information about themselves to voters, so that candidate information was provided primarily via a website, was a mistake. (Electoral Commission, 2013, p. 3)

As the government had ruled out paying for a leaflet drop to all households in England and Wales on the grounds of cost, candidates perforce had to make use of a government website on the forthcoming elections that was neither well known nor 'hit' in any substantial numbers. There was a consequence to the frugality of this approach. Watson went on to observe that one of the outcomes of the government's strategic decision was that:

> Lack of information was cited as a reason for not voting in the election by more than five times as many non-voters at the PCC elections than at the May 2012 local elections. (Electoral Commission, 2013, p. 3)

Simply put, people did not know enough about the election; why it was happening, what it signified, who was standing and why, and as a consequence some may have been unable to make informed choices. As for the Home Office playing the major role in structuring the PCC elections, this was also regarded by the Electoral Commission as a blunder, because:

> the Home Office does not have the necessary expertise to set the detailed legal framework for holding elections. As a result some of the rules were confirmed too late, which caused confusion or a lack of certainty for candidates and electoral administrators. This is unacceptable. This expertise resides with the Cabinet Office, and they [sic] should have played a greater role. (Electoral Commission, 2013, p. 3)

The synapses of 'joined-up government' simply did not connect in this instance; there was confusion, a distinct lack of expertise and a degree of improvisation that characterised the Home Office's preparations for the election. There were other factors that also seemed to bedevil the election process, noted both during and after the event by academic psephologists and the specialist electoral bodies. Significant among these additional impacts was the timing of the election and the size of the vote. Toby James[2] noted that:

> Low turnout would not be a surprise because voter turnout is generally low or declining in many countries. It also tends to be lower in elections other than general elections. (James, 2013)[3]

James went on to observe that the timing was technically problematic too:

> November is a bad time for electoral officials who are busy updating the electoral register. This means that their resources are drained and they cannot invest in public awareness activities, as they might at other points in the year. (James, 2013)

Jess Garland and Chris Terry, in an Electoral Reform Society Report, noted acidly that:

> From the start, *the PCC elections looked set to be an exercise in how not to run an election.* [...] Candidates were kept away by huge deposits, unclear eligibility rules, vast electoral districts and high campaign costs. (Garland and Terry, 2012, p. 7; our italics)

We look at the issues of eligibility in more detail in a moment but it is worth noting here that the Garland and Terry analysis indicates that the costs to candidates of this election campaign were of a different order to those normally incurred. It is not clear why this should have been the case, unless the government was intentionally making the hurdles

---

high at the outset to discourage political extremists.[4] Nonetheless, Garland and Terry noted deprecatingly that:

> The deposit for [each candidate to contest] the election was set at £5,000; 10 times that required to stand as an MP or elected mayor. The size of constituencies also created additional sizeable costs. Our survey found that 93% of candidates experienced difficulties associated with campaigning over large electoral districts. (Garland and Terry, 2012, p. 13)

The 'large electoral districts' were, of course, the constabulary areas, which constituted whole counties or dense metropolitan districts like the West Midlands or Greater Manchester, and, in the cases of Devon and Cornwall or Avon and Somerset, much wider geographical areas still. These compare unfavourably with the much smaller constituencies for MPs or city mayors.

The size of the election territory was one thing; costs, as we have noted, were another; then the government raised the bar even higher for candidates. No one could stand who had a criminal record, even when that record entailed offences committed long ago. Among others, the Falklands War veteran Simon Weston stepped down from his candidature after it was revealed that he had had a conviction in his teenage years.[5] Others were excluded on the grounds of cautions incurred when they were young. The relevant legislation notes that:

---

[4]   When the notion of Police and Crime Commissioners was first mooted in the Conservative Party manifesto, a number of senior police officers, including Sir Hugh Orde (ACPO Chair) and Sir Peter Fahy (Chief Constable, Greater Manchester Police), commented that extreme right groups such as the British National Party or the English Defence League would seek to become PCCs and that this would have dire consequences for policing. See Kelly (2012); and Lord Imbert (2011), former Commissioner of the Metropolitan Police, who commented in a Lords' debate that: 'Those who are of the same political persuasion as the Bill's originators will, understandably, no doubt vote for this part of the Bill, but how will they feel when we have the first National Front, British National Party or other extremist party-political commissar?'

[5]   Michael Crick, a political commentator, brought the likelihood of disqualification to Weston's attention in June 2012, following which Weston withdrew: http://blogs.channel4.com/michael-crick-on-politics/teenage-crime-set-to-disqualify-war-hero-simon-weston/1179. Crick commented: 'In most other fields, of course, Simon Weston's teenage offence would be regarded as a "spent conviction" and disregarded, but the 2011 Police Act is extremely tough and makes no allowance for spent convictions.' See also Brookes (2012).

A person is disqualified from being elected as, or being, a police and crime commissioner if –[...]

(c) the person has been convicted, in the United Kingdom, the Channel Islands, or the Isle of Man, of any imprisonable offence (whether or not sentenced to a term of imprisonment in respect of the offence)

(Section 66, clause 3 of the Police Reform and Social Responsibility Act 2011)

It was pointed out to politicians that such youthful misdemeanours would probably not have excluded the candidates from consideration as police officers, all other things being equal, but the government stood firm on the principle that a PCC must be absolutely above reproach, even though the Home Secretary expressed regret that Simon Weston had withdrawn from the contest (see Crick in Note 5). Garland and Terry noted dryly:

Several of the disqualified candidates were disqualified for fines received as teenagers, some as low as £5, many decades previously. (Garland and Terry, 2012, p. 14)

Such exclusions bordered on the petty (see Travis, 2012a; Weston himself had been fined £30 for his offence) but the regulations as set out in the Act of 2011 have not been repealed or modified, so it is possible that they will still apply when the next rounds of PCC elections take place in 2016 and 2020.

Phil Mackie, a BBC election analyst, noted that:

When the original PCC elections took place in 2012, the overall turnout across England and Wales [...] was just 15%, the lowest in an election since World War Two. (BBC 2014)

The percentage turnout was less than half that normally obtained for county and local elections (held in May of each year when a third of councillors retire and elections are held to return or replace them); between 30% and 36% of the electorate turns out to vote.[6] The basic statistics of the voting in November 2012 looked like this:

---

[6] See the Electoral Commission's *The European Parliamentary elections and the local government elections in England and Northern Ireland, May 2014* and Chart 1 on p. 11, www.electoralcommission.org.uk/__data/assets/pdf_file/0010/169867/EP-and-local-elections-report-May-2014.pdf

Some 192 candidates stood for the 41 posts covering England and Wales [...] in the elections held in November 2012. Labour and the Conservatives fielded candidates in every area, with the Liberal Democrats putting forward 24 candidates. The results were: Conservatives – 16, Labour – 13, Independents – 12, Liberal Democrats – 0. (BBC, 2013)[7]

The Association of Police and Crime Commissioners (APCC) later made its own analysis of the results, noting that a number of successful candidates had previously served on police authorities, or with the police and some had been MPs. The gender split was also noted (see Table 1).

Table 1: Analysis of 2012 election outcome

Breakdown of PCCs	Percentage
12 members and 1 staff member previously in police authorities	31.7%
8 former Police Officers	19.5%
6 women	15%
19 current or former Councillors	46%
6 former MPs	15%
Overall vote share	
Labour	33%
Conservative	27%
Independent (Independents did not contest 7 of the 41 areas)	22%

Source: Adapted and modified from the table on APCC's website, available at http://apccs.police. uk/?s=elections+2012

The *Telegraph*, normally supportive of the Conservative party line, noted rather testily (and inaccurately) that:

---

[7]   The full list of candidates, together with notes on those who proffered themselves and then withdrew, can be found in a *Police Foundation* document, dated 31 October 2012, at http://thewomensresourcecentre.org.uk/wp-content/uploads/ pcc_candidates_update.pdf

The elections [...] had been planned for two and a half years and cost more than £75 million to stage. But widespread indifference among voters led to some of them [PCCs] winning office, and a potential salary of up to £100,000 a year, with the support of less than 10 per cent of electors. (*Telegraph*, 2012)

The dismay at the low turnout was echoed by the Electoral Reform Society:

Unfortunately on 15 November 2012 less than 1 in 5 members of the public chose to take up this opportunity [to vote]. This flagship policy was poorly delivered and failed both candidates and voters alike. (Garland and Terry, 2012, p. 7)

Worse was to come:

A poll, conducted by Populus in the last week of January 2013, showed that only 11% of respondents could correctly name the person elected for their area. In other words, after spending £75 million holding the elections and millions more [on] staff and resource office holders, nearly 90% of Britons have no idea who their elected police and crime commissioner is. (Garland and Terry, 2012, p. 7)

Garland and Terry concluded with damning succinctness that:

It is clear that voters were suspicious about the nature of the post, confused about the reasons for conferring election upon it and in the dark about those standing for it. A failure to engage voters in this election meant that many simply chose not to participate. (Garland and Terry, 2012, p. 11)

All this suggests that the pithy assessment by Interviewee 51, that the 2012 election was "a typical British cock-up", may not have been far from the truth. When the subsequent elections take place in (May) 2016 and 2020, it is evident that some reform must be introduced to the voting and electoral procedures if candidates are to have, in treasured governmental phrase, 'a level playing field'.

Party invitations

Garland and Terry went on to analyse the political party involvement in the 2012 election and produced an interesting table (recreated in Table 2) that highlights the relative political party inputs into contested 'seats', and that showed that only Labour and Conservative contested *all* the available posts; the other parties were selective about where they fielded their candidates. The Liberal Democrats, perhaps already smarting from an electoral drubbing in the May 2012 elections,[8] fielded slightly more than half the available posts (23), exceeded by UKiP (by one, 24), with other right wing and single issue parties and organisations registering candidates in single figures. Of most interest, perhaps, was the appearance across 34 of the 41 electoral areas, of independents, some of whom in some cases (including Lincolnshire), ran against each other in the second round play-offs.

Table 2: PCC candidates, by party

Party	Total candidates
Labour	41
Conservative	41
Lib Dem	23
UKIP	24
English Democrats	5
Other	58*
Total	192

Note: *54 of 58 'Other' were independent candidates, of whom 12 were elected.

Source: Garland and Terry, 2012, p. 15; reproduced with their kind permission.

In a later report for the Electoral Commission, Colin Rallings and Michael Thrasher noted that total votes cast in the PCC election were almost 5.5 million, out of an electorate of some 36.3 million in England and Wales. Differentiating the two countries gives these outcomes:

> Of the 37 Police and Crime Commissioner (PCC) contests in *England*, 15 were won by the Conservatives, 12 by Labour and 10 by independent candidates.

---

[8] and, perhaps, their 'wipe out' in May 2015.

In *Wales* [with four available seats], independents won two seats, and Labour and the Conservatives one each.

The electorate for the PCC contests was nearly 36.3 million – 34 million in England and 2.3 million in Wales. Nearly 5.5 million votes were cast, making the overall turnout 15.1%. This is by some way the lowest turnout ever recorded in a nationwide election.

The police authority area with the highest 'ballot box' turnout was Northamptonshire (19.8%) and that with the lowest was Staffordshire (12.0%). (Rallings and Thrasher, 2013; our italics)

The results for the various 'seats' can be seen in Figure 1.

James Cousins, an Associate of the Local Government Information Unit, made a general analysis of the results of the PCC elections in the course of which he asked whether the PCCs will be seen as the first of what may be a number of local services' commissioners. Might there be 'educational commissioners' and 'health commissioners' following where the PCCs had led? He also made this thoughtful comment on the nature of politicised elections:

> In modern times the UK has tended to elect generalist politicians to collective bodies, any specialism from a portfolio comes from appointment, not election, to that portfolio. Even the relatively recent innovation of directly elected mayors has only changed the election to that of an executive, rather than deliberative, position – the mayor still has general responsibility for a range of public services. (Cousins, 2012, p. 16)

In some ways, the presence of 12 independents within the 2012 body of PCCs bucks the trend that Cousins observes; because, as we saw above, some of the independents are well versed in policing, having been police officers or having served on police authorities, so they would be seen as having specialist knowledge or 'insider experience' which a generalist politician would not. We cannot see the election of the independent PCCs in isolation; they have to be at least part of the expression of disillusionment with mainstream politics that has been evident since about 2008, not least of which was sparked by the MPs' expenses scandal (see Martin, 2014).Cousins was upbeat about what the 'independent' vote signified:

Figure 1: Results of the PCC elections, England and Wales, November 2012

Legend: Dark Grey = Conservative
Mid-Grey = Labour
Light Grey = Independent

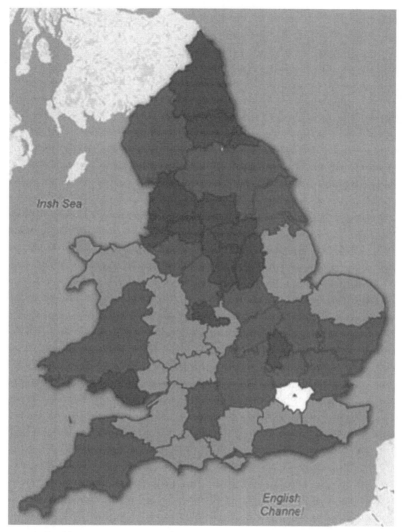

Note: London did not vote.

[...] that 55 independent candidates managed to clear a fairly significant nomination process shows there remains a strong feeling that the position [of PCC] should be independent. Nomination requires a deposit of £5,000 and 100 signatures of support, a significant hurdle before you even consider the costs of running a campaign in some incredibly large constituencies. (Cousins, 2012, p. 7)

What might turn the 'significant hurdle' of a one-off event into a more general trend of some political impact would be the election of more independent PCCs in 2016 and 2020, or their significant presence in other local polls, such as for mayors in conurbations. That currently does not seem likely, despite an evident ground-swell that rejects conventional party nominations and a continuing rumble of public dissatisfaction with Westminster.

The Police and Crime Commissioners: a question of one's standing

Useful though the steady emergence of statistics and hindsight analysis has been in the wake of the 2012 PCC elections, the data only tell part of the story. We must consider something more immediate, that is, the individual Commissioner's 'take' on his or her election to the role and ascertain what, looking back, struck them as important about their candidature. There are qualitative questions about their experiences to which it would be helpful to know answers:

- What motivated them to stand?
- Was this a one-off chance to govern the police?
- How was the opportunity to 'throw one's hat into the ring' created?
- Were they approached or was it their own decision?
- What factors influenced them locally?
- What was their experience of the election itself and their competition with other candidates?
- Do they have any regrets?
- How do they feel about being returned by 'the lowest turnout ever recorded in a nationwide election' (Rallings and Thrasher, 2013)?
- When they look back on the experience, how do they assess what they went through?

We may not get all the answers we would wish for, but the PCCs' responses in interview were sufficiently detailed about this aspect of the process to give us 'rich detail' that is lacking in the purely quantitative analysis.

First, the trenchant view of an independent, one of the 12 elected:

'I threw my hat in the ring and was amazed to get in on the first ballot by some margin.[9] I thought it would go to play-off but it didn't. I beat the openly political candidates out of sight – even with their party machines behind them. I'm not a political animal really, but I am vocal and articulate, and I know that I speak for the communities, not to a party manifesto. That gives me huge independence of judgement: I don't have to tread any line formulated elsewhere.' (Interviewee 58; our footnote)

Modest expressions of astonishment at winning are fairly constant in our interviews of both party and independent candidates, so we should aim off for such typical self-deprecation as being a characteristically British trait, but, as we have already observed, a number of the successful candidates were well known locally, some are former police officers or ex-military who spoke to their electorate with some authority,[10] and in some areas there is no doubt that the election of an independent was the result of genuine anger against the established political parties and a desire by some of the electorate to reject all political affiliation in the local ballot.[11] So too, it seems in retrospect probable that the fears about formidable party machinery steamrolling over all alternatives were exaggerated.[12] The situation was different in reality. Many of the constituency level party organisations, geared to returning MPs, were ill-suited to county-wide campaigning, and having to cut across conventional administrative boundaries caused them procedural problems.[13]

---

[9]   This was fairly unusual. The Electoral Commission (2013, p. 7) noted that 'Thirty eight of the 41 November 2012 PCC elections were held using the Supplementary Vote electoral system, and of those, five were concluded without having to proceed to a second round because the winning candidate received more than 50% of valid first preference votes cast. Three PCC elections were held using the first-past-the-post electoral system as they had only two candidates standing.'

[10] Matthew Davies (2014b) noted that PCCs from the police or the military tended to conceive their role in quite narrow management terms; PCCs from a political or business background saw themselves in broader and more conceptual terms as crime reducers. We detect that these roles have now more or less fused (see Chapter Six).

[11] Others, even more recalcitrant than these, spoiled their ballot papers deliberately; see Travis (2012b), who noted 'there is evidence of more deliberate spoiling of ballot papers as a protest than is usual' in the PCC elections.

[12] See Peachey and Lee (2012).

[13] See for example Cousins (2012), p. 7.

By contrast, the comments that follow are by a PCC who was his party's choice and who is adamant that, however small the percentage polled, his election was valid and acceptable:

> 'I was already in public service. I had lived in this city area for the best part of 30 years, I know the place really well and my family grew up here. I know what blights our communities and I know how prevalent crime, serious, real, major crime is and I am determined to do something about that. Fortunately the good citizens of [...] agreed and elected me in 2012.'

> [*Interviewer:* 'what was the percentage of the public who voted?']

> 'About 14%'

> [*Interviewer:* 'do you regard that as a mandate?']

> 'One vote would be a mandate if there were no others against, and though it was a small percentage it was nonetheless a clear mandate.'

> [*Interviewer:* 'involving only a third of those who normally vote in local elections']

> 'Yes, but the election was rushed and ill-considered in 2012 and the ruling coalition government was determined to force the issue through come what may, and holding it in November, divorced from the usual local elections in May, meant that fewer people knew about it and, because it was a cold winter's day here, not so many turned out. I expect far bigger percentages will vote in 2016.' (Interviewee 60)

There is a tone of assertive self-justification in this PCC's comments which reflected the almost stereotypical responses from PCCs when pushed by us to respond to a charge that they were elected by too small a percentage genuinely to claim a governance mandate. Many, though, were evidently disappointed that the entire populace had not rushed to the polls to elect them on a tide of popular fervour:

'I secured a full nomination and election on the first count, which was excellent.'

[*Interviewer:* 'what was the percentage of your potential electorate that voted?']

'Just over 16%. Not huge, I grant you [...] but I got more than anyone standing against me got, and as a result I feel perfectly justified in acting on behalf of the people. And that's the point: I represent *all the people*, not just those who voted, even those who voted for me. And, I might add that the percentage that voted for me personally is larger than that which has returned many county councillors, so I am not going to take any moralistic nonsense from them about my election.' (Interviewee 62; speaker's own emphases)

Criticism of the election results and the size of the turnout was largely generated by the media rather than by local councillors (some of whom probably could not resist a sly dig), but the suggestion of the 'aggressive/defensive' in Interviewee 62's reply is echoed in another PCCs' comments. This response, from one of the six former MPs to stand in 2012, is of interest when he was asked about his characteristic and rather weary defensiveness:

'I was quite surprised when I got in, but this was because people knew me and knew what they were getting. I'm plain spoken and have a high local profile.'

[*Interviewer:* 'would you call 15% a mandate?']

'It was more than that in proportionate terms: a greater proportion of people voted for me as PCC than voted for me when I was an MP. The principle is precisely the same and this is what you have to remember: I represent the people, whether they voted for me or not, just as when I was in Parliament; and a majority, however small, is enough in a democracy, to return a candidate to elected office. Indeed, with PR [proportional representation] in Europe you can gain disproportionate representation, like the minority right wing parties and the Greens.'

[*Interviewer:* 'Forgive me but you sound defensive']

'I probably am, because I have had to defend my election a number of times and it gets wearing. No disrespect to you, but it can seem impertinent to suggest or imply that somehow I should not govern because more people did not vote for me. One vote is enough if it constitutes the majority.' (Interviewee 70)

It may be that, following extensive criticism both in the media and from academic analysts about the low numbers turning out to vote, PCCs have rehearsed to themselves, and others, some robust defences of taking office through a small mandate. Our experience in posing such questions in interview was twofold: most PCCs disliked being challenged in this way, repeating the mantra that one vote in majority was a mandate, and many thought that things would be different next time (May 2016 and again in May 2020). Nearly all appeared uncomfortable when pressed about the size of their share of the vote.

Another former MP seems to relish the absence of party discipline in his new post and evidently enjoys his "strong voice locally". Nonetheless, he is not particularly persuaded of the value of what he calls the "glued-on" PCC role:

'I knew in 2012 that the elections for the PCC role would give me a strong voice locally on crime and the police and I wanted very much to be the person who spoke to the police on behalf of the public. Even if I didn't actually rate the glued-on role of the PCC very much.'

[*Interviewer:* 'is it a come-down from being an MP?']

'It's certainly different; but in a sense I am the public's representative in a much more immediate way than I was as an MP: I have no party line, no Whip and no national agenda to get in the way of or modify what I represent.' (Interviewee 65)

A number of PCCs, and not only those who stood as political party candidates, expressed a degree of uncertainty about the closeness of the PCC role to "political affiliations", principally because their feedback from the public has suggested strongly that its preference, at least within their force areas, is for independent non-political approaches to the job, rather than party candidature and national party 'line'. This next PCC commented that his motivations to become a PCC were "quite complex", and although the notion of democratic oversight of the police appealed to him as a paradigm for local governance, his uneasiness about the "emphasis on political affiliations" persists:

> 'The reasons for my standing as a candidate PCC were quite complex and I was unsure at the outset whether this governance model would work. We had not tried democratically-elected oversight of the police before and I wasn't certain that this was the right way to do it. I'm still uneasy about parts of it; particularly the emphasis on political affiliations. David Cameron declared that the role would not be political when it was first suggested, but he has gone back on that and the party machines have taken over. That's what I'm against: there's enough politicking in policing already, we don't want more of it under some party banner or other. It's not what the people want either: they tell me that they want an independent person dealing with them and the police, not a party member.' (Interviewee 66)

By 'politicking', Interviewee 66 appears to mean politically motivated interference in or influence upon policing, usually from the centre and personified through the Home Secretary or Policing Minister. Yet the notion of the PCC itself, as we explored in Chapter One, was a political creation, and its adoption by the Conservatives was a political act. It may seem somewhat eccentric therefore, to deprecate the 'politicking' of the PCC in policing when that was its fount and origin. We might note in passing that the police have always been the subject of political comment and 'interference' from 1829 when a 'Tory' Home Secretary[14] created the 'New Police', through to Labour Party leader Tony Blair promising in 1995 to be 'tough on crime and

---

[14] Sir Robert Peel, later Prime Minister.

tough on the causes of crime'.[15] Political engagement in policing, in other words, is nothing new and the police are used to it, as they are used to cross-examination in court or the preparation of case files: it is not necessarily something they relish, but it comes with the job. It is probably true to say that 'politicking' in the police becomes more evident the higher in rank you go, but no one is immune and most chief officers as well as their PCCs have come to realise that it would be impossible to remove the politics from policing in any meaningful way. This chief officer confided to us that:

> 'I have no fear whatever of accounting for what I or my officers do and I have great pride in the police. The worry for me has been the intrusion of party politics into the democratic accountability of the police, which must usher in partisanship.' (CO3)[16]

The worry about political "partisanship" is expressed frequently and freely by chief officers, of whom this comment is characteristic, and it seems to stem from concern that the police themselves will be sucked into supporting a particular political 'line' or platform:

> 'The main contention is when party politics intrudes to attempt to influence the mode of policing and we won't have that. There have been some strong disagreements about the PCC trundling into departments with tame politicians in tow and we've had to make it perfectly clear that we are

---

[15] In 1995, this was Tony Blair's second speech as Leader of the Labour Party, two years before he won the election and became Prime Minister. He declared in Brighton at his party's Conference that: 'It has always been absurd that the debate about crime in this country has some talking of its causes and others of the need to punish criminals. Sweep away the dogma - *tough on crime, tough on the causes of crime*: reform of the criminal justice system; a comprehensive programme to deal with juvenile offending; tackling drug abuse; proper treatment of victims and witnesses; tougher penalties on violence or guns; a crackdown on those who make life hell in their local neighbourhoods through noise or disturbance and, for the first time, a nationwide crime prevention policy in which in each community, police, schools, businesses and local government plan together how to beat crime.' [our emphasis]. The full speech is archived at www.britishpoliticalspeech.org/speech-archive.htm?speech=201.

[16] It may be helpful to note again that police chiefs (COs) who were interviewed are numbered from 1 to 19; PCCs from 51 to 74. The numbers are arbitrary but the distinctions are important.

not about re-electing PCCs and we are certainly not about re-electing [a political] party.' (CO3)

There is probably a necessary distinction to be made between 'PCC-as-local-governance' and 'PCC-as-political-animal', but it can be disingenuous of the police to suppose that, as here, they "won't have" party politics intruding "to attempt to influence the mode of policing", when most of the 'modes' of local policing, particularly Neighbourhood Policing Teams (NPT), are political in origin anyway, and some of those undertaking NPT tasks, the PCSOs, are arguably 'political' creations.[17] Nonetheless, the point that Interviewee CO3 makes is a valid one: it does not behove police forces to endorse a *party* political stance, and chief officers have to be as alert to deflect party political interference in their world as they are acutely sensitive to deflect external interference away from policing operations.[18] This echoes the views of many prominent police officers in both speech and print, the most notable of whom was probably Sir Robert Mark, Commissioner of the Metropolitan Police, when he wrote in 'Peelian' terms in 1977 that:

> We [the police] discharge the communal will[;] not that of any government minister, mayor or public official, or that of any political party. (Mark, 1977, p. 12)

As Robert Reiner observed: 'an important ingredient of the legitimation of the British police was non-partisanship' (Reiner, 2010, p. 32); it would seem that such a view is not only still prevalent, but is insisted upon by the current generation of chief police officers. All the same, the general political influence within and upon policing is something that has always been there (Reiner, 2010[19]). Fraser Sampson commented on the inevitability of policing being mixed with politics:

---

[17] We may include rural Wardens and Community Support Officers, who may not have a police function or ambit. Nonetheless, PCSOs and their ilk were very much joint products of the Labour government and the Metropolitan Police Deputy Commissioner (Sir Ian Blair as he then was) in 2002, given statute under the Police Reform Act of that year. See Caless et al (2014), p. 99.

[18] See Caless and Tong (2013).

[19] Robert Reiner sagely observed in *The politics of the police* (2010, p. xiii) that 'The concern of politics in a just society should be with minimizing the need to resort to policing, not to compete in its enhancement as the parties do today'.

the undeniable effect of law enforcement activity on people's lives, liberty, and livelihood makes the confluence of politics and policing in maturing societies not only inexorable but also inevitable. (Sampson, 2012, p. 5)

Sampson suggests that those who decry political 'interference' in policing are simply intransigent or unrealistic in supposing that the clock can be turned back. The fusion of the two aspects of 'policy' and 'police' has gone too far for that (for a contrary view, see Stenning, 2007[20]). However, this did not prevent one PCC claiming that his motivation to stand as a candidate came about because he wanted to end interference in policing by the government:

'I thought that the government approach to policing is flawed and only demoralises officers and I wanted to do something about that.' (Interviewee 54)

Another PCC denied that party politics played any real part in the PCCs' approach to their job; rather, commissioners nobly put their party politics aside and concentrated on being genuinely representative:

'I do think that the PCC role is more politicised by outsiders than by PCCs themselves. I know half a dozen fellow PCCs well and although they are generally a different political complexion from me, I have never, ever, seen their views get in the way of their representative role: they simply don't follow any party diktat.' (Interviewee 64)

We have no reason to doubt this PCC's sincerity, and if PCCs *are* able to set their party politics to one side while they exercise their due governance of the police, then that is something to be applauded. What might be apt would be to visit this statement again when the re-election campaigns of 2016 or 2020 can be assessed.

One PCC, responding to our questions about the size of the electorate that voted him into office, was robust in his defence of the "pitiful" numbers involved, but asked in his turn whether not taking office would have been missing "the chance to make a difference".

---

[20] Phillip Stenning (2007, p. 32) argues that 'the idea of "police independence" in England and Wales remains today, as they always [sic] been, unclear, and open to contestation and debate.'

Answering his own (rhetorical) question, he concluded that his duty was clear:

> 'Of course turnout was poor – we all know that, but we have to make the best of it. I got elected by some margin, but the overall numbers were pitiful, I know. But does that mean I should turn down the chance to make a difference and to improve relations between public and police just because some people were not prepared to turn out on a wet November night? No.' (Interviewee 66)

Another PCC described "a number of bases" that were influential in his motivation to stand for office, noting that the newness of the Commissioner's role entailed inevitable teething problems. He told us, rather breezily, that he:

> '[...] was persuaded to [become a candidate] by my [political] party on a number of bases that I found persuasive: one was that I know this area really well, having lived and worked here for years. Another was that I have strong views about the police which I have aired in the past and which chimed with my party's approach, the third is that I was willing to stand and the fourth and last is that I was known in the area as an honest broker and that probably got me elected.'

> [*Interviewer:* 'it was a small percentage that voted wasn't it?']

> 'Absolutely, but that doesn't bother me. I got in on first preference and that is what was important: I didn't have to run off against the other candidates. Besides, this is a pioneering job; no one has tried to do it before.' (Interviewee 68)

It is not entirely apparent how the novelty of the PCC role is of itself a justification for a small turnout, but the Commissioner is more concerned that he "got in on first preference" and can use that as a matter of pride because he "didn't have to run off against the other candidates". In other words, accepting the small percentage of voters from the beginning can be translated into a personal virtue because there had been no requirement to count second preferences. Evidently, the world of politics takes such somersaults of logic in its stride.

One PCC with a military background had already served on his police authority and was convinced that his "shoe-in" election to office resulted in a drop in crime, a factor stemming from his determination "to make a difference to people's lives". This was the exchange we had:

'[...] when the opportunity arose to stand as a candidate for the PCC job, I was pretty keen. I knew about policing because I had been a member of the police authority and I knew about disciplined service because I had served in the Armed Forces. I was a shoe-in you might say. When I was elected I was determined to make a difference to people's lives and I can successfully claim to have done that. Since my election, crime has fallen here by more than 10%.'

[*Interviewer:* 'how is that attributable to you?']

'Because I have insisted that the police respond to community concerns about crime, get out of their cars and actually engage with people. For far too long now, the criminal justice concerns have been with the offender and not with the victim, and I don't exclude the police from this kind of thinking. Now, with my new emphasis on community policing and response to the public, the police focus is properly on the victim of crime – where it should be.'

[*Interviewer:* 'That may well be, but where is the causal link between your election and the fall in crime?']

'It should be obvious.'

[*Interviewer:* 'Not to me. Crime fell elsewhere in England and Wales by 9%. Is that attributable to you too?'][21] (Interviewee 59)

It seems to be a common mythology among PCCs that the general fall in crime is directly because of their interventions in policing rather than being any part of a general trend.[22] What is indisputable, of course, is

---

[21] See ONS (2013).

[22] Sir Clive Loader, PCC for Leicestershire claimed the same in a letter to *The Times*, see Chapter One.

that the trend has been downwards for some years in recorded crime, and this has happened across England and Wales in a uniform manner, beginning well before the election of PCCs.[23] That makes it unlikely that a force initiative or a PCC's Police and Crime Plan, however assiduously implemented and executed, was a causal factor. It is of a piece with the hubris of the claim by the Commissioner of the New York Police Department, Bill Bratton, that

'Crime in New York is down; blame the police' (Bratton and Knobler, 2009).[24]

Since the noise and tumult of the 2012 election have long subsided, a more sober approach in England and Wales has determined that the statistics suggest more widespread, and probably more complex social, explanations for the fall in crime than the individual interventions of PCCs (see McKee, 2014).

Another example of what might be called 'aggrandisement of office' is found in comments (given verbatim below) by a PCC who both wanted to keep politics out of policing but at the same time intended to subject the police to close scrutiny by "their masters":

> 'I'm passionate that politicians shouldn't run a police force. I don't like the police, I don't trust them and I want to get rid of the police culture. I want to change them. [...] They forget who the public are and who their masters are! They need watching. I don't trust them.' (Interviewee 61)

There is a level of anger here that is not entirely explicable, especially as the speaker is a former police officer whom you might expect to have a little fellow feeling for his erstwhile colleagues. But the comments verge also on the incoherent, confusedly bracketing together a visceral distrust of the police and their 'culture', with an adamant assertion that those in the role of PCC should not have a party political affiliation.

---

[23] In ONS (2013), the summary reads: '[...] figures from the Crime Survey for England and Wales (CSEW) estimate that there were 8.6 million crimes in England and Wales, based on interviews with a representative sample of households and resident adults in the year ending March 2013. This represents a 9% decrease compared with the previous year's survey. This latest estimate is the lowest since the survey began in 1981 and is now less than half its peak level in 1995.' The trend downwards is very clear.

[24] A number of commentators (principal among them Bowling, 1999) noted that crime had fallen elsewhere in the USA and that, although Bratton's incisive approach was having a public impact and was generating headlines in plenty, the causal factor was missing, as here. See Walsh (2001); and Willis et al (2007).

The PCC's sense of the Commissioner's own office is shown in his use of the word "masters" to describe himself and his PCC colleagues,[25] but he admitted later in his interview that some of his confusion may arise from the fact that he is "a poacher turned game keeper". A chief police officer observed of another independent PCC that:

> '[...] he is overwhelmed – the consequence of being one individual. Sometimes he can't see the wood for the trees. He works really long hours, inordinately long hours.' (CO13)[26]

It is possible that standing as an independent brings in its train an absence of peer support or a lack of machinery for consultation and advice which party affiliates may enjoy. Indeed the same chief officer went on to say:

> 'Our PCC is independent so doesn't have an affiliation with a party to support him. Political influence would give much more support to [him] and it would be easier for [him].' (CO13)

Other independent PCCs have not raised this with us as an issue, and most seem to relish their sturdy self-reliance. Another (party political) PCC made much of how considerable persuasion was needed to make him stand for the election, particularly because he "knew nothing about the police" and thought his standing for election "a crazy notion". What decided him appears to be his perception that the police were well intentioned but "didn't have even a faint clue about being businesslike". He described the process of persuasion like this:

> 'I got into this via local politics where I ran a large department after a background in private industry where I ran my own company. At the time the role was first discussed I had no intention whatever of running for the PCC post; I thought it was a crazy notion, but that was because I knew nothing about the police. Then someone rang me up and asked me to think about standing. She suggested that I went along and had a good look at my local

---

[25] It was evident in the context of the interview that he did *not* mean that the public was the 'master' of policing but only the PCC.

[26] We examine the PCCs' 'long hours culture' in detail in Chapter Seven.

force before I made a decision one way or the other. I did this and found a police force that was absolutely determined to do the right thing but that didn't have even a faint clue about being businesslike.' (Interviewee 57)

Another PCC entered the fray willingly as a candidate but found himself subject to the 'second preference' round, from which he emerged victorious, believing robustly that he speaks for the people despite a small mandate. Interestingly, this PCC describes the transfer of the levers of power from the police to the Commissioner's office, the consequences of which, he declares, make him "unassailable":

'I stood as a candidate and actually got the election on the "2nd preference votes" beloved of the Liberal Democrats (though I am not myself a Liberal Democrat).[27] [...] I speak for the people.'

[*Interviewer*: '15% of them?']

'Yes, if you want to be picky; it was a low-ish turnout, but I was elected [...] and the police had better listen. [...] As the elected representative of the people I am unassailable except by them or if I break the law. Actually, I'm unassailable by the police as well: they can see that I have the real power now and that power has moved from them to me.' (Interviewee 53)

We examine the mechanics, meanings and effects of this transfer of power in greater detail in Chapter Three, but the point to make here is that the police appeared to be slow in acknowledging a change in the *realpolitik* of local accountability, and that in turn may explain, in part at least, the abrupt departure of some chief constables within a year or so of the PCCs taking office. The sense of a lack of quality in police leadership, noted above by Interviewee 53, led another PCC to decide to stand after he had carried out a reconnaissance:

---

[27] The speaker means that s/he failed to get an overall majority on the first ballot, but when 'second preference' votes were counted, s/he won on the second ballot. Voters were able to indicate, in order, their preferences among the candidates; a measure proposed and introduced by the Liberal Democrat Party in 2012.

'I was approached by the county rep of the [...] political party and asked if I'd stand. I wasn't a party member, but they thought I could do it. So I went to talk to the serving chief constable (and was frankly not impressed) and also the President of ACPO (ditto).[28] What I saw made me want to stand as a candidate and want to make a difference to the way that policing was done to people.' (Interviewee 52)

The motivation here was evidently one of dismay at the calibre of the status quo, and that was an inducement for a number of candidates to seek office, though not many have explained to us what attracted them to the job with the frankness of this PCC:

'I had a pre-existing interest in politics and the police, as a state agency, was inevitably part of that interest. The PCC job though, had other inducements which included being a really substantial activity, locally based and it was one where I could see myself making a difference to the quality of people's lives. Therefore it was very attractive as a prospect. It was also very new. [...] I don't think I expected to get elected so I thought I'll give it a go and see what happens. It was a bonus that I got in, really.' (Interviewee 54)

In a sense, with this observation, we have come full circle to those repeatedly modest expressions of surprise at being elected at all. Perhaps the last word should be given to the same PCC with whom we began who, asked about the nature of political influence within the office of the Commissioner, replied with characteristic, even predictable, robustness:

'The role should not be based on party politics. The only proper stance for a PCC is as an independent.' (Interviewee 51)

Regrettably, only time will tell whether "the proper stance" is reflected in the psephology of elections, whether it is in the return of an elected

---

[28] Sir Hugh Orde, former Chief Constable of the Police Service of Northern Ireland. The President of ACPO was elected by the chief officers of the police service of England and Wales until its demise in late 2014, after PCCs had withdrawn 'top sliced' funding. It was replaced by the National Police Chiefs' Council (NPCC) – see Glossary.

panel of overseers of the police (along the lines of the Stevens' Inquiry) or whether we retain the existing model of a single Commissioner with the remit of governance of the police, moderated through a Police and Crime Panel.

Summary

The election of PCCs in November 2012 was a flawed business and the shortfalls in organisation, publicity, legislation, candidature and timings may all have contributed to a low turnout in the polls. PCCs are practisedly robust at defending their meagre mandate but there seems to be a whiff of siege mentality about their repetition of the mantra that 'one vote is enough if it is a majority'. Clearly, they would have liked more. What is also clear is that the police were slow to catch on to the fact that power had been transferred very tangibly from them to the PCCs after the election. An inability to cope with this new regime may have been the primary cause for the departure of many serving chief constables. The long-running debate about the politicisation of the police has been re-catalysed by the advent of commissioners and many relish their new challenges in purely party political terms. Some of their claims to have reduced crime in their first years of office need to be interpreted in the context of a general fall in crime levels over a much longer period.

It is time now to find out what the PCCs think of his or her chief police officer teams, and reciprocally, what members of those chief officer teams think of their commissioners. It is not a place for the faint of heart.

THREE

Is the law on my side?
Relationships between the PCC and the chief police officer team

'The PCC came into this job on the back of a tiny number of people who voted obediently with their party machine and he has no proper mandate to control the police at all. And we're stuck with this party hack who now tells us that he is empowered to make changes and that we'd better all look out. He actually said that in our first chiefs' team meeting. You can imagine what the comments were afterwards.' (Chief Officer 1)

'I think that this PCC has made a difference already and working with him is exciting and different. He really does have a finger on the pulse and he is frighteningly intelligent. What I really respond to is that you only have to explain once and he remembers. And once he tasks you he lets you get on with it – unlike most police chiefs I've ever known, who normally stand over you breathing heavily and saying that they wouldn't do it like that.' (Chief Officer 6)

'Most chief constables in 2012 were rampant egoists or else on some kind of personal power trip which would not acknowledge any mandate of the people to hold them to account unless it was flourished under their noses, because of scandal, error or ineptitude.' (PCC Interviewee 51)

'I was pleasantly surprised to find that most of my chief officer team is not at all averse to change; they listen well and they challenge back to me, which is healthy and stimulating.' (PCC Interviewee 64)

This chapter will explore in some detail the nature of the relationship between the PCCs and the 'top team' of chief police officers. The range of opinions is demonstrated graphically by the citations with which we begin this chapter: there is a spectrum of opinion on both sides – Commissioners and Chief Officers – that is worth closer analysis. It would be helpful at the outset to consider the differences, from the *police* perspective, between the Police and Crime Commissioner and the police authority s/he replaced. We will then consider the seismic effects on the chief officer team of the PCC's arrival, examining the dynamics of the relationship between PCCs and chief officers and how practical day-to-day contact is handled, as well as charting a tangible, if occasionally grudging, change (on both sides) from hostile resistance to qualified approval, as the PCCs bed into the role, and the police in turn take their measure of the incumbent. The chapter concludes with an exploration of the practical ways of working together the chief officer teams adopt to respond to the PCC.

'Paradise Lost' or the 'New Jerusalem'? The demise of the Police Authority and the rise of the PCC

'I've done 23 years as a cop and this is my first PCC so, like nearly everyone else, what I can offer are first impressions only. All that I can compare her with is the old police authority and she has a bigger IQ than all 17 of them had added together. I think that she is dynamic and businesslike in a way that the police authority, seeking consensus and compromise, never was.' (Interviewee CO5)

Police officers who have served more than five years are familiar with police authorities (PAs), and those at or near the top of policing will have had considerable dealings either with the authority in formal session, or through hosting visits by the authority, singly or collectively, to policing specialisms, or through interactions with individual authority members. The response of the chief officer quoted above pretty much encapsulates the general police view of PAs as well-meaning locals who largely left policing intact. The cleverer and more dynamic PCC who has replaced Interviewee CO5's police authority seems an altogether different proposition.

We noted in Chapter One that the prevailing 'central political' view of the PAs of England and Wales was that they were 'invisible', unelected and largely ineffectual. What we did not explore then was the attitude of the police themselves to the PAs, nor, in any detail, did we capture the PCCs' views on what they replaced. What were police authorities? How did they come into being?

Force area or county police authorities, established by the 1964 Police Reform Act, replaced local 'Watch Committees', whose function had persisted over many centuries as a quasi-judicial body, often consisting of lay magistrates and justices, overseeing the work of parish constables and shire officials charged with keeping the King's Peace.[1] The establishment of county police forces, following the Municipal Corporations Act of 1835, required a more formal oversight, and Watch Committees were empowered to appoint 'constables to keep the peace', and also took on a formal, local governance role, which persisted for more than a century[2] until the reforms contingent on the Royal Commission on the police in 1962. The Police Reform Act of 1964 grew out of the Commission's findings (Taylor, 1997, pp. 12–43; and Emsley, 2009, Ch. 3, pp. 67–90). Floyd Millen and Mike Stephens summarise this historical transition with admirable conciseness:

> The transition from watch committees to police authorities, the role of the Justices of the Peace and their powers to appoint chief officers along with the significant impact of the various Acts of Parliament all provided the foundation for the current structure of policing and police authorities. (Millen and Stephens, 2011, p. 7)

In 1964, PAs consisted generally of an indeterminate but small number, of whom two thirds had to be elected councillors and the remainder were drawn from the magistracy. We may note here that even half a century ago, those with an elective remit were preferred, by a proportion of two to one, above those who were simply appointed. Subsequent legislation in the 1990s established 17 members of a police authority as the norm,[3] nine of whom were elected councillors (often, but not always, from across the political spectrum) and seven were 'independent' appointees, of whom three were magistrates, plus a chair who could be any of these (Rawlings, 2002, pp. 212–21).

---

[1] Phillip Rawlings has particularly good coverage of the history of policing before 1829, see Rawlings (2002), Chapters 3 and 4. Clive Emsley covers the modern period well in his histories of policing (1999, 2009, 2014). The best treatment of modern policing in England and Wales is Tim Brain's (2010); while a general popular history is by Richard Cowley (2011).

[2] This is true of local borough-type police forces. County forces were overseen by 'Standing Joint Committees' which contained both elected councillors and appointed Justices of the Peace (Rawlings, 2002; Emsley, 2009).

[3] London and some of the larger metropolitan forces had 23, as did amalgamated forces, such as Devon and Cornwall.

The proportions have changed from those in the first authorities, but elected councillors still held the majority. It is important to observe that these were not direct elections to the authority. Members were already-elected county councillors who, for a variety of reasons, were assigned to or made part of, the shire police authority. Appointees, by contrast, had to be approved by the Home Office (nominally the Home Secretary) before they could take up post (Myhill et al, 2003). There seems to have been a lack of assessment or challenge about the degree to which central political influence was exercised in such appointments and a tacit silence locally about who was assigned to the police authority from among the elected councillors, and why. We have searched in vain through various county archives and police authority minutes for *any* standard criteria by which elective councillors were appointed to the PA. Indeed, aside from their being worthy citizens, resident in the county, the required 'profile' for appointed members is similarly opaque. Commentators seem equally baffled by the imprecision within selection or appointment decisions. Matthew Flinders argues in his cogent 'Distributed Public Governance in Britain' (2004) that local governance is 'largely devoid of an underpinning rationale' and, in an article in 2006, Adam Crawford notes in an extended nautical metaphor that 'networked governance' in policing is a matter of 'steering, rowing and anchoring', but he does not laud the role of the police authority in doing any of this work. Even the 1964 Act itself was vague about who would serve on a police authority and why. Section 2 (4) merely notes that:

> The magistrates to be appointed members of a police committee or watch committee shall be appointed at such times, in such manner and for such term as may be prescribed by rules made by the Secretary of State; and the other members of a police committee or watch committee shall be appointed at such times, in such manner and for such term as may from time to time be determined by the council responsible for appointing them. (1964 Police Reform Act, Part 1, Section 2 (4))

Might there have been, as one sceptical chief officer observed in 2011, a very restricted 'gene pool'[4] from which either elective or appointed police authority members were drawn, and that:

---

[4] Tellingly, the same phrase is used of the available pool of police officers for promotion to chief officer rank, by PCCs, see later in this chapter.

> The police authority is the last major bastion of white, male, middle-aged, middle-class, conventional do-gooders who have finally made it beyond Neighbourhood Watch. (Caless, 2011, p. 133)

Caless (2011) goes on to show (pp. 133–4) that this view, while trenchantly held by some in the police, was not always supported by the statistical data for police authority membership. Nonetheless, he concludes that, as a matter of preponderance, 'the majority of authority members *are* male, white and middle-class' (Caless, 2011, p. 134; his emphasis). It would seem that few left-wing radicals, independents or mavericks, outside the metropolitan forces, were appointed to their respective PAs and that therefore neither political impartiality nor political diversity were much in evidence in those who oversaw the police (Reiner, 2010).

PAs controlled the policing budget, held their chief constables (nominally) to account for the actions of the police and could hire and fire incumbents (subject to Home Office agreement).[5] But even early in their existence, PAs were derided for the rather ineffectual way they oversaw local policing (Millen and Stephens, 2011), and for the inherent weakness of the system established under the 1964 Act, whereby they could only 'call for reports' from the police in instances

---

[5] Which could be problematic. Relations between Police Authority and Home Secretary could be strained, or even diametrically opposed, when it came to the forced removal of chief constables. Two instances in the early part of the 21st century may be illustrative. The first involved the Chief Constable of Sussex, Paul Whitehouse, who reluctantly resigned in the wake of a shooting scandal after having been hounded publicly by the Home Secretary – though supported by his pressured Police Authority (Johnston, 2001). The second concerned David Westwood, Chief Constable of Humberside Police, who refused to resign after his force had failed to pass on intelligence to Cambridgeshire Police (which might have prevented the employment of school caretaker Ian Huntley who murdered Jessica Chapman and Holly Wells in Soham in 2003). Despite being heavily criticised (by Bichard, 2005) and suspended after pressure from the Home Secretary, David Westwood was reinstated in post, supported by his PA. Westwood eventually retired seven months later (Home Office, 2004; Reid, 2005). It may have been these instances, coupled with similar clashes in the Metropolitan Police (Caless and Tong, 2013), that led politicians to seek new ways to deal with autonomous and sometimes immovable chief constables. The abolition of Police Authorities might be traced back to David Blunkett's impatience (Home Secretary in both the examples outlined above) with the cumbersome Police Authority machinery that was needed to 'hire and fire' chief officers. This led to Labour calls for 'elected authorities' who would oversee policing (2003), which later transmuted into the Conservative Party's 'directly elected PCC' in 2010.

where the authority was perturbed.[6] Chief police officers themselves could be scathing:

> 'Police authorities were pussy cats; you could do anything with them. My old boss in my previous force used to take the entire 17 of them to the skidpan or to the dog kennels so that they could play about with cars or puppies. He always said that he could then do anything he liked with them. They were certainly not the brightest or most able of people, but I thought them well-intentioned.' (CO4)

Bryn Caless, in his 2011 empirical study cited previously, noted that some of the wilier chief police officers had brought manipulation of the police authority to a high state of sophistication and method. One commented directly:

> 'It's well worth wooing the police authority with lots of attention and giving them small 'victories' which don't really matter but which make them feel good about themselves. I always give them choices – carefully constructed so that it is a win–win for me – and they feel so happy at making a decision, that they're easy to manage.' (Caless, 2011, p. 135)

Such manipulation may not have been universal, but it was widespread and may have contributed to the occasionally rather contemptuous attitude of many police officers towards the body supposed to hold them formally to account. The general failure of PAs properly to challenge the police is well documented (McLaughlin, 2005; Myhill, 2007). Millen and Stephens undertook a comprehensive empirical survey into PAs in 2010–11 and concluded bluntly that:

> The evidence from our interviews, questionnaires and the literature shows that whilst the functions and the responsibilities of police authorities are important, the current structure and arrangement has resulted in police authorities being unfit-for-purpose. (Millen and Stephens, 2011, p. 20)

---

[6]   Mike Brogden criticises this rather constipated and tentative approach to police governance in an incisive 1977 article.

They also noted that a principal difficulty lay in the anonymity of police authority members: the public simply had no idea of the PA's function or who was a member. This was compounded by police authority deference to police operational priorities and a tendency not to challenge what they were told:

> One of the key challenges for police authorities is that many people are not aware of their existence. This problem is augmented by the fact that police authority members see themselves as having minimal power to influence policing. (Millen and Stephens, 2011, p. 19)

The researchers' findings are corroborated by a comment to us from a chief officer who had served a number of PAs:

> 'The old police authorities were not remotely businesslike, but were almost unthinkingly supportive of the police. They brought a range of pretty modest talents [...] bickered a lot in their meetings and were phenomenally slow to make decisions and were hardly ever strategic. They seemed to divide up their time between work in committee and getting involved in internal force governance. We didn't like that, and it was never really part of their remit to be down among the weeds of policing, but they wanted to feel that they belonged, I guess.' (CO3

Ian Loader (2000) placed the anonymity and general failure of the PAs to challenge in the context of 'the fragmentation and pluralization of policing' that cast doubt on the mechanisms of local governance. He went on to argue that questions about democratic legitimacy lay more with disengagement from the public than with the growing complexity of what constituted 'policing' (Loader, 2000). HMIC was apt to agree (2010, para 10, p. 7).[7] Yet, however much we contextualise the role of police authorities within a general disregard for the public voice locally (Rix et al, 2009), the PAs' failures robustly to challenge the

---

[7] HMIC following an inspection of ten police authorities in 2010 observed: "*Police authorities are not yet demonstrating that they can respond effectively to the demands being placed on them. Police authorities need to improve their understanding of the risks and threats to policing and their scrutiny of value for money if they are to provide effective governance in the future.*" (HMIC 2010, p.7) Prescient thoughts indeed, if not already nudged that way politically.

police seemed to be born of their faith that the police were doing a difficult job 'in difficult circumstances'. Members of authorities were not impressive individually, said the police, but as far as the service was concerned, PAs 'wanted what was best':

> 'I had a soft spot for the old police authority: it didn't have the sharpest knives in the box, and I guess that some of the time we got away with bloody murder, but essentially you know they were supportive. They largely believed that the police did a good job in difficult circumstances and at public meetings went out of their way to make sure there was unanimity of views and supported us 100%. OK some of them were time servers, some didn't really know the time of day, and a couple were on a massive ego trip (especially the JPs [Justices of the Peace]), but by and large they wanted what was best for both the public and the police.' (CO1)

The well-intentioned but rather amateurish approach of police authority members observed by this chief officer chimes with academic analyses undertaken in the period leading up to the abolition of PAs. Andy Myhill et al (2003) noted that the 'structure of accountability had no meaning for the public, as they had no or little understanding of the Police Authorities', (p. 16). Those engaged in such research might have negatively influenced wider political opinion about the efficiency and effectiveness of local 'platonic guardians' (Loader, 2006). From the police point of view, however, there existed plenty of machinery already to ensure accountability. Dermot Walsh and Vicky Conway noted a 'bewildering mixture' which included:

> [...] administrative mechanisms for handling citizen complaints; civil actions and criminal prosecutions in the courts; the exclusion of improperly-obtained evidence in criminal trials; internal disciplinary procedures; whistle-blowing mechanisms; judicial enquiries, inspectorates overseeing professional standards; local police-community consultation fora; and democratic oversight from local/regional assemblies and national parliaments. (Walsh and Conway, 2011, p. 62)

This catalogue does not excuse the police from accountability to its police authority, nor does it excuse the police authority for less than rigorous implementation of challenge (Myhill et al, 2003; Gravelle and

Rogers, 2011); but it is surely permissible to suggest that, in the context of the 'bewildering mixture' of means to ensure their accountability, the police may have ducked or discouraged robust challenge from PAs because they saw it as yet another hurdle to clear. That exculpation, however, presupposes that the challenge when it came from the authority was indeed 'robust'. The opposite is more likely to have been the case (Smith, 2009). Millen and Stephens noted that:

> Our research identified that police authorities were increasingly preoccupied and focused on managerial and organisational issues rather than the strategic policy issues governing local policing. (Millen and Stephens, 2011, p. 5)

It is not surprising then, that PCC Interviewee 57 thought that his arrival in post signalled a radical sea change in the relationships between the police and direct local oversight:

> 'I am not the police authority, I am the people's representative. The old police authority function was to rubber-stamp what the police did and to be excited by fast cars or helicopters. My job as a PCC is to ask why and how, not to be diverted by shiny equipment or cute puppies. I have refused all such trips and inducements, because I know what the police are trying to do when they inveigle people into going on them.' (Interviewee 57)

Here speaks the authentic voice of one determined not to be manipulated by devious but plausible police officers into 'rubber-stamping' anything, and it resonates with the observations by CO Interviewees 1 and 4 cited earlier, where the equivalents of "shiny equipment and cute puppies" were commonly used to "inveigle" the police authority. Of course, it may be of point that the PCC cited here is a former police officer: far from being diverted, he may have been a former 'diverter' in precisely the way described. (In interview, his detailed knowledge of the tricks and stratagems used to manipulate PAs suggests that he had employed them himself.)

Where does this leave the police, vis-à-vis the old police authority and the current PCC incumbent? One chief officer described the change in succinct staccato:

> 'The PA were elected councillors who had other things [that they had] to do, the PCC is *one* role – this is

significantly better. Scrutiny of the CC [chief constable] is better, healthier for a public service.' (CO1; speaker's own emphasis)

The action of holding the police to account by a full-time, salaried and elected person is self-evidently more rigorous than that provided in the past by a police authority (Gravelle and Rogers, 2011; Millen and Stephens, 2011), and, in the view of the officer cited, "healthier"; but the opinions of chief officers on the benefits of a PCC replacing a police authority are by no means unanimous:

'I never had any problems with the old PA because essentially they were pro-police and easy to manipulate to get what you wanted. To be fair, that was usually more kit, more people or more cars and the authority usually played ball. They were so on-side that they fell over themselves to understand us and "the hard job we do". Also, nobody knew who they were – even sometimes on their own councils – so being on the PA gave them status and authority which they didn't have anywhere else. Naturally they were supportive. Now it is different and you find yourself edging into a room to get past the PCC's ego and it is all or almost all confrontational.' (CO2)

Others are far less nostalgic for the days of the police authority and its amateur ways:

'Police authorities were pretty tedious groups; I have served two and I did not find the membership of either very impressive. They were some of them elected and some of them appointed, which made a strange mix and they often saw the PA job as explaining and defending the police to the unruly populace. They didn't do this well and we didn't like them doing it. Meanwhile the public had no idea who they were and cared less.' (CO6)

Indeed, a negative view of the quality of the people who served on police authorities is more common among the chief police officers whom we interviewed than any praise for the PAs' existence or regret at their demise. Here is a typical view from a chief officer who began his close observation of PAs at a lower rank:

'The police authority was worthy and well-meaning but quite ineffectual. The old chiefs used to run rings round them. I had been Staff Officer to one of the top team and saw how easily the PA was manipulated by experienced cops, used to getting their own way with HMIC, the Home Office and everyone else: a sweetener here; a day out on the firing range there and the police authority would practically nod through the precept rise.[8] It was quite painful to watch sometimes, because the members of the PA were so eager to please and so convinced that the police were the only hedge against anarchy.' (CO5; our footnote)

Perhaps an epitaph for the last amateur or 'lay' oversight of the police can be given by this chief officer:

'Police authorities were quite poor at what they were supposed to do. I've had two in my time as a copper, and they were not really very impressive. Some of the members clearly only thought about the role on their way to a meeting, whereas others were trying (and failing) to use membership of the police authority to advance themselves within the county council. Some undoubtedly used their status to get preferential treatment: one we had in my old force was a landowner, and he'd be forever ringing up because local builders and others would fly-tip on his land. Because he was in the PA we had to turn out every time: it was a joke!' (CO9)

One might be tempted at this point to say that the disappearance of PAs was less 'Paradise Lost' and more 'Brave New World'[9] as the PCC was ushered in, yet even here there is blend and compromise, since some individual police authority members made a fairly seamless transition from PA to PCC. Despite what some police officers and PCCs have suggested to us, the differences between the two modes of police governance were never simple or stark. One chief officer put it like this:

---

[8] An increase in local council tax to supplement the police budget.

[9] 'Paradise Lost' is a poem by John Milton (1608–74) and *Brave New World* is a dystopian novel by Aldous Huxley (1894–1963). Huxley's novel's ironic title is from Shakespeare's *The Tempest*, where the innocent Miranda exclaims: 'O brave new world / That hath such people in't' (Act V, scene 1).

'The real difference between the PCC and the police authority is that now everything is demanded immediately. The PA could be kept sweet with interim papers but this PCC wants it straight away, or there is hell to pay.' (CO20)

It is appropriate that we should now turn our attention to the relationship between PCCs and their chief officer teams, and chart police responses to the elections of 2012 and what impact the arrival of the PCC had.

"Some kind of magic PCC bullet": the ebb and flow of views

We can chart a slow change from the original dismay and defensiveness with which chief officers greeted the arrival of PCCs, through the steady departure of 'old school' who did not feel, or whose PCCs did not feel, that they could cope with the changes, through to (a sometimes unwilling) admiration for the PCC and his or her approach to the job:

'I see my job [as] not simply to do the PCC's bidding, but to make his ideas work in practice and also to remind him when necessary that there are other kinds of policing that are equally important. But *there isn't some kind of magic PCC bullet*: we still have plenty of crime, we have attrition,[10] and we have slashed budgets. The picture isn't easy and it's going to get worse, but essentially I feel that the PCC is on our side, with one inquisitive eyebrow cocked. I can live with that.' (CO10; our italics and our footnote)

How the police move from, in many cases, marked hostility to the PCC to, in some contemporary interviews with us, cooperative admiration, is a journey of unwilling culture change and a slow acknowledgement of the *realpolitik* of power in policing having slipped from the police's hands into those of PCCs, whose firm grasp is now unmistakeable. We look first at the comments from a chief officer who has already worked

---

[10] The interviewee is referring to the notion of the 'attrition of crime' where there is a progressive diminution of effective 'brought to justice' outcomes in reported crime: in, say, 100 crimes that take place, fewer than half are reported to the police at all, and of those a very small percentage make it to the courts and to a judicial outcome. See Burrows et al (2005).

for two PCCs and who notes a marked difference, "wildly varying" between them in terms of approach and personality:

> 'I have worked for two PCCs and the contrast between them could not have been greater. On one side, there was intelligence, commitment, understanding and the willingness to visit and listen. A pleasure to work with and to serve. On the other side was a brazen personality cult, a refusal to understand the complexity of policing (particularly major and serious organised crime) and a person who hardly ever visited the 'harder' bits of policing, such as covert investigation, homicide, or public order, and who concentrated instead on a rather fatuous self-promotion of simplistic 'beat bobbies'. This means that even between two constabularies in different parts of the country – one urban, the other rural – you could get wildly varying PCCs with very different approaches and talents.' (CO7)

The stark contrast in personality and approach in different PCCs observed by this chief officer is inevitably a reflection of the varied make-up of those who were elected to office; there is almost a 'Jekyll and Hyde' character in the differences between the 41 PCCs. We saw in Chapter Two how wide the spectrum of candidates for election was,[11] and it should come as no surprise that there is variation between the personalities who were returned,[12] just as there is between the 'constituencies' that the PCC represents. The PCCs themselves acknowledge the variety in their number, one commenting to us on his colleagues, like this:

> 'You must not assume that being eccentric and having lousy judgment are prerequisites for the job, even though some of my PCC colleagues exhibit these characteristics in spades.[13] There are six or seven really good PCCs who are transforming the policing landscape, perhaps up to a dozen who have opened up the system and made policing

---

[11] Though 99 of the 192 candidates (52%) had had prior experience as an elected politician (see APCC, 2012).

[12] A House of Commons Library Research paper (Berman et al, 2012) notes, for example, that the *successful* PCCs were local politicians (19), ex-military (7), national politician (MP) (6), police officer (6) and magistrate (5) (see HASC, 2013c).

[13] A card-playing metaphor that means plentifully or immoderately

transparent, and about 22 who are absolutely bleeding hopeless.' (Interviewee 58; our footnote)

Such gleeful venom is uncharacteristic of most of those we spoke to in the PCC ranks, but there is general agreement that their role is more dynamic and far-reaching than anything envisaged or accomplished by a police authority. PCCs themselves went on to note that, in some instances, the police responded to the change with belligerence:

> 'The police are highly political with a small 'p', internally and they thought that I'd respond to bullying by the chief officer team. They were right: I bullied back. The police are paradoxically brutally powerful in their professional actions but painfully sensitive personally to criticism or attack. Time after time, these great blustering bullies caved in when I stood up to them and collapsed when I went on to the offensive.' (Interviewee 54)

A number of commissioners remarked on the aggressive reception they had from their chief police officer teams when they began work after the November 2012 election. In plenty of cases, like that cited above, the aggression was reciprocated and there were some fraught encounters. Here is one PCC's recollection:

> '[Relations between me and the chief officer team] did not begin well. We started like fighting dogs, snapping and snarling at each other. I was wary and so was the chief officer team: we sort of circled each other for a bit with hackles raised. It is simple enough to see why. I was the new boy, the new broom come in to call them to 'democratic account' for the first time ever, and they were very, very cautious. (Interviewee 69)

The original reception given by the police to some PCCs bordered on the overtly hostile:

> 'I saw this in the first meeting, the sort of disguised belligerence that underlay everything they said. They even sat aggressively: jaws thrust forward, arms folded, lots of eye contact – like preliminaries to a fight or an arrest. Well, they'd got a fight all right.' (Interviewee 53)

Other PCCs looked on with some incredulity as chief officers seemed to embark on a course of wilful self-destruction, occasioned by their reactions to being criticised:

> 'There's something self-destructive about the way that chief officers, when criticised, run full tilt, head down, into a brick wall and then look surprised when they hurt their heads. The chief looked amazed when I sacked him: I was astonished that he was astonished. How wet did he think I was?' (Interviewee 57)

Although there was much reserve in the general police attitude towards the new 'governor', most of the real dismay and dislike was located at the chief constable level it seems; the rest of the chief officer team was often more content to watch and wait. This comment is typical of many we heard:

> 'The police chief team seemed to resent me, and I was mistrustful of them. The "sitting" chief constable left soon afterwards – it just blew his mind having to answer to a politician elected by the people, instead of deciding himself what was best in his nannying way.' (Interviewee 70)

Other PCCs encountered resistant and obstinate obstruction further down the police ranks. One PCC characterised the 'blocking mechanism' like this:

> 'It's actually further down that the genuine resistance to the PCC role is felt most strongly. I don't mean at superintendent rank, because there they are either at the top of their professional expertise and content to be recognised as leaders in their specialty or they are looking for a promotion to the strategic ranks, and so have an interest in how things operate at the higher level. I mean really from sergeant upwards: cynical, suspicious, hard to convince and doggedly immovable if they choose to be. The inspectors are the worst.' (Interviewee 64)

Another PCC confronted police resistance by cutting the middle management layer out of his consultations. He believes that this tactic was highly effective:

'There was soft resistance at the ACPO chief officer team level; some harder resistance at the 'Head of Profession' level (Chief Superintendent) and some rather spiky resistance at Inspector/Chief Inspector level. So I instead went straight to sergeants and constables and met more than 700 of them in the first two months. I fixed lots of small niggles – ranging from poor equipment to badly organised shifts – so the front line eventually said "Bloody hell, we can work with this bloke" and they backed me.' (Interviewee 57)

Having police 'rank and file' backing the PCC, led (asserted Interviewee 57) to the chief officer team deciding that they would have to work with him after all, and the "soft resistance" ended. Another PCC observed that he had to engage in "tough conversations and some arm-twisting" to get his way and ensure that his views prevailed, even though parts of the chief officer team had already left. He saw the situation in this way:

'The real problem was not the old chief officer team because they went relatively quietly; it was the layers below them that posed the biggest obstacle because they were really resistant to all and any change. There were lots of pretty tough conversations and some arm-twisting to register the transfer of power to me and that this would require a change of police habits as a result.' (Interviewee 54)

By contrast with the handful of PCCs who saw the lower ranks as being the major obstacle to change, a substantial number of our PCC interviewees commented that once "the incumbent chief constable" had departed, the commissioner could begin with "a clean sheet" and bring in a leader with whom it was possible to work. The signals that such departures sent, and the new appointments that followed, were unmistakeable:

'I had to let the incumbent chief constable go and there were anyway hard questions about the chief's time in office that were nothing to do with me. It is clear that I was seen by him as the last straw. His angry departure gave me a clean sheet and a chance to put someone into the job that I could have confidence in.' (Interviewee 64)

Another remarked:

'It has helped that I had my own choice appointed as chief constable and that has strongly influenced the success of what we have put in place. We think alike and we want the same things. He worries more than I do about budgets and targets, and he's very picky about detail, whereas I am very broad-brush, but I guess we complement each other.' (Interviewee 70)

A newly-appointed chief constable told us with a grin that:

'My PCC is brilliant and does nothing badly. She is just fantastic at selecting chief constables!' (CO20)

All the same, the often abrupt, occasionally acrimonious, and sometimes media-featured departures of chief constables, encouraged a general feeling of unease in the police:

'At first, all chief officers were very wary of the PCCs across the country. I suppose it didn't help that the incumbent chief constable here departed in short order.' (Interviewee 64)

The same interviewee continued:

'some chief officers went because they were not willing to operate in a hot kitchen. Some felt that they were not equal to the new demands that PCCs would make of them – mostly the sitting chief constables – and their departure has been largely unmourned.' (Interviewee 64)

It is not entirely true that the departing chief constables were "unmourned". One chief officer to whom we spoke remembered the departure of his 'sitting' chief constable with some sadness and empathy:

'I was sorry to see the Chief go; it was like watching an old battered stag going off to die because a new and younger rival had replaced him. The Chief was old school of course, and I had often been impatient with him when I was serving lower down the scale, but it was still sad. He was so bitter. The PCC was quietly ruthless about it, and very soon had her own choice in as replacement, and then things really started to move.' (CO5)

Quiet ruthlessness characterised the actions of many PCCs in encouraging those who opposed them to go. The PCCs of course, as we have noted in our title for this chapter, had the law on their side, in one sense at least. The normally impassive House of Commons' Home Affairs Select Committee (HASC),[14] looking quizzically at the right of PCCs to dismiss chief constables, registered some astonishment at the unfettered powers that had been granted to the commissioners under the Police and Social Responsibility Act 2011:

> [...] it is very easy for a police and crime commissioner to remove a chief constable, even when the stated concerns of a PCC are about operational policing matters or are of an insubstantial nature. The statutory process provides little safeguard [...]. (HASC, 2013b)

There have since been suggestions that the role of the Police and Crime Panel be enhanced so that statutory consultations, together with greater powers to scrutinise and perhaps delay a PCC's decision to sack a chief constable, can be invoked (May 2014). At the time of writing, no such amendments have been made (and may indeed require further legislation, since fettering or modifying the legal powers of an elected individual cannot be undertaken lightly). A chief officer, observing his PCC narrowly, noted that the incomer was as capable of manipulating his Police and Crime Panel as some chief police officers had been at manipulating their PAs:

> 'I don't mourn the police authority at all: what makes me hoot is that some of them now serve as the Police and Crime Panel to advise the PCC. He runs leisurely rings round them and clearly doesn't take them seriously, which pisses them off no end, but there isn't a thing they can do about it.' (CO11)

Police and Crime Panels apart (and many of them do indeed contain former members of the police authority),[15] it was the departure of incumbent chief constables that really triggered change and signalled

---

[14] A very powerful group of cross-party politicians, chaired at the time by the occasionally maverick Keith Vaz MP. For an example of the HASC's accountability and oversight work, see HASC (2014).

[15] We look at the PCPs in more detail in Chapter Six.

to the police at large that PCCs meant business.[16] Some 18 chief constables (8% of all chief officers, but 44% or nearly half of the chief constable rank; *three times the norm*) departed within the first year of the arrival of PCCs. This compares with 15 chief constables who 'did not complete their fixed-term contracts' over the three-year period 2008–11 (Winsor, 2013). A few of those who went in 2013 were due to retire anyway, but undoubtedly the arrival of PCCs was a catalyst for 'churn' in the topmost police rank. [17]

Others in the chief officer team quickly adapted to the new *realpolitik*:

> 'Well, I didn't know what to expect, so I planned for the worst possible contingency. Then things started to change. This PCC listened, and listened very carefully to what we told him. He sought our views. Decisions were made quickly. My ideas and those of my colleagues were encouraged and acted on (for the first time, to be honest). [...] Of course the incumbent chief constable was heavily resistant to the idea of being called to account: he was of the school who hated his judgments being questioned. He didn't do 'challenge'. So he went – extremely swiftly. I blinked and suddenly there was an interview process in place for his successor.' (CO10)

Another chief officer thought that the changes contingent on the arrival of the PCC were for the better, echoing a well-known lager advertisement:

> 'This PCC reaches parts of the community that the old PA never did.' (CO12)

Another chief officer seems to relish the fresh, upbeat qualities that the elected PCC brings to the equation, including being "dynamic and inexhaustible":

---

[16] That, and their determination that they would no longer allow Force top-sliced money to finance ACPO.

[17] Nearly 7% of all chief officers and about 36% of chief constables, spread over three years. So in an average year about five holders of the chief constable rank are 'churned'. The change in 2012–13 was just over *three times above the norm*; a significant drift of experience out of the rank.

'The PCC is a real contrast [with the police authority]: he is dynamic and inexhaustible. I have never seen him downcast or at a loss (though I suppose he must be sometimes; we all are). He is professionally well-briefed and commands language well: he can say the same thing ten different ways to ten different audiences, each tailored to suit. He is a real go-getter. What's most important about him is that he is elected, and is therefore legit[18] in holding the police to account. I know it was only 15% but that's more than the PA ever had.' (CO4; our footnote)

The PCCs themselves seemed to be in no doubt what was involved in the adaptation of the police to their new system of 'democratic accountability'. One PCC, noting what a difficult job policing is, nonetheless made it clear that he would not tolerate 'an "I don't need to be told" attitude' on the part of his police officers:

'Look, I am a champion of the police: what they have to do is very difficult, and they are required to do what ordinary citizens do not: if there is a fight, the police have to go in and sort it out. They can't stand at the side and wait for it to finish. If there is a major pile up on the motorway, they can't beg to be excused; they have to get in and sort it, however hard that may be.

'But there can also be a kind of arrogant self-sufficiency in the police sometimes; it's an "I don't need to be told" attitude that I rock up against now and then, and that makes my blood boil. I will *not* be told what to do and I will *not* be told that something is not possible. I will *not* be palmed off with excuses and blame-shifting.' (Interviewee 60; speaker's own emphases)

Such determination to have their way eventually was understood and largely accepted by the police, though PCCs continued to notice a residual reserve or resentment that persisted for some time:

'There is a residuum of resentment, carefully suppressed but there all the same, which derives from the police being held firmly to account. They preferred it when they could divide and rule the old police authorities, who were amateur

---

[18] Legitimate; that is legally empowered (an important consideration for the police).

part-timers with other concerns and [other] jobs. That doesn't work with the PCC: I'm full time, full-on and fully committed to the role I do. That means in practice that the chief constable daily or weekly is held to account for his and his force's actions on a much closer, tighter, more sceptical scrutiny than ever before. And sometimes they don't like it.' (Interviewee 69)

PCCs noticed that after about a year, during which time the police and the PCC began to bed down together in a more amicable way, "things started to change round":

'[...] things started to change round because they realised (and to be honest, so did I) that we were both on the same side and wanted the same things. Perhaps the ways we each went about getting those things was different and that is what worried them, but I hope and believe that they have since come to trust me and to realise that I will deliver on my promises.' (Interviewee 69)

The identity of purpose and the desire to address crime and community issues may have reconciled some chief officers to their new masters and mistresses. Certainly the PCCs welcomed the new atmosphere of cooperation and, however grudgingly, a police acknowledgement that PCC and police were, in the last analysis, on the same side:

'[...] everyone now knows where the power has moved and who has control of the levers. Within that, we all work well together and I have no complaints (unlike some of my colleagues who see police plots and chief officer conspiracies behind every corner).'

[*Interviewer*: Such as?]

'Nice try. No, I'm not saying. You'll know who I mean anyway.' (Interviewee 65)

Other PCCs acknowledge that what they bring to the police is constant access and quick decisions, both of which the police at all levels and ranks appear to relish:

'The major thing is that the police can get a quick decision about things from me and they like that. It is such a contrast with the old fuddling lay approach of the police authority. Lots of cops have told me how much better in terms of access, efficiency and decisiveness the PCC role is than the PA.' (Interviewee 67)

At the same time, the austerity in public expenditure, coupled with the pain of implementing cuts in resources, has helped to make the police allies of the PCC rather than opponents. For their part, the PCCs declare that they are prepared to cooperate whole-heartedly with chief officers as long as the police know who is really in charge:

'What I have is a transparent, professional relationship with my chief officer team. I expect to challenge the chief constable and to be challenged in my turn, but that is part of the important dynamic in our relationship. I do not expect it to be dysfunctional, but I did not scruple to get rid of the previous man, once he had served out his time.' (Interviewee 56)

Yet sometimes, despite everyone's best intentions, the relationship remains one of wary cooperativeness and the best that can be achieved is "a working compromise":

'[...] the chief constable and I see eye to eye on most things, but it would be daft to pretend that we agree about everything. Of course we don't. On some things we are diametrically opposed and probably always will be, but on the majority of things, the things that really matter in the delivery of policing, we can obtain a working compromise. On some parts, like victim focus and violent crime, we are exactly aligned. On others, like division of the policing budget, we have manoeuvring room and a robust exchange of views.' (Interviewee 68)

All the same, a number of chief officers believe that PCCs tend to the monothematic; that is, policing is seen in simple terms as only or entirely community focused. The police argue, of course, that there is much more to policing than that and that PCCs should make more effort to understand the many facts of police work:

> 'The office of PCC has trivialised what the police do and has reduced it to the lowest, simplest denominator, taking no account of the complexity of policing and the multiplicity of tasks we do.' (CO7)

adding:

> '[There is by the PCC] a refusal to understand the complexity of policing (particularly major and serious organised crime) and [he is] a person who hardly ever visited the "harder" bits of policing, such as covert investigation, homicide, or public order, and who concentrated instead on a rather fatuous self-promotion of simplistic "beat bobbies".' (CO7)

By contrast, PCCs are impatient for local change and for responsiveness towards communities from their police teams. It is less a concern with different branches of policing or the specialisms of crime that concern them, so much as a clear appreciation of what the public wants to be done:

> 'What I have done, and still do, is say: "this is what I want: how soon can you deliver it?" and mostly that's all the chief officer team needs to galvanise them. If they don't deliver, I'm on to it very quickly and they know this. It's like learning to adapt the way you play to the individual referee in a rugby match: the more you oppose his decisions or try to get away with sly infringements, the more you will be penalised, the more inevitably you will lose the game and the more the rest of your team gets pissed off with you. (Besides, I can always send the offender off.)' (Interviewee 52)

While the PCC here is observing that the police are slow to adapt to new ground rules and a different game, others have noted that even 'long-serving and very eminent' chief officers are more likely to cooperate whole-heartedly when their interests and those of the PCCs are aligned:

> 'I don't always agree with the chief constable or he with me but we discuss things in a mature and sensible way. It wasn't always like that. I inherited him and there was

a difficult period at the beginning for oh, the first nine months to a year when we were edgy; eyeing each other like boxers waiting to land a first punch. We now know how to handle disagreements and we negotiate compromise in a sophisticated and professional way.' (Interviewee 67)

On police leadership and direct entry

One PCC thought that police leadership is lacking in edge and focus and noted that generally the police are not reflective:

> 'No one holds a mirror up to the police so that they can see themselves as the public sees them. Well that's what I try to do. If they don't like what they see, then it's their reflections that they are looking at and the option to change is within them and is for them to initiate, or take the consequences. I still think that the police are badly led, and too often lack integrity.' (Interviewee 52)

Other PCCs agreed with this suggestion that police leadership is lacking in quality, and speculated whether this might be rooted in the 'climb from the bottom' police career system which produces too few genuine candidates for the top jobs:

> 'The chiefs are threatened, of course, and because they come from a very shallow gene pool there isn't much to choose between them. I hope that direct entry will broaden the skills sets and proffer candidates who know something of the world outside policing. It's a rarefied world that the chief officers grow up in, and whilst the police may know the worst that human beings can do to each other, they don't always understand how things work outside policing and how people think who are not police officers.' (Interviewee 64)

Another PCC drew attention to a worrying dearth of candidates for top posts in policing, noting that a number of vacancies had had single applicants:

> 'I inherited a chief constable who did not accept the principle of democratic governance, and mine was one of the 18 chiefs who went in the first year. Interestingly, five

consecutive CC posts thereafter had only one candidate applying to become chief constable. That tells you something about the available pool of people for the top jobs, and maybe something about how PCCs were regarded at first.' (Interviewee 66)

In addition to the currently very limited supply of candidates for chief constable posts across England and Wales, the PCC may be right to suppose that the character of the individual commissioner may determine to some degree how many chief officers will apply for vacant chief constable posts,[19] as this senior chief officer observed:

'You asked whether I am going to go for any other chief constable's job in the future. Well, if I do, considering the character and nature of the incumbent PCC will be 80% of my consideration of going for it. If the PCC has the wrong value-set, wrong for me or wrong for the police; no, I would not apply. It is 'one-to-one marking', this relationship and it has all to be related to the PCC's and one's own styles of working.' (CO3)

The PCC cited above went on to say:

'This means of course that candidature is sparse and I welcome the idea of bringing in people from outside the police. Provided that they quickly assimilate what policing is (without necessarily taking in the prevalent culture) and can make operational decisions effectively, have good business credentials and understand budgeting and can run a highly complex organisation with an elastic remit, AND deal with a picky PCC, then I'd welcome "outsiders" warmly! They'd have to be exceptional people.' (Interviewee 66)

This raises dual concerns about the leadership potential within the police and the decision made in 2014 to embark on direct recruitment to leadership positions. One PCC remarked laconically, when looking at replacements for a chief constable who had abruptly left, that:

---

[19] Bryn Caless detected much the same 'personality calculation' among chief officers applying for jobs in other forces when police authorities held sway. Then, a reception with authority members was part of the selection process, and many police officers detested the artificiality of the process (Caless, 2011, p. 34).

'The original pool of applicants was very poor, I thought, and it showed me graphically that the reservoir of potential chief officers is in practical terms just more of the same.' (Interviewee 68)

In September 2014, the first cohort of nine 'outsiders', recruited initially at superintendent level, began their induction into policing with the national College of Policing and completed Phase 1 in March 2015. They have embarked on a modular development programme, interspersed with practical experience in a police force (including patrolling as a constable), all of which continues for 18 months, as does the candidates' probation (College of Policing, 2014).[20] What currently matters to the police, however, particularly in selection processes for leadership or command posts, seems to be the candidates' operational experience. In other words, what matters is what jobs they have done and whether they have acquired 'street credibility' in policing (Caless, 2015). On this basis, and given the prevailing experiential culture (which outclasses intellectual or professional qualifications by some margin), direct entrant 'guinea pigs' may be received in forces with as much rancour as were the first graduates of Lord Trenchard's officer school in the 1930s.[21]

Still, this experiment with direct entry is a bold one, aiming to 'attract highly talented leaders from outside the [Police] Service' and it remains to be seen how well the graduates from the direct entry programme are assimilated into police forces and how quickly they make it to chief officer rank. Indeed, if they do, what is equally important is whether they then make a tangible and positive difference at that level of

---

[20] According to the development rubric, direct entrants will study and practise being a constable, a sergeant and an inspector in their designated police force, as well as learning the 'command' role of superintendent, together with learning blocks that cover police service, community policing, policing operations, investigation and leadership. The 'graduation' from the programme has to be certificated by the chief constable of the parent force, together with the College of Policing. There appears to be no role for the PCC in any of this. The world of policing and the academic world of commentary upon policing, is watching this pioneering work with considerable interest and some misgivings.

[21] Tim Brain, author of an article on Trenchard's scheme to produce an 'officer class' within policing, commented: 'Trenchard was seeking to ensure that the Service produced its own leaders rather than rely on the mosaic of backgrounds, often after military or colonial service, from which many chief constables were then drawn.' Cynical police officers in the Met and other forces treated the 'graduates' of the Trenchard Scheme with scorn and derision, and it was abandoned soon after (see Brain, 2015, and Caless, 2011, p. 47).

policing. PCCs indicated to us that, if their own role still exists when the 'Class of Direct Entrants, 2014' become chief officers, each side ought to find the other reassuringly innovative and businesslike. Time will, inevitably, tell.

Summary

There has been a tangible but positive movement in the opinions of chief police officers, and to a lesser extent in the ranks below them, about the Police and Crime Commissioner. It does not seem to be born entirely of expedience or manipulation, and it is inconceivable that any chief officer would have said this two or three years ago:

> 'I can't think of anything this PCC does badly. He's competent, accessible, clever and very, very conscientious: I think we're lucky to have him, especially as there are some real nightmares as PCCs out there.'

> [*Interviewer:* like whom?]

> 'No, no: you won't catch me with that!' (CO10)

Approbation is still individual rather than generic and that is probably par for most innovative actions. Police officers, trained to be sceptical, experienced in deflating pomposity, mendacity and self-importance, continue to regard the mass of PCCs with some disfavour (no doubt influenced by their own 'grapevines' and by some instances of critical or negative publicity surrounding PCCs). Often, by contrast, they see 'their own' PCC in a favourable light and, in some cases, prefer the PCC's scrutiny and challenge of them to their own superior officers' querulousness. Acceptance of independent oversight comes with the territory and much of the manoeuvring and jostling that characterised the first two or three years of PCC incumbency may well have been merely adjusting to the new forms of democratic oversight and seeing what differences PCCs made to the old, often rather too comfortable, relationships that the police had with their local watchdog. What the police are in no doubt about now is that their new watchdogs have teeth, and most have accepted that the power centres in policing correspondingly have been relocated:

'Real power had very clearly moved from the Chief Officer Team to the PCC. Those who couldn't see that, and who butted up against it, were going to lose.' (CO5

and this can have unexpected but beneficial consequences:

'[The PCC] challenges us all the time, and I actually relish having to justify what I want to do, and know that if it gets past him, it must be pretty robust.' (CO10)

For their part, some PCCs believe that the apparent accommodation of their challenge to the police is window-dressing, and some suspect that that the police may be going back to their old ways:

'The previous CC left in something of a huff and some of that legacy persists. I appointed a new chief constable almost immediately and he's been dutiful and says he believes in what I am doing, but I'm beginning to have my doubts. Things are slowing down, we're not getting to issues quickly enough and I wonder if this CC is doing a Sir Humphrey[22] and deliberately delaying or obstructing progress.' (Interviewee 58)

There will continue to be some rumpling of the normally smoothly-made bed of policing while the PCC and the police get used to each other and try to find ways not just to understand each other, but work together for the good of those who pay them. There may continue to be private spats and 'confessional' comments about each side to researchers. A prevailing uncertainty during 2014–15, when most of our interviews were conducted, was whether PCCs would continue if the government changed,[23] and this was the case until May 2015, when the future of the role until 2020 was assured. In general terms

---

[22] Sir Humphrey Appleby, a master of delay and obfuscation, is the fictional top civil servant in Yes Minister and the later Yes Prime Minister written by Antony Jay and Jonathan Lynn, televised by the BBC over 1980–84; see www.yes-minister.com

[23] The Labour Party adopted Lord Stevens' recommendation for the abolition of PCCs and replacement with an elected Board (a sort of Police Authority in elective miniature) while the Conservatives intended to keep PCCs but make challenge to them easier probably through enhanced powers for the Police and Crime Panels. The outcome of the 2015 general election secured the PCCs' future to 2020 at least.

and judging by the preponderance of responses we had from chief officers, the police can live with their PCCs:

> 'At first (and partly because of the attitude of the previous chief constable), I was prejudiced frankly, because the PCC knew nothing about policing and had not served as a cop in any capacity. It was the standard police contempt for anyone not from 'the job'. However, when the old CC went, I was among the first to realise that the old power bases had shifted too and that no appointed police officer could gainsay the importance and influence of someone who had been elected.' (CO5)

Plus ça change? Perhaps police adaptability is the *même chose*.

In the next chapter, we examine the PCCs' wider relationships in the world of policing: the Home Office, the Prosecution Service, HMIC and the machinery of criminal justice.

FOUR

Partners, colleagues or rivals for oversight? The (PCC) art of making friends and influencing people

Emerging from the transformed local policing landscape are new ways of working, negotiating, and of 'getting the job done'.[1] We have already examined the relationships that PCCs have with their chief police officer team; in this chapter we explore the corollary of how PCCs work with and alongside significant key partners who impact either nationally or locally on their role: the Home Office, Her Majesty's Inspector of Constabulary (HMIC), and local partnerships like the Community Safety Partnerships (CSPs). We focus on the nature of those relationships and what PCCs want from them (and indeed what others want from the PCCs). It is occasionally a landscape of opposition and hostility, sometimes an area of cooperative enterprise and mostly a place in which PCCs are feeling their way carefully as they secure their places in the local hierarchy of emergency service and criminal justice.

In 2008, a review of policing chaired by Sir Ronnie Flanagan (then HM Chief Inspector of Constabulary) proved influential with Whitehall and police alike in bringing about changes to the nature of governance that has since dominated contemporary policing. A White Paper (Home Office, 2010) proposed that the responsibility for local policing was 'moved out of Whitehall' and returned 'to Chief Constables, their staff and the communities they serve' (Home Office, 2010, p. 2). It was not quite as simple a process as this bland statement suggests. As we noted in Chapter One, the Police Reform and Social Responsibility Act 2011 tried to establish a new 'quadripartite' model of police accountability, replacing the old centralised tripartite system with a new decentralised structure without much Home Office involvement, and also heralding the introduction of two entirely new bodies: PCCs and the Police and Crime Panels (PCPs) intended to oversee the PCCs' work. In other words, moving the primary governance of the police out of Whitehall and back to local and parochial control was seen as

---

[1] For example Webster (2015); Foster and Jones (2010); Millie and Bullock (2013).

a positive move,[2] and one that was welcomed initially by the police, though reservations were expressed about the whole notion of the PCC, as we have noted in the preceding chapters.

From our discussions with PCCs about their relationships with these largely national organisations, some clear themes have emerged, the most controversial of which is 'control':

> 'The Home Secretary has said that she wants to be hands off local policing. Suits me. She's let the genie out of the bottle and has to take what follows; having created the PCC, you don't keep a dog and bark yourself.' (Interviewee 51)

There is a sense in which the PCC role was ill-defined at the outset (as might be supposed when it subsequently proved difficult for PCPs to restrain the more exuberant spenders and talkers among the PCCs), and in some respects this has allowed the PCCs to define themselves.[3] Not least of these was the various ways in which PCCs initially tackled local governance of the police but then started to look further afield to the rest of the emergency services and beyond to the wider criminal justice arena (aspirations which we will critically examine in Chapter 7). It is not surprising therefore that Interviewee 51 should regard the undefined role of the PCC as the "genie [let] out of the bottle" by the Home Secretary; who has struggled since to impose control (particularly in respect of mechanisms to restrain or curb PCCs).[4] Some of the more political PCCs, especially those from opposition politics, have cheerfully exceeded their initial remits and evidently enjoy the autonomy that being a PCC gives them, content at the same time to be undermining the Home Secretary's control. One commented acerbically that:

> 'We are not to be herded into voting lobbies at the Home Secretary's say-so and to that extent I think the notion of the PCC has backfired on the Tories.' (Interviewee 66)

---

[2] and one that is characteristic of a Conservative-dominated Coalition. Very broadly, the Labour Party tends to centralise control when in power, the Conservatives tend to devolve control locally; but of course there are variations; not least in the larger powers devolved to Scotland and Wales by both major parties when in power.

[3] A point we look at in more detail in Chapter Six.

[4] Especially in the aftermath of PCC Shaun Wright's drawn-out departure from South Yorkshire.

One PCC observed that he had both more power and more freedom as a PCC than he had had as a Member of Parliament.[5] The cynical might remark that he has more money too.

By contrast, some PCCs have expressed strong support for the Home Office and HMIC, with a number noting that such partnerships give impetus to the growth and development of their police forces and the community each serves. However, there have also been significant expressions of concern and mistrust, particularly in terms of a perceived lack of support and unethical practice. We shall examine this in more detail later, but "the genie out of the bottle" is a concept we should first explore a little more. Was the PCC always going to outgrow the original rather amorphous remit? Could such development not have been predicted? A delegate at the Association of Police and Crime Commissioners (APCC) Conference in Harrogate in November 2014 said:

> 'It's interesting how Police and Crime Commissioners have modulated their views and ambitions in order to fit the role and make it work. There is no doubt that the role has expanded beyond what the Conservatives originally designed. The key point is how do you control the PCCs once in post? There is no equivalent of a party whip to keep them on the straight and narrow.' (Anonymous delegate at the APCC Conference in November 2014, in conversation with Bryn Caless)

What is needed, the delegate said, was someone:

> '[...] who could respond robustly to a PCC performing inadequately, ineptly or contrary to the principles – but falling short of criminality – for which s/he was elected. IPCC can investigate criminal activity; the electorate can have its say every four years: what's missing is how you can intervene if a PCC goes off his or her head between elections. (Anonymous delegate at the APCC Conference in November 2014, in conversation with Bryn Caless)

---

[5]   Interviewee 65, who went on to remark: "I am the public's representative in a much more immediate way than I was as an MP: I have no party line, no whip and no national agenda to get in the way of or modify what I represent."

Stuart Lister and Michael Rowe have proposed that the 'arrival of 'strong' and 'visible' locally elected leaders [...] would not only empower local communities but also overturn antiquated political structures and cultures' (Lister and Rowe, 2013). They appear to be referring mostly to local police force structures, functions and practice, but there is also a sense in which county council political balances are overturned by the installation of a PCC who may well be of a different political complexion from the governing body of the council (as in Kent or North Wales for example). From our own research it seems probable that Lister and Rowe have identified some genuine local impacts, but these do not seem necessarily confined to local policing alone. According to most of the PCCs we have interviewed, change seems to be more about the relationships that local forces have with their partners rather than any deliberate or systematic attempt to dismantle cultures and political structures.[6] Perhaps that could be because we are looking at a comparatively new system which is not yet fully embedded but which was also fully aware of its possible demise as May 2015 approached.[7] Dr Samuel Johnson remarked that

'Depend upon it, sir, when a man knows he is to be hanged in a fortnight, it concentrates his mind wonderfully.'[8] It could be that PCCs, in addressing ideas about the expansion of their remits and wresting governance to themselves not just of the police but also control of strategic and community partnerships, parts of the criminal justice system and the other emergency services, may be quietly fearful of the impermanence of their office.

Control, partnership and influence: PCCs, the Home Secretary and political colour

The respective roles and responsibilities of Police and Crime Commissioners, PCPs, Chief Constables and the Home Secretary are defined in the Policing Protocol, a separate document (Statutory Instrument (SI), 2011b) attached to the original 2011 Act. It sets out to all PCCs, Chief Constables and the PCPs, how their functions will

---

[6] We explore this in more detail towards the end of the chapter.

[7] In the event, and quite unexpectedly, the Conservative Party won a small overall majority. This is discussed in more detail in Chapters 6 and 7.

[8] Dr Johnson was a major eighteenth-century man of letters and the compiler of the first comprehensive dictionary in English; see Boswell, James (1986) Hibbert, Christopher (ed.) *The Life of Samuel Johnson* (original publication 1791), New York: Penguin Classics.

be exercised in relation to each other (SI, 2011b, c.13), and goes on to declare that:

> an effective, constructive working relationship is more
> likely to be achieved where communication and clarity of
> understanding are at their highest. Mutual understanding
> of, and respect for, each party's statutory functions will serve
> to enhance policing for local communities. (SI, 2011b)

In order to understand who has which controls and who exercises what influences, it may be helpful to examine in more detail the statutory functions specified in the Policing Protocol, where clear demarcation lines apparently exist. The PCC 'has a statutory duty and electoral mandate to hold the police to account on behalf of the public' (SI, 2011b, c.15). The PCC additionally has control over all sources of police funding, including the central government grant and local precept (SI, 2011b, c.16). Section 17 of the Protocol (SI, 2011b) lists 14 legal powers and duties for PCCs, some of which could seem to be in conflict, such as setting the strategic direction and force objectives at the same time as scrutinising, supporting and challenging overall performance of the force. Might this not lead the PCC to be 'judge and jury' of its own case, or to exercise unwonted control not only of the direction of policing but its means and outcomes? The dichotomy thus created seems to suggest that the urgent impetus to create local democratic accountability for the police in 2011 may have unintentionally created ambiguity and a fuzziness at the heart of the respective functions:

> 'Time was, when the Home Office would control policy
> for the police. No longer; that's my job and the jobs of the
> other 40 PCCs in their own localities.' (Interviewee 65)

This in turn, while a typically robust PCC response to any attempt at direction from central government, does not acknowledge that within the same Statutory Instrument that specified the PCC's duties, the Home Secretary actually has "reserved powers and legislative tools that enable intervention and direction to all parties" (SI, 2011, c.28). However the SI goes on to declare that the Home Secretary may only exercise these powers when:

> action is necessary in order to prevent or mitigate risk to
> the public or national security. Such powers and tools will

only be used as a last resort, and will not be used to interfere with the democratic will of the electorate within a force area. (SI, 2011, c.28)

For all the suggestion that the powers would be used only in extremis, it is evident that, within the law, the Home Secretary retains the ultimate power of 'intervention and direction', while routinely devolving local police oversight to PCCs and 'the democratic will of the electorate'. The essential fuzziness noted earlier remains, because the declaration of any 'risk to the public or national security' will presumably be a political act by a serving (not necessarily the current) Home Secretary and not something judicially or objectively defined. In other words, nothing legally prevents the Home Secretary from declaring a state of public crisis in order to override the autonomy of a PCC or to dismiss the incumbent.[9] This is the same power, essentially, that a Home Secretary used to override a police authority or dismiss a Chief Constable before 2011.[10]

For their part, some PCCs seem to feel that any strategic or national considerations about policing are not their concern:

'I saw Hugh Orde[11] and he was going on and on about the strategic policing requirement. I'm not interested in that – I have more pressing problems.' (Interviewee 73)

Such parochialism may be excused on the grounds of expediency but this PCC's attitude is one that is often deplored by chief officers, since many find it difficult to interest their PCCs even in matters of serious crime within their force areas, let alone the concerns of, say, the National Crime Agency and its remit to counter transnational organised crime.[12] The point is made a number of times by chief police officers

---

[9] Though interestingly, not exercised in the case of Shaun Wright, the former PCC for South Yorkshire.

[10] This was known in Whitehall as the 'Turbulent Priest Syndrome' after Henry II's declaration of frustration with Thomas à Becket, Archbishop of Canterbury, who had persistently opposed the King: 'will no-one rid me of this turbulent priest?' (Three knights did so by murdering Becket in Canterbury Cathedral in 1170.) One of the authors well remembers seeing 'TPS!' written in the margins of a Home Office document about a particularly recalcitrant police authority in the mid-1980s. David Blunkett when Home Secretary was especially exercised by his encounters with police chiefs whom he could not sack.

[11] The president of ACPO until the organisation was dissolved in 2015.

[12] We discuss this in more detail in Chapter Six.

that PCCs occasionally need to lift their heads above the parapet to see what is going on nationally and what political or criminal events may impact upon them locally. It means, of course, that we need to ascertain the nature of local relationships with national bodies and to determine what governs contact between PCCs and the Home Office. There is some evidence, despite PCCs' occasional protestations to the contrary, of a close and operationally fairly effective relationship between the two, built on partnership working and a shared goal in providing a quality policing service to the communities of England and Wales. For some, it is a question of the mechanics of office:

> 'I know how Whitehall works and I know how important it is to get alongside the permanent officials in the Home Office if you want to get things done or if you want to influence policy. Talking directly to the politicians simply gets you another slice of the bland. I don't want sound bites or stock political answers, I want a dialogue. That means talking *to* each other and not *at* each other, which too often happens. That's why I focus on the officials: they'll still be there tomorrow.' (Interviewee 67; speaker's own emphasis)

For others, the relationship with the Home Office is personal, 'productive' and respectful:

> 'I see a lot of the Home Office and the Home Secretary. Relations on the whole are productive, based on respect.' (Interviewee 57)

Some take a slightly more detached view, based partly on how they perceive the evolution of their own roles as PCCs:

> 'I have a close relationship with the Home Office and the Home Secretary. The officials and Ministers there are supportive and equally well-meaning, though I suspect that they are not entirely comfortable with what they have created.' (Interviewee 58)

Others report that relations with the Home Secretary can be difficult, varying between "fairly prickly [...] with [...] constant negativity about the police" (Interviewee 69) to "a tad strained, even frosty" (Interviewee 60), while some indicated that relationships with officials were "hands off", where "the Home Office [does not] impact on me and is unable to tell me what to do, so I tend to ignore [it]" (Interviewee 65). Some felt that this latter 'detached state' arose from compliance with the guidelines concerning relevant powers laid out in the Policing Protocol (SI, 2011b):

> The establishment of PCCs has allowed the Home Office to withdraw from day-to-day policing matters, giving the police greater freedom to fight crime as they see fit, and allowing local communities to hold the police to account. (SI, 2011b, c.27)

A perception of the deliberate lack of control by the Home Office featured in some PCCs' comments about their sense of autonomy:

> 'I'm an elected PCC with nothing left to prove, so there is very little real pressure that the [Home Office] can exercise over me.' (Interviewee 52)

This next observation came from a PCC who evidently thought that the creation of the role had exceeded the original expectations:

> 'If the Home Office thought they could control PCCs at the beginning, they now understand that they can't.' (Interviewee 58)

This assertion is not entirely true since there are some examples of the Home Office holding back from taking control. In 2013, for example, pressure was placed on the Home Office by the media to create a national register of PCCs' financial interests, covering 'pay and perks', packages, gifts, hospitality and second jobs. The Home Office refused to take responsibility for this action, declaring that it was not its place to do so (HASC, 2014). PCCs, however, agreed that this was a fair way to hold them to account and promptly established their own register. The Home Secretary declared to the Home Affairs Select Committee that it was 'the responsibility of the electorate to decide whether PCCs had done a thorough job'.

Equally, there have been examples where the Home Secretary and other politicians appear to want to exert overt pressure on PCCs. In 2014, Shaun Wright at first refused to heed calls for his resignation as South Yorkshire PCC over his previous role as councillor for children's services during the Rotherham child sex abuse scandal (Whitehead, 2014). The Home Secretary, along with the Prime Minister, the then

Deputy Prime Minister, Nick Clegg, and the then Labour Party leader (Ed Miliband), in a rare show of unity, demanded that the (Labour) PCC resign his office. Mr Wright did subsequently resign, after some weeks of stubborn resistance (Whitehead, 2014). The Home Secretary has since attributed his resignation to the fact that he was 'held to account by the people who elected him' (May, 2014a).

The picture is actually much more complex than the Home Secretary suggests. The media were instrumental in the resignation of Wright, with most newspapers backing calls for him to resign. The *Guardian* even urged the Home Secretary to launch a police investigation into Wright's 'fitness for office' (Weaver, 2014). The APCC issued a statement in September 2014 which concluded that '[Wright's] decision to resign is the right thing to do in the interests of the communities that PCCs are elected to serve and to protect.'

The APCC went on to discuss the 'need for legislation governing PCCs to be strengthened in several areas', and noted that this work was being scoped by Home Office officials and a group of PCCs.[13] The main areas requiring change were cited as 'rules for elections and sharper mechanisms to scrutinize the work of PCCs' (APCC, 2014). That the APCC should seek to limit PCCs' powers is laudable, but it is also reminiscent of turkeys voting for Christmas.

Interestingly, PCCs did not make any comments to us in the course of our research interviews about a need for an outside entity of some kind to scrutinise or constrain their role; in fact, some of their comments tended to the opposite:

> 'I think they (PCCs) are a fantastically excellent constitutional innovation that serves the public well [...] At the moment I can't say there are any obvious drawbacks to the role. We are in a highly political and sensitive arena.' (Interviewee 73)

Michael Rowe has commented on the 'huge influence' that the Home Office exerts on police forces, particularly through the issue of funding – the Home Office is the financial guarantor of police forces, providing '51 per cent of funding' (Rowe, 2012, p. 138). Now that the PCCs control their local police budgets (made up of the government 'grant' and what the PCCs can raise from the local precept), and the Home Office decides what general savings should be made in line with the government's Comprehensive Spending Review, there is at least the

---

[13] The Home Secretary made a statement at the APCC Summit in November 2014, that she was 'looking at how PCCs can be held to account' (May, 2014a).

potential for a clash between local and national interests. Some chief officers have noted, approvingly, the PCCs' attempts to loosen the Home Office's tight hold on the purse strings[14] but the fact remains that central control is maintained through the national setting of the amount of the annual policing budget, and some PCCs saw this as an attempt to control them by the 'back door':

'I have resolutely opposed all the budget cuts to policing [...] and I simply cannot see how anyone can expect the same level of policing to be delivered with a quarter of the available budget slashed.' (Interviewee 60)

Another PCC commented that his persistent lobbying for a moratorium on budget reduction had got him nowhere, and he expressed his frustration like this:

'I'm tired of banging on at them about budgets and cuts. Why the police? We are placing public safety at grave risk through cutting funding by another 25%–30% between now and 2020 in real terms – yet it's a drop in the government's ocean of spending.' (Interviewee 70)

Interviewee 70 may have a point, since the government's "ocean of spending" in 2014[15] included the creation of an incentive scheme for PCCs to develop efficiencies in policing, to encourage innovative practice and provide a better service to the public. At a time of considerable fiscal restraint, the Home Office allocated £50 million in 2014–15 for a 'Police Innovation Fund' (Home Office, 2014). The message sent by this action is, at best, ambiguous, given the more than 30% cuts in police budgets imposed in successive tranches of public services' austerity since 2010.

Although most of the time the Home Office appears actively to encourage PCCs' independence of central governmental control, there are examples to be found elsewhere of other government departments

---

14 For example: "The PCC's help with the reducing budget is really helpful and supportive and I know we think as one on the inadvisability of reducing the police budget any further." (CO3). The decision by the Chancellor of the Exchequer in his autumn statement (December 2015) not to seek further cuts in policing budgets may reflect PCC lobbying as well as a concern about the possible proliferation of terrorist attacks.

15 Including 'ring-fenced' budgets for the NHS and for Department for Education.

seemingly wanting to be involved in oversight of the work of PCCs or at least to act in some sort of regulatory or inspection role. It gives us an interesting sidelight on 'joined-up thinking' in Whitehall which continues to be as elusive as ever.[16] An example of central control is a recurrent concern about PCC 'transparency'. The Electoral Local Policing Bodies Order 2011 places a statutory duty on PCCs to publish 25 primary statutory disclosures about themselves and their work, including who they are and what they do, what they spend and how they spend it, what their priorities are and how they are progressing towards them, how they make decisions, what policies and procedures govern the operation of the PCC's 'Office' and lists of gifts and donations, 'Freedom of Information' requests, and registers of interests.

The Home Affairs Select Committee reported in 2014 that even though the Home Office had reminded PCCs of this statutory duty for 'transparency', commissioners continued to fail to meet those requirements, adding:

> The Home Office and the Association of Police and Crime Commissioners provide relatively little comparative analysis that might help the general public to assess the actions and decisions of their commissioners against each other. (HASC, 2014)

It has also been suggested by the Committee on Standards in Public Life that PCCs should publish a register of meetings held with external stakeholders, since 'lobbying activities may bring conflicts of interest' (2013, para 13).

PCCs seldom noted to us that 'transparency' was a continuing issue for them, and there was a sense in some of our discussions that PCCs ignored what they saw as additional Whitehall demands, citing that they are elected to account locally not nationally. Others made no apology for systematic lobbying of their own, both to parliament: "I network a lot with MPs – it is hugely important to me that I get on well with them" (Interviewee 61) and to Whitehall generally and the Home Office in particular:

> 'I serve on some Home Office committees and often brief the [Home Secretary], so I'm close to the central levers of

---

[16] One of the authors, then working in Whitehall, remembers 'joined-up thinking' being mooted as a desirable aim of governance during John Major's administration in 1992–97.

power and often know what the thinking is there ahead of the game. That helps me to do my job here and to articulate the future of this role.' (Interviewee 59)

Another PCC, well versed in the ways of government and experienced in how influence operates in the civil service, suggested that his unseen activities yielded dividends that more overt activities would not:

'I know how the civil service machine works and I know how to influence those officials so that the message gets through more or less obliquely to the Minister. I prefer working that way, as it is low profile and is not headlined as it is when you talk to the politicos directly. It's really a matter of being able to read the runes.' (Interviewee 64)

There is evidence to demonstrate that the work and role of PCCs and the operational functionality of police forces continues to be driven by the government machine, albeit opaquely. Yet the Home Secretary remains adamant that PCCs are delivering 'a level of transparency, visibility and accountability that did not exist before 2012' (May, 2014a). Our interviews with PCCs suggest that they agree that they have the power to run their local police force, but they stress their concerns that tight budgets will restrict how they can achieve this successfully. Attempts to influence are by no means a one-way process from central government to the local PCC. There are indications that PCCs persistently exploit their connections with political parties to try to influence areas like budgets and research.[17] Some academics have foreseen the problems that might arise with too emphatic a governmental control of both policing budgets and policy. Some have even suggested that PCCs might actually have been set up to fail (Newburn, 2011; Lister and Rowe, 2013). The Association of PCCs does not accept any such suggestion, stating forcefully (if inaccurately) that PCCs 'are responsible for the totality of policing' (APCC, 2015b).

---

[17] It may of course be of point that a number of PCCs are politically Conservative and some espouse a 'party line' on public issues, including reform of criminal justice. It is not surprising that many of them get on with the Home Secretary and other government ministers.

Collaborative working: PCCs and other national agencies

Operating under the auspices of the Home Office, it appears that Her Majesty's Inspectorate of Constabulary also possesses significant power and influence over the functionality of police forces, and therefore can have an impact, at least indirectly, on the work of the PCC. During our interviews with PCCs we found clear opinions on the role of HMIC vis-à-vis PCCs:

> 'HMIC – very good. As long as they understand that they are not there to inspect me. I get on well with them. I've never used their service. There is some sensitivity with PCCs because they think the Head [the Chief HMI[18]] has ambitions to scrutinise PCCs.' (Interviewee 73)

HMIC was first established in 1856, with the remit to report on the 'efficiency and effectiveness' of police forces. This remit continues today with the function made statutory in the Police Act of 1996 that HMIC inspects police forces in England and Wales. In 2014, the Home Secretary expressed the government's support for the agency and declared, rather unconvincingly, that she had made the HMIC 'properly independent of government' (May, 2014a). HMIC echoes this on its website where it claims that 'it is independent, appointed by the Crown and possesses powers to seek information from police forces and access their premises'. This assertion is undermined somewhat by a parallel declaration that 'HMIC's annual inspection programme is subject to the approval of the Home Secretary in accordance with the Police Reform and Social Responsibility Act 2011' (HMIC, 2014a), which does not sound much like being 'properly independent' of government. It has always been the case, of course, that the Home Office called HMIC's tune and that the agency operates for and on behalf of the government at large and under the direction of the Home Secretary in particular. That there is political influence on HMIC is undeniable, not least because the appointments of the Chief HMI

---

[18] Sir Tom Winsor is HM Chief Inspector of Constabulary and is the first non-police officer to be appointed (in 2013) to the role. His appointment has not been without controversy, especially among chief police officers, but he has not stated on the record that he wishes to look at PCCs themselves. That has not stopped some PCCs believing that he intends to.

and all other HMIs are decided by the Home Secretary[19] (Mawby and Wright, 2008).

One of the 'new' roles of HMIC is to work in partnership with PCCs. In a survey of PCCs conducted by the House of Commons' Home Affairs Select Committee, this comment was made by a PCC about the importance of partnership working and the role of the PCC in coordinating such work:

> [O]ne PCC described partnership working as 'perhaps the most exciting frontier for commissioners to explore', noting that they are in a unique position to bring partner agencies together in the public interest. (HASC, 2014, p. 12)

PCCs offered many examples of how they work in collaboration, however most of this evidence revolved around police forces working together (HASC, 2014) and this evidently did not impress those looking over PCCs' shoulders. In July 2013, the HMIC declared that:

> the picture on collaboration is deeply disappointing. Despite HMIC highlighting the untapped potential that exists in collaboration, the pace of change over the last year has been too slow and only a minority of forces (18 of 43) are delivering more than 10% of their savings through collaboration. (HMIC, 2013b)

The pace of collaborative working between PCCs and HMIC itself also appears to have been slow to develop. That said, it is important to note that HMIC does not have a role in inspecting PCCs,[20] but in 2012 the Inspectorate published details of what it can do to support them. This includes 'sharing expertise and information in a timely, targeted and useful way with police and crime commissioners'; proposing a 'mix of scheduled meetings and as-required updates for PCCs'; and consultations on 'how to best work together in the future'. None of this really amounts to more than a pious intention to be of service and it is not at all surprising that little in this publication has openly resonated

---

[19] 'Crown appointments' based on the Home Secretary's recommendations.

[20] Indeed, it is hard to see how constitutionally they could have such a role. It would entail the politically appointed inspecting the democratically elected, and any interference in the work of PCCs by HMIC could well be judged as beyond its remit or illegal, as we noted in Chapter Three with the plans to enhance the powers of PCPs.

with commissioners. However, HMIC also set out in the article its purpose 'to fully support the PCCs' in holding their Chief Constables to account. If the HMIC guidelines are accepted and utilised by PCCs, we may yet anticipate a relationship between them that is built on a shared understanding of police accountability. PCCs themselves seem more intent on preserving their freedom to act as the sole judges and arbiters of effectiveness and efficiency in their police forces:

> 'HMIC does not impact on me and is unable to tell me what to do, so I tend to ignore them. They used to attest to effectiveness and efficiency of each police force; no longer: that's my job (and the other PCCs too).' (Interviewee 65)

Some of this has to be in the context of a general dislike of outside 'interference', which characterised the police for decades, extended in its turn to the old Police Authorities, and now, as we have seen in Chapters 1 and 3, to the PCCs as well. We did not get the impression from the PCCs we interviewed that there is either as widespread a mistrust of HMIC's intentions as there is among chief police officers, or that there is the same cynicism about the political drivers which influence what HMIC inspects.[21] That should not be surprising: PCCs are not inspected by HMIC and so in a sense are inviolate. They have little to fear from HMIC's inspections of their police forces and indeed could use outcomes to galvanise or extend their own reform agendas, but, as characterised by Interviewee 65's comment above, there appears to be a developing sense of indignation that 'their' police force should be assessed by anyone but them.

One of the HMIs, Zoë Bellingham, was interviewed on the record by Bryn Caless in 2014 and it was put to her that the 15% public mandate for PCCs was not impressive. She responded that "they are more accountable than the old Police Authorities", clearly indicating that HMIC was inimical to the PAs in line with the Home Office's own policy approach. In *public* statements, PCCs respond apparently appreciatively to the information that HMIC supplies on how forces can improve their efficiency and effectiveness, including 'thematic inspections' – seven were conducted in 2013 and nine in 2014. Here is a flavour of the published comments on HMIC by PCCs:

---

[21] As registered in Caless (2011, Chapter Four), in which chief police officers were witheringly negative about the usefulness of both HMIC and the Home Office.

We are pleased that the Chief HMIC says that public accountability through PCCs (and the media) is the "proper price" for the powers and funding that the police receive. We welcome HMIC's PEEL[22] inspection process for contributing rigour and transparency to police performance and accountability. (Sussex PCC Katy Bourne, Chair APCC Performance, Standards and Accountability Group, 2014a)

and:

PCCs believe the HMIC report provides further evidence that lends weight to their case for funding and expertise for the pilots. (Dorset PCC Martyn Underhill, Bourne, 2014a)

Yet, our research suggests that this is not what many PCCs feel privately about HMIC; some have strongly indicated an element of mistrust:

'HMIC is a quango[23] that has certainly not proved to me that it does anything that an enlarged IPCC couldn't do.' (Interviewee 65)

and:

'They should be carrying out an important role – helping us to hold our chiefs to account and telling us how well we are doing. Unfortunately I think they have lost sight of it and are playing all sorts of games which are elaborative and destructive. [...] I'm not prepared to engage with them until they engage with us objectively.' (Interviewee 73)

There is then a discrepancy between what is said publicly (with the APCC collectively also declaring 'support and gratitude for the work

---

22 On 27 November 2014, HMIC published its first 'PEEL assessment', which is a new way of conducting inspections based on all the information about a particular force that HMIC has amassed in the previous 12 months. The Inspectorate uses this 'to produce an assessment of how the force has performed, which in some areas will include a graded judgment of outstanding, good, requires improvement, or inadequate' (HMIC, 2015).

23 A quango is 'a quasi-autonomous government(al) organisation' that deals nationally with specialist activities. Most quangos were abolished or dismantled in the course of 2010, but some have since been replaced. The National Policing Improvement Agency (NPIA), for example, was replaced by the College of Policing in 2013.

of the HMIC') and what PCCs have said to us anonymously. This may have to do with a perception that, together with democratic oversight 'of the totality of policing' (APCC, 2015b), PCCs have taken on the role of scrutiny of 'their' force, and do not willingly surrender any of that to any outside body over which they cannot exercise control. At the same time, there is a parochialism in the PCCs' private responses which indicates a rather grudging attitude to larger national interests and indifference to the provision of data on police performance across England and Wales. There is also a possibility in all of this that PCCs are strangling at birth any notion that they themselves might be subject to HMIC comment or scrutiny.

More fundamentally, there may be a misunderstanding by some PCCs as to the role(s) of HMIC, or perhaps HMIC is not communicating effectively with them. It has been difficult to peel away the layers and determine the precise nature of any issues between the two, other than an apparent general dislike by PCCs of any external scrutiny of or 'interference' with the force which they oversee. For all that, according to HMIC (2014b), its duties encompass the acceptance of 'commissions from local policing bodies', which can include PCCs. There have been examples of this happening in the recent past. In 2012, Kent PCC Ann Barnes instigated the very first such 'commission' and asked HMIC to review crime recording in her force. The subsequent report published by HMIC in June 2013 resulted in Kent Police taking strong action to deal with identified failings. There have been only a further six commissions to date (December 2015). Objectively, we may suppose that this could be a wasted opportunity: HMIC is apparently willing to respond to the PCC's 'commissioning' in a positive way. On the other hand, PCCs would probably not want to invite HMIC's 'thematic' scrutiny of their police force unless there was an overriding need to do so: HMIC inspections are not part of 'nice to do' and they can be disruptive of force routine. Given such a requirement however, the considerable resources afforded to HMIC could provide the PCCs with an opportunity thematically to scrutinise their own forces and at the same time demonstrate 'national service delivery' to their critics and public alike. There could be kudos in this for PCCs because HMIC would probably be regarded by local media at least as an objective assessor. This was emphasised by Zoë Bellingham in her 2014 interview, when she claimed that "

HMIC is independent of everyone, and is accountable only to parliament. HMIC may act in a collegiate way, but it is entirely independent of all influences" (Bellingham, HMI, on the record conversation with Bryn Caless, 2014).

We may not accept this assertion entirely at face value (certainly many PCCs would not) because the claim that HMIC is "independent of all influences" is patently not the case, but the government itself has stated in terms that, even though there are plans to extend the remit of HMIC, this is not likely to include PCCs. Indeed, in a consultation exercise for a Home Office report in 2015, PCCs were in the majority of those who objected strenuously to an extension of HMIC's powers, believing, it seems, that PCCs could fall under HMIC control in such an instance. Responding to these concerns, the Home Office observed with magisterial weight that:

> Allowing HMIC to inspect PCCs would undermine the democratic accountability of PCCs to their electorate. The Government does not believe that accountability should be mediated by a third party and so the Government will not enable HMIC to inspect PCCs directly. Scrutiny of PCCs will continue to be provided by PCPs [Police and Crime Panels]. (Home Office, 2015, p. 15)

The report goes on to say that 'HMIC will continue to retain the ability to inspect the efficiency and effectiveness [of the police]' (Home Office, 2015, p. 15), and expresses concern about how the transparency and accountability of PCCs can be managed. We share this concern; especially where the direct actions of a PCC may lead to: frustration of court processes,[24] allegations of dishonesty,[25] reluctance to resign despite intense public pressure to do so,[26] 'stacking' the support office with campaign staff,[27] participating in a controversial documentary film[28] and making decisions that were 'perverse' and 'irrational'.[29] However, it is unlikely that HMIC could legitimately have investigated any of these instances, which leaves PCCs possibly subject to enhanced scrutiny, perhaps by an Ombudsman figure or senior member of the

---

[24] PCC Olly Martins, Bedfordshire, gave details of a police investigation to his partner.

[25] PCC Antony Stansfeld, Thames Valley, was accused in 2013 of expenses irregularities (which he denied).

[26] PCC Shaun Wright, South Yorkshire, 2014.

[27] Claimed of PCC Adam Simmonds, Northamptonshire, 2013.

[28] PCC Ann Barnes, Kent, 2014.

[29] PCC Alan Hardwick, Lincolnshire, was described thus by a High Court judge on 28 March 2013, after suspending his Chief Constable, Neil Rhodes, without making the reasons for his actions public. All these allegations and reports are listed at the end of this chapter.

judiciary (Lister, 2013; Painter, 2013; Davies, 2014a). We discuss this in more detail in Chapter Six.

Other partnerships, other stakeholders

On 1 April 2015, with an ironic timing lost on most observers, official approval was given by the Home Secretary to the formation of the National Police Chiefs' Council (NPCC),[30] which replaced ACPO. The decision to establish the new body was made after a review conducted on APCC's behalf by General Sir Nick Parker[31] was published in 2013. Getting rid of ACPO was a conscious early decision by many PCCs, who objected, often strenuously, to being 'top-sliced' to pay for it, without any say in the running of what was a limited private company. ACPO did profess a remit to speak nationally on police and crime matters and had a role in coordinating police responses to national crises (however they were defined). Funding was taken from forces' budgets; at a time of budget reduction, this was too much. General Parker's *Review* (APCC, 2013) was critical of ACPO's purpose and its 'private' membership and as a result of this, many PCCs began to withhold the funding for ACPO during the course of 2013–14. In private conversations, PCCs were sometimes vehemently critical of ACPO:

> 'Their cosy little private enterprise shop is doomed – and was from the moment PCCs were elected. The power base has shifted from them to us, though some of them can't see that yet. They will. For far too long, ACPO was a Mount Olympus where the chiefs had God-like status, and all you could see were egos jostling for space and smell the power-broking.' (Interviewee 51)

Another remarked: "I hate ACPO. They have to go. I think it is a corrupt old boys' network" (Interviewee 61), supported by this acid

---

[30] The NPCC started in April 2015, and is currently chaired by Sara Thornton, former Chief Constable of Thames Valley Police. The role of the NPCC is to coordinate operational policing at national level.

[31] General Sir Nick Parker produced *The independent review of ACPO* under the auspices of the APCC in 2013; effectively proposing ACPO's abolition and hiving off its functions variously to: the College of Policing, the National Police Chiefs' Council and the Home Office or to individual PCCs (APCC, 2013). See also http://apccs.police.uk/press_release/implementation-board-launched-wake-parker-review-acpo/

observation: "ACPO is a waste of space. Chiefs deserve a better spokesperson mechanism than this" (Interviewee 53).

However, the need for a "better spokesperson mechanism" at the top level of policing was recognised by a number of PCCs who agreed that the police needed a "joined-up voice" of some kind to represent them. One characteristic comment from PCCs was:

> 'The police need a joined-up voice on matters to do with policing and crime; I'm not sure that ACPO is the right means to deliver that. Many PCCs agree that ACPO should be more transparent and answerable outside its narrow, private company remit. Otherwise – as is already happening with some of its remits going to the College of Policing – more of ACPO's functions will be taken away and it will become even more of a talking shop than it is already.' (Interviewee 52)

We found that generally the PCCs whom we interviewed did not respect ACPO as an agency, and most wanted to see it abolished. However, it was recognised that there is a need for a supporting "body to speak for the police", and the College of Policing and the NPCC will partly fill that void in the interim. A professional 'Police Council' is envisaged in time:

> 'There will have to be something else, some body, to speak for the police but that won't be until the police themselves decide that they want to become a profession, and currently there are too many obstacles in the way of their doing that – not least that policing is not yet a graduate occupation. The College of Policing[32] is not the whole answer either, as it has too many other things to do. The police needs something like the GMC[33] as its representative and powerful body to deal at national level with government.' (Interviewee 65)

---

[32] The College of Policing website (2015) contains a section entitled 'What do we offer Police and Crime Commissioners?' It lists 'information, evidence, guidance and support' to help PCCs; among which is to 'understand how your force is performing against national standards' and 'identify and address the local policing needs in your area'; see www.college.police.uk/About/What-do-we-offer/what-do-we-offer-police/Pages/Police_and_cc_offers.aspx

[33] The General Medical Council speaks nationally on all medical issues on behalf of doctors.

The NPCC now speaks nationally for the police, can broker directly with government and acts as a lobbyist on behalf of chief police officers. The essential difference from the time of ACPO is that research, 'portfolios' of police knowledge, expertise and national commentary on issues are now firmly with the College of Policing, while an oversight role on police integrity and probity goes to the Independent Police Complaints Commission.[34] The NPCC has become, essentially, the "talking shop" that PCC Interviewee 52 predicted, funded solely by its members and a government grant. No levy is now taken from force budgets. The PCCs have emphatically won this opening battle.

So much for national bodies and representation at the highest strategic level; what about PCCs' partnerships at the local and tactical levels?

'Sweating the small stuff'[35]: working with local partners

At its annual Conference in Harrogate in 2014, the APCC chose as its theme *Working in partnership to keep communities safe* which reflects the twin themes of focus on community relations with the police and the PCCs' determination to engender positive outcomes from those relations.[36] Privately, PCCs seem to think that 'sweating [this] small stuff' is not as simple to attain as they may claim publicly:

> 'The way forward for the PCC role itself is to get the small bits right in policing first, then move progressively to each of the bigger reforms. Then, you could expand the role to embrace the rest of the criminal justice system. The other emergency services, particularly the Fire and Rescue Service, are in dire need of instant reform. They really are appallingly badly run and focused: they need huge

---

[34] The IPCC investigates complaints against the police and, inter alia, against PCCs if there are allegations of criminality. This has provoked a testy response from some PCCs, of which this, from Interviewee 55, is a typical example: "I have particular issues with the [...] IPCC which I think takes too long to resolve issues and should not discuss police conduct. That is my job; theirs is to find the facts and they should not comment on those findings."

[35] A phrase first used by the life-style guru Richard Carlson (1961–2006) in his best-selling book *Don't Sweat the Small Stuff*, Hyperion (1977).

[36] See http://apccs.police.uk/about-the-apcc/ in which this summary of the importance of partnerships is made by the APCC: 'Across the country, PCCs are delivering better scrutiny of police forces. Day by day they are building the strongest possible partnerships between police and the agencies and volunteers who work to keep communities safe.'

reform and compared with them, the police are brilliant!' (Interviewee 57)

The ambitiousness of this statement probably needs a moderating context, but there is no doubt that some PCCs, content that they now have policing properly on track and under their own tight scrutiny, have turned their attention to other areas, particularly in local partnerships (or strictly, oversight of local partnerships) in which they can play a part.[37] There is already a background to the police being central players in local partnerships, participation in which may have whetted the PCCs' own appetites to do more and oversee more. The context for the PCC's comment above lies in what were first called Crime and Disorder Reduction Partnerships (CDRPs), but which are generally now known as Community Safety Partnerships.[38] The police response to public enthusiasm for renewed law and order within communities extended to the challenge of working in partnership, as one chief police officer commented:

> '[...] if you want to reassure the public it isn't enough to be a blue uniform at the corner of the street – despite what the newspapers say. You have to do something about what is troubling people, and sometimes that isn't always crime – just disorder, or a few antisocial characters making other people's lives a misery, or problem-solving. We've had to learn how to intervene and work in partnership.' (CO5)

CSPs were introduced almost a decade ago by the Labour government as part of its Crime and Disorder Act of 1998, and are intended to address local issues of crime, vandalism, criminal damage and disorder. The original idea was that local authorities, rather than the police on their own, would have the remit to organise and coordinate partnerships between those organisations that had a part to play in crime and disorder. The 'standing' membership of the CSP originally consisted of: the local authority (usually in the chair, because it carried the statutory duty[39]) the police, the police authority, fire and rescue, the health sector (primary healthcare) and probation. Others, such as

---

[37] and it is of a piece with our discussion of the future of PCCs and their remit, in Chapter 7.

[38] They always have been in Wales; see Caless and Spruce (2013).

[39] Local authorities are required 'to do all [they] reasonably can to prevent crime and disorder in [their] areas[s]', Section 17 of the Crime and Disorder Act 1998.

housing or social services, might be seconded on an 'as needed' basis as part of the local authority input.

As long ago as 2007, Gordon Hughes and Michael Rowe were suggesting that the political and policy discourses on community safety were unstable and contested as a 'terrain' (Hughes and Rowe, 2007). In time, too, the Home Office turned its attention to concerns about local relationships and intervened to provide some adjustments to the role and composition of CSPs. Steve Savage observed the effects of these interventions on frontline policing, and saw, in Neighbourhood Policing Teams, the planned emergence of a police officer who specialised in community work and who gave impetus locally to the formation of community-specific partnerships,[40] and who was conceived of as a community leader, rather than the old multi-functional 'bobby' of the past (Savage, 2007).

Even with observable changes of the kind Steve Savage talks about, it is not an easy matter to assess the impact of CSPs on local issues around crime and disorder. One of the problems may be that no one is looking systematically at what is involved. Caroline Thwaites (2013) found no evidence of research into or assessment of the impacts that CSPs were having on communities' crime and disorder problems. She also noted that there was an over-reliance on measuring partnership effectiveness through recorded crime data. Most of the partners in the CSPs had heavy workloads but there was little in the way of evaluation of the usefulness or impact of that effort, compounded by a tacit acceptance by participants of the inherent value of partnerships, whether or not these had assessed outcomes (Thwaites, 2013). This then, was a partnership 'terrain' greatly in need of some form of evaluation, a sense of direction and a greater clarity of purpose.

The arrival of PCCs in 2012 threw some of these issues into the air (not least the rather passive police participation in local authority targets), because the PCC not only expected to work in place of the police authority, but also he or she would take a pro-active role across a whole spectrum of partnerships:

---

[40] The Police Community Support Officer (PCSO) fulfils this role in place of warranted police officers in many community models across England and Wales (see Caless et al, 2014), but increased financial stringency in police forces may see the end of the PCSO. The Metropolitan Police seems set to shelve all its PCSOs (*Times*, 10 September, 2015). The same report suggests that the Home Secretary will try instead to galvanise volunteers to do the PCSO job.

'I chair a strategic board where the Crown Prosecution Service, the Prison Authority, Health, Youth Offending Teams and the top local authorities all attend. These are people with their hands on the levers of criminal justice and it is a very powerful body – especially for me, as I can help to direct their partnerships and purpose.' (Interviewee 56)

In this context, Stuart Lister observed that:

'[...] the introduction of PCCs continues the long-term project of marginalizing local government in the framework of police institutional accountability.' (Lister, 2013, p. 241)

That said, a chief police officer sounded a note of caution, based on her experience of handling partnerships, in which she acknowledges that PCCs can occasionally be naïve about the motivations of those around the partnership table:

'He grasps very readily that policing is part of the larger social context, and as a result, he is very sold on partnerships but I'd like him to learn that some partnerships are more equal than others. The police often work disproportionately hard at partnerships, whilst some of those attending – like Health and often the local authority – sit back fat, dumb and happy and expect the police to make all the running. It's abandonment of responsibility at best and negligence at worst. I want the PCC to understand the frustrations inbuilt into the processes we have to undergo, and when he does grasp that, I think he'll be a formidable champion for us.' (CO12)

What is it that the public wants from CSPs and the PCC's own Police and Crime Plan? Could it be something like that articulated by this PCC, who identified a strong consistency of views from people across his force area?

'You know, wherever I go in this area, people are saying pretty much the same things. They want to feel safe and secure, they want to be able to go shopping, go to work, travel, take leisure, visit friends and relations and go on holiday, all without being threatened, hurt or being the victims of crime. Is that too much to ask? The security to conduct your everyday affairs in a peaceful and orderly society is very fundamental, I think.' (Interviewee 69)

Acting so uncompromisingly as the public's spokesperson on crime and disorder, the PCC might very well be seen as undermining quite directly the local authority's duty and responsibility to coordinate CSPs. What Daniel Gilling (2014) calls a 'hybridised model of local governance' is emerging alongside PCCs' focus on community policing and on partnerships with those who have an interest in a "peaceful and orderly society" (Interviewee 69). What this produces in turn is a PCC who is often in the driving seat of local initiatives, and according to Megan O'Neill (2014), is 'play[ing] nicely with others'. Linda Reid (2014) has noted, from her incisive study of partnership responses to domestic violence in Greater Manchester, how a new partnership model is emerging there consisting of strategic leaders from the police, the Office of the PCC, local authorities and voluntary not-for-profit agencies.

If PCCs continue to develop Police and Crime Plans, not just through consultation with chief officer teams but also through CSPs, the resulting tactical level impact may indeed be measurable, as Thwaites (2013) has proposed, but something akin to the Greater Manchester 'strategic partnership model' may replace the CSPs, predicated as the latter are on public service participants operating in operational/tactical modes rather than at a strategic level. There is a strong probability that the strategic lead for these initiatives will be firmly with PCCs. The power has already started to move from local authorities (who, admittedly, never quite had their hearts in the lead against crime and disorder) and other formal public partnerships, to PCCs. The views of a chief police officer in this context, are telling. The officer notes "that the old power bases had shifted" from police to PCC:

> 'I was among the first to realise that the old power bases had shifted too and that no appointed police officer could gainsay the importance and influence of someone who had been elected. Real power had very clearly moved from the Chief Officer Team to the PCC.' (CO5)

It may not be too much to read across from CO5's comments of how he perceives the impact of the PCC, to the seismic disturbances caused by PCCs in wider partnerships. It is not always clear to what extent the PCC continues to need formal partnerships of the kind offered through the community safety parameters.[41] Many commissioners seem entirely self-sufficient, building up contacts but always focused on the nature of the problem and certainly not always respectful of local 'vested interests' or custom-and-practice, as this keen-eyed chief police officer observed of his PCC at work with local communities:

> 'The PCC is really into contact with communities and it's something he works very hard at, and I think he does it well. He never promises them the earth, and never says that he can solve everyone's problems. But I've seen him at public meetings with self-important councillors or [Neighbourhood Watch] people, patiently explaining to them that the fear of crime is often exaggerated and telling them straight that the remedies for most of their problems lie in their own hands.' (CO10)

Such messages might not be what everyone locally wants to hear.

Summary

This chapter has explored some of the significant partnerships of Police and Crime Commissioners with the Home Office, the Home Secretary and HMIC. It has also noted relationships with ACPO and now the NPCC, and touched very briefly on relationships with the College of Policing and the IPCC. CSPs and other partnerships at a local and parochial level also exist, and some PCCs might argue that these are the really important ones, since they impact (perhaps) on the day-to-day community work which is the PCCs' primary focus, rather than the vaguer and broader national picture. It is at least possible that organisations at local levels can have a significant influence on the Police and Crime Commissioner. Without the continued support and guidance of partners of all kinds, PCCs would be much less informed and supported in their roles of being responsible for the 'totality of policing', providing the voice of the people and holding the police to account (APCC, 2015b).

---

[41] Barry Loveday (2013) had observed that PCCs represented a threat to CSPs, but precisely how that threat would manifest itself over time was unknown. We suggest it may be in exactly this way, with PCCs taking over and supplanting the CSPs, while creating new partnerships which may become more dynamic. One full-time 'catalyst' of partnership working may be all the impetus that local coordination requires.

Control and influence have emerged as significant themes for this chapter; the PCCs' relationships with their partners appear to be mostly strong, however it has been noted that some are indifferent and some border on the superficial. Comments concerning the personalities with whom they sit down to work, were made by many PCCs and this perhaps reflects the general air of honesty that PCCs and chief police officers alike afforded us in our investigations. Throughout the research for this book, both during interviews and through an exploration of the written word by academics, on websites and in legislation; the word 'independent' has appeared in many guises and with varying levels of emphasis. Some posturing came from PCCs keen to state that they are now in control. The Home Office and Home Secretary have issued statements to support this independence and limited evidence supports the Home Secretary's reassurance to PCCs that she does not want to 'step on their toes'. The reality of those relationships has been difficult to fully evaluate. Although an interview with the Home Secretary was requested a number of times, we were not granted a meeting. There is, though, some evidence to demonstrate that the relationship between the Home Office and PCCs is moving, at a glacial pace, towards shared goals and outcomes, in the interests of the public they both serve.

Research into the PCCs' relationship with HMIC has elicited a similar picture, although it was evident that there was less direct involvement and only limited partnership working. Some PCCs had little to do with HMIC while others valued its contribution to effective scrutiny of their forces. Personalities appeared to play a role in whether or not HMIC was considered to be of value. Axiomatically, it would benefit both parties if a shared understanding of how they can collaborate and work together more effectively could be achieved, as originally recommended in the *Policing Protocol* (2011).

PCCs focus most on their communities: not only is this where their legitimacy as elected representatives comes from, it is also where the PCC has focused the Police and Crime Plans for his or her force. The CSPs and other local partnerships are what the PCC seeks to influence, and in many cases, take control of. The 'local levers of power' are clearly where the PCC sees most potential impact and where partnerships can have immediate outcomes. It is by no means clear that CSPs will survive the PCC in terms of coordinating local effort, but if CSPs can have a strong and supportive input to the PCC's Police and Crime Plan, there may yet be another mutation in local partnerships to counter crime and disorder. We continue to see the likelihood of PCCs taking on the formal coordination of *all* local crime and disorder partnerships, as part of a deliberately extended remit. If that happens, CSPs, like ACPO, will wither on the vine. It remains to be seen if that remit embraces more of the criminal justice system.

We turn our attention in the next chapter to examining what the media does with the PCC's messages and how s/he sustains access to the public at large.

Note

For ease of reference, here, in constabulary order, are the reports in which allegations and criticisms were made of PCCs.

Bedfordshire: *Daily Mail* (2014) No action against PCC over 'leaks', 17 September, www.dailymail.co.uk/wires/pa/article-2759199/No-action-against-PCC-leaks.html

Cumbria: Pidd, H. (2013) Police panel questions commissioner's response to expenses leak, *Guardian*, 19 April, www.guardian.co.uk/uk/2013/apr/19/cumbria-police-inquiry-chauffeur-leak

Lincolnshire: Williams, M. (2013) Lincolnshire Police and Crime Commissioner Alan Hardwick: "I will not quit", *Lincolnshire Echo*, 31 March, www.lincolnshireecho.co.uk/POLL-Lincolnshire-Police-Crime-Commissioner-Alan/story-18555685-detail/story.html

Kent: Francis, P. (2014) Kent crime commissioner Ann Barnes accused after Kent Police press office takeover move, 14 April, *Kent Messenger Online*, www.kentonline.co.uk/kent/news/ann-barnes-kent-police-press-office-15820/

Northamptonshire: Glynane, B. (2012), The ludicrous story of Northamptonshire's new Policy and Crime Commissioner, *Liberal Democrat Voice*, 21 December, www.libdemvoice.org/the-ludicrous-story-of-northamptonshires-new-police-and-crime-commissioner-32298.html

South Yorkshire: South Yorkshire Police and Crime Commissioner (2014) Shaun Wright Resignation Statement, 16 September, www.southyorkshire-pcc.gov.uk/News-and-Events/News-Archive/2014/Shaun-Wright-Resignation-Statement.aspx

Thames Valley: Jennings, T. (2013) I'm not fiddling expenses says police and crime commissioner, *Oxford Times*, 13 May, www.

oxfordtimes.co.uk/news/10414718.I_m_not_fiddling_expenses_says_
police_and_crime_commissioner

FIVE

"Putting yourself about": PCCs, the media and the public

'I know the power of the media and how it [sic] can change minds, influence people and pursue to destruction those in public office who cross them. But I also know how trivial, shallow and petty the media can be, and I am never complacent or unwatchful in my dealings with them. Popularity can turn on a very small issue from warm and friendly to bitterly cold and hostile, so I am careful not to antagonise. At the same time, I will not pander to journalists or help them if they insist on pursuing something irrelevant, counter-productive or silly.' (PCC Interviewee 68)

'[J]ust like you have to work the media, so you have to work the public. There's lots of apathy and indifference out there (though people shout loudly enough when they're burgled, mugged or have things stolen from their cars), and I have to put myself about to make sure that I am constantly in the public eye.' (PCC Interviewee 59)

This chapter examines the outward-facing roles of the PCC in responding to and developing relations with the media, and in representing and responding to the public as its elected representative. How well do PCCs handle a frequently hostile media and how do they develop positive relationships with the press, TV and radio, as well as mastering the social media functions like Whatsapp, Twitter and Facebook? What is their impact through social messaging? Can we measure or estimate it? How much of the PCC role is spent in interacting with the electorate and what can PCCs do to influence a sometimes indifferent or critical public? These are not just questions about function: the PCC needs positive relations with both media and public if he or she is to make a positive impact, especially among the leaders of influence and opinion in communities all over the PCC's 'constituency'.[1]

The media[2]

We might argue that, from the start, Police and Crime Commissioners need to have some skills in handling media relations, need a polished self-presentation and must pursue a persistent profiling of their views and achievements, or they would never have been elected in the first place. We noted in Chapter Two how the elections in November 2012 entailed a presentation of prospective PCCs on TV and in the press as well as appearances in person, which were necessary firstly to have the candidate's face recognised and secondly to ensure that his or her policies and views received differentiating coverage, especially as the government had ruled out the static but comprehensive communication of a candidate's views through a leaflet drop.

One chief officer, observing the adroit way in which his new PCC handled the media, commented on her assured touch:

> 'She is really, really good at this, and I have learned a lot from watching her. She has a very retentive memory and can recall people's names well. So she greets journalists by name and they love that; makes them think they have an inside track or something. And she is charming. You can't play down how well she works groups of journalists and cameramen: she'll smile sweetly as she ducks a question yet she'll be quite steely in getting her point across.' (CO5)

It was this kind of confidence in handling the media that helped to secure the PCC's election in the first place, because "she knew how and

---

[1] Matthew Davies argues in a 2014 paper that one of the main 'constructions' of a PCC is to be a *Crime Reduction Coordinator* engaged with many different parts of a community and its leaders (Davies, 2014b). But this is only one among a number of 'roles' (including 'crime manager') played by the versatile PCC. None of those roles could be performed adequately without thoughtful and dynamic strategies that characterise the PCCs' relationships with the media and the public.

[2] There is no extant analysis, to our knowledge, of the PCCs' relationship with the media. In what follows, we draw extensively on the published canon about *police/media* relations and attempt to relate that to the similar, but often more sophisticated, PCC/media contact. In line with the prevailing presentational mode throughout this book, we try to relate the PCCs' views to those of others (including chief officers), contextualised by academic research and the published literature.

who to brief" and understood "both the volatility and the aggression" (CO5) which characterised the media approach to the November 2012 election. Others did not fare as well.

> 'The PCC has an arrogant and unfortunate style: the media don't like to be patronised or feel that they are being manipulated and they buck against it with hostile coverage and emphasis on PCC error rather than PCC success. The PCC has a really hard time trying to get achievements across, whereas any and every shortfall is reported gleefully and at length.' (CO7)

Such a prickly and apparently counter-productive relationship is surprising, given the inherent self-publicising that goes with the role and the need for every PCC to cultivate positive media coverage for his or her policies and actions. Yet the PCC described above by CO7 is not alone. Others too are observed to have an antagonistic rather than an emollient relationship with the media:

> 'He doesn't handle the serious papers or TV journalists well. And is too easily flustered by persistent questioning. He was asked what he thought about the Channel 4 portrayal of that Kent PCC – the [...] woman with the dogs – and he said something vapid and bland and got quite upset when the questioner persisted. He started on about 'undermining the authority of the PCC' which was just a red rag to the press that gave him very scant treatment.' (CO9)

It is not an accident that the PCC commented upon by CO9 is an independent. While many of the PCCs display thoughtful sure-footedness in dealing with the media, there are some who lack confidence in being questioned or who seem to bring a kind of defensive combativeness into play, like that observed by CO9, and the result is really a foregone conclusion because it engenders more hostile coverage. Matthew Davies has observed that, of the range of PCCs:

> Those with expertise and networks in politics came into the job with a different perspective of the scope of the role compared to [sic] those coming from the police or the military. (Davies, 2014b, p. 29)

We might expand Davies' observation to suggest that the more sure-footed of the PCCs in handling the media probably come from a political or business background while the more guarded or defensive responses may come from those who served with the police and the military.[3] A chief police officer noted that the business background of his PCC directly contributed to "a consummate act" denoting the confidence with which the media were handled:

> 'The PCC does this sort of thing really well. Having a business background, he knows what "sells", what to feed and what to avoid. He always has a fund of good examples and ideas to inform the stories that the media take from him with grateful eagerness. Quite a consummate act, really.' (CO20)

By the same token, in being a media resource of some weight, one PCC observed ruefully that, having begun badly, with considerable media hostility to his election, his only route had to be upward to "a different relationship", especially as he has become "a huge source of information", at least to his local newspapers:

> '[The media] hated me when I was elected but I am a huge source of information for them – now I have a different relationship. I give them a story and I write it. I wrote a story recently and they put it on the front page – we work together.' (Interviewee 61)

This idea of a conduit to the media, where the PCC 'feeds' stories to the press and TV and attempts to cultivate thereby a positive image for both the PCC office and for the police, is echoed by others as a deliberate strategy. This is a representative approach:

> 'Most of the time, I have a strategy for dealing with the media which is every bit as important as my strategies for resolving policing problems. The dealings between us have

---

3   That said, the PCC for Gwent (Ian Johnston, a former Superintendents' Association President and senior police officer) has experienced a vigorous media – initially hostile and now guardedly cooperative – while his neighbour PCC in Dyfed-Powys (Christopher Salmon, ex-Army) is adroit in all forms of media encounter, from tabloid to serious investigative journalism (based on personal contact with the authors at the APPCs' Conference in Harrogate in November 2014).

to be honest, they have to be frequent and they have to bear repetition. I have a message to get across, and I will use every possible media opportunity to do that, whilst at the same time I will see that the media get what they want – which is stories and profiles of crime and policing which sell their TV/radio programmes and papers.' (Interviewee 69)

There are some points made in this comment that will repay analysis. The PCC notes that he has "a message to get across" and the nature of that message will determine, to some degree, the frequency of his contact with the media and the formulation of what is offered to the media as "the story". At the same time, he is aware that the media generally have a need for "stories and profiles of crime and policing" which help to sell their newspapers, or radio or TV programmes, to the wider public. Indeed, it is almost axiomatic that these days there is an insatiable diet for crime stories and police-related news in the media. Commentators have explored what this diet consists of, and Ian Loader was among the first to note that the police remain 'a principal means by which English society tells stories about itself' (Loader, 1997, p. 3). In other words, the media and the public 'fuse' as an entity that describes crime and assesses what is to be done about it, while engaged in a continuous narrative that reflects social interaction at a more basic or fabular level. The PCC appears to sit somewhere in the middle of this as a modulator, explicator, facilitator and narrator of stories about society.

Some interesting research by Michael Welch and others in the late 1990s showed that the media responded to and cultivated expert (or at least 'pivotal' law enforcement officers') opinions on crime as part of a more emotive portrayal of 'moral panic' in the population at large (Welch et al, 1997). To arrive at their judgement, the researchers analysed the content of four major newspapers over a three-year period, during which time they made a 'content analysis' of more than 100 articles on crime and criminality (Welch et al, 1997). This (now a little dated) investigation of how 'crime becomes news' is very interesting, but if we were to repeat the exercise 20 years later, it is probable that we would now need parallel research into social messaging sites and visual media coverage to obtain reliable data on how the range of the population responds to such 'stories about itself'.[4] The PCC, as revealed by our own research, is central to this process of reporting 'low' crime in contemporary society:

> 'I decided from the off that the media and I would have a symbiotic relationship, by which I mean that I would feed them stories I wanted to appear and they would get plenty of other stories through me. Over the 18 months or so since I formulated this media plan, we have created a climate of dependence. [...] It's performance management in a sense: in this job you need highly attuned antennae for a positive story and to know what the media will run with and what they won't.' (Interviewee 57)

Another noted that 'feeding the media' entailed careful analysis of what would work in each medium, so much so that the 'crime and reassurance stories' were deliberately tailored to this end:

> 'The more thoughtful journalists in the press, TV and radio engage in debate, while the wilder tabloids and 'gutter' TV wants tits and titillation. So I have a double strategy for the media – carefully selected to suit what they want – for the populist end: plenty of stories where cops are brave and come to the rescue, and for the responsible end: debate and discussion about crime types and accountability.' (Interviewee 58)

This recognises as a deliberate methodology, what Garth Crandon and Sean Dunne called the simultaneous 'symbiosis and vassalage', that can exist between the police provision of crime news and the use that the media make of the supply (Crandon and Dunne, 1997). It does not matter, in this context, whether the provider of crime news is a police

---

[4] Not just because the younger generations (15–29, 30–44) obtain much of their 'crime picture' from such social messaging sites, where minor 'moral panics' surface from time to time, but because PCCs have proven adroit in some cases in feeding stories into social media, including use of their own blogs and websites as sources of information, and in responding to comment sites of the kind that accompany nearly every online media story. See good analyses of the role of social messaging in Lewis and Fabos (2005); Shao (2009); and Quan-Haase and Young (2010). We know of no parallel or published analysis of the PCCs' use of message sites, so these more general analyses must serve for the moment, though we offer our own analysis of PCC usage of social messaging media later in the chapter.

source or the PCC's office; what is important is that the relationship between 'crime and reassurance stories' and media reporting, is sustained. In turn, this evidently requires a sophisticated briefing machinery within the PCC's office and sometimes a professional media adviser working with the PCC to ensure consistency of 'line':

> 'I have a full time expert media adviser who is a former journalist and between us we cover most of the bases. We work together on stories so that the right level of fact and human interest are covered, without compromising police information.' (Interviewee 60)

Rob C. Mawby (2010) acknowledges that such a relationship is in some ways 'asymmetric' in favour of the police or official side, but characterises it nonetheless as being 'in a healthy tension'. He commented in an earlier study that the media are central to promoting positive images of policing, but that the 'level of trust' between the two of them has been constantly in the balance (Mawby, 1999, p. 280). Robert Reiner noted too that the relationship between 'the odd couple' of police and media has always been 'vexed and complex', (Reiner, 2003, pp. 313–14), going on to quote former Met Commissioner, Sir Robert Mark, as saying that the relationship is "an enduring, if not ecstatically happy, marriage" (Reiner, 2003, p. 314). We can extrapolate these observations to the relationship that has grown up between the PCC and the media in the last three years or so, and suggest that the contacts between PCC and media are reasonably sophisticated and based, if not on trust, then at least on reciprocation. Each appears to 'need the other':

> 'The trick is that we each need the other: I need an outlet that sends a message swiftly and broadly; they need a reliable source to confirm stories and reports.' (Interviewee 68)

One chief officer expressed his admiration of the adroit way in which 'his' PCC approached the media/police relationship:

> 'I think the PCC handles the media very well indeed and I wish I was half as good at doing it as he is. He charms them, briefs them, has them in for drinks and [police] displays, feeds them stories, suggests angles for a story, gives them 'human interest' access to my officers – especially the photogenic ones – even supplies pictures. They love him

to bits because he's almost certainly their major supply of local information and news stories.' (CO8)

A canny PCC, "under no illusion" about the strength and power of the media, noted that getting to grips with their drivers and motives was "halfway to accommodating" them, and therefore to being able to deal with them on a daily basis:

'I am under no illusion: the media are powerful and they can be recklessly irresponsible, but they are driven by deadlines and a yen for novelty just like the rest of us. If you understand that, you are halfway to accommodating the media's demands of you, and the relationship can develop.' (Interviewee 69)

Using the PCC's sophisticated media interface as a preferred conduit for 'spin' on policing activities, rather than through the often antagonistic or tetchy relationship between the police and those doing the reporting, clearly appeals to the more thoughtful of chief officers. A number of them commented privately that 'their' PCCs handled the media with consummate professionalism. So widespread is this view that we might suppose generally that the role of PCC brings with it a requirement to service the media in order to gain positive coverage of policing as well as of the policed. That many PCCs can do this consummately well as part of their job does not mean that the police should think that they are similarly able:

'My police colleagues do not yet understand [the need to deal professionally with the media] at all. They labour under the fond delusion that they can control the media. They can't: they're not intelligent enough and they are not powerful enough. What they need to learn (and it isn't my job to teach them) is that dealing with the media needs a CRBN suit,[5] gloves, tongs, body armour and ears the size of elephants.' (Interviewee 69)

---

[5] The speaker is ex-military, where this cover-all clothing, claimed to be resistant to chemical, radiological, biological and nuclear contamination, is known as the 'Noddy suit' after clothing worn by the children's character created by Enid Blyton. The 'onesie' CRBN suit is always worn with a respirator. One of the authors can say from experience that wearing a CRBN suit is a prolonged experience in perspiration.

Indeed, one PCC noted that:

> 'I have to say without boasting that my office of PCC is better at media relations that the police; we work at it all the time and we are professional. I sometimes get the impression that the police think of media relations as a necessary evil rather than a relationship that has to be worked on.' (Interviewee 60)

Another PCC, looking critically at his police colleagues, thought that their methods for dealing with the media were too one-dimensional and inadequate in an age of mass communication. Their tactics seemed mistaken, and predicated on a default to the defensive. He found that:

> 'When I took over, the police corporate communications machine was brilliant in defence but had no attack at all. Editors and programme makers were ignored or never seen, journalists were fobbed off and information was either leaked or grudgingly admitted. The tactic seemed to be say nothing and deny everything. That simply doesn't work in this media-savvy age, and in the end I had to bring in my own manager of communications and open a separate channel to the media.' (Interviewee 66)

This suggests that the PCCs are 'media-savvy' but the police are not, though that is often too simplistic a reading, as this chief officer makes clear when drawing a distinction between what the PCC can say and what constrains the police:

> 'I've watched him handle a Q and A[6] with TV and press over a community event and it was a real exercise in good briefing and tact. I tell you we could learn a lot from his media strategy and his honesty in his dealings with editors and reporters. Mark you, he *can* be [open in his dealings]; he doesn't have confidential information to protect as we do sometimes. No, nothing sinister, I mean like a serial killer's MO or the details of a sexual attack, best not made public.' (CO11; speaker's own emphasis)

---

[6] Question-and-answer session, usually on the record.

while another chief officer noted that dealing with the media was not an end in itself for police officers, beset as they were with many other calls on their time:

"[I]t's the PCC's bread and butter to have a high profile and endless sound-bites, but to us relations with the media are simply another angle in a busy job" (CO6).

This "bread and butter" familiarity leads some of the more seasoned PCCs make distinctions about the kinds of media with which they are comfortable:

> 'The print media are only occasionally challenging, largely because they seem content with a press release and very little else. The TV and radio tend to challenge more and are anyway much more interactive. I use them a lot and ensure that my face is as memorable as my message – or even more so. People often come up to me and say that they have seen me on TV or have heard me on the radio, and that's nice. It means that the message is out there. Of course only constant repetition will get it across.' (Interviewee 64)

Another PCC agreed, adding that his "decades of public speaking" gave him an insight into which of the media streams most suited his talents:

> 'Some papers are negative whatever you do, such as the *Daily Mail*. Others are almost uncritical. The TV is least intrusive and most superficial; radio is often the hardest to do, because you only have your voice to paint a picture or to come across as reassuring or confident. I have decades of public speaking practice, so I think I now understand the power of the media.' (Interviewee 65)

Reach and range

We should not exaggerate the effects and power of the media. Most media coverage of most PCCs is local; comparatively few of them have come to national notice for their work despite the APCC's attempts to feed stories to the media simultaneously at national and local level[7] (though some PCCs have achieved nationwide prominence for what

---

[7]   See the APCC website, where stories are arranged by PCC force area: http://apccs.police.uk/

they have done outside the role).[8] This may suggest that local coverage would be geared almost exclusively to local issues and that a wider perspective is not always required. That in turn seems to mean to PCCs operating locally, that media opinion can adversely or positively affect their standing and 'name'. Yet analysts like Kenneth Newton have shown that the impact of the (relatively weak) mass media can be offset or moderated through other powerful factors, such as strong distrust, solid 'bedrock' opinions based in religious belief, education, class or age, as well as personal experiences (Newton, 2006, p. 225).

The powers that the media have to criticise institutions and organisations probably remain local, temporary and limited – though it may not seem like that at the time to harassed PCCs. Things pass and what seemed to be a major issue will fade over time, such as the notorious Channel 4 documentary which dominated the early (2013) period in office of Ann Barnes, PCC of Kent.[9] As one PCC remarked

"Remember that today's scandal covers tomorrow's fish and chips!" (PCC Interviewee 53).

It remains the case that the PCC handles public relations well and many of the police chief officer team are content that s/he should do so, always assuming that the outcome is positive coverage of the police. The caveat is that in turn this may hand to the PCC the entire PR remit for the public image of the force. That may not always be something that the police would want to surrender to someone who has a political agenda, within which the image of the police may become a tool to be used like any other:

> '[The police need] to keep party politics out of policing: we wouldn't be drawn into any of the preparations for the

---

[8] One might instance the PCCs of Kent, Bedfordshire and Lincolnshire and the former PCC for South Yorkshire among others, as we noted in more detail in the previous chapter.

[9] Mrs Barnes was followed by a Channel 4 documentary team for four months in 2013 (see www.channel4.com/programmes/meet-the-police-commissioner) and the resulting film entailed considerable criticism of her performance, and even of the wisdom of her agreeing to the documentary in the first place. See www.bbc.co.uk/news/uk-england-kent-27711638, and www.theguardian.com/uk-news/2014/jun/05/kent-pcc-ann-barnes-police-crime-commissioner-channel-4-documentary for representative coverage. Characteristic was this acid comment from Ceri Radford, of the *Telegraph*: 'As Barnes was shown trying to make sure that the police put people before targets, she came across as well-meaning, attention-seeking, patronising, and the worst public speaker on our screens since Bridget Jones.' (29 May 2014, www.telegraph.co.uk/culture/tvandradio/tv-and-radio-reviews/10863213/Meet-the-Police-Commissioner-review-farcical.html)

general election [May 2015], nor for the local elections next May [2016]. We won't allow the interference or intrusion: it is not our job to get the PCC re-elected nor to help in any way the PCC's party.' (CO3)

It is an invariable theme with police officers that they do not want themselves or their forces to be seen as espousing any party political line and that they should always be seen as above or detached from political viewpoints. But that presupposes an idealised world in which PCCs do not seek re-election on a political platform, in which the making party political points is never allowed and where temporary and expedient advantage is never sought. In reality, of course, PCCs will (and do) exploit the police to reinforce a political line, even where the incumbent is nominally an independent, because so many elements of policing are politicised in the media (McCombs, 2013). These range from issues about police funding to community engagement, from mental health issues to criminal profiteering, and from phone-hacking to election and ballot rigging. It would be a rare state of affairs where the police were divorced entirely from the political issues of the day, and one that might not necessarily be productive or helpful (Bradford et al, 2009). The role played by the media, whether 'weak' or not, is key to public perception of the police, and that includes consideration of both local and national politics. Stuart Lister noted a couple of years ago that politics was now inextricably part of policing and this impacted in turn on 'constabulary independence' (Lister, 2013). Such a perception is often interpreted through the media and its 'enduring, if not ecstatically happy, marriage' with policing. We might add that this has now extended to a love affair with the PCC as well.

The PCC and the public: wooing the reluctant lover?

In interview, many of the PCCs talked at length about how they paid considerable attention to the public, their electorate, and many characterised their relationships with communities and citizens as the most important things that they do. Some told us what they did to engage people, others described the spread and familiarity they had with social messaging, and many outlined the sheer amount of time they spent in public engagement of one kind or another. This part of the PCC role, 'putting yourself about' to enhance the PCC/public interface, has not been the subject of much analysis or commentary to date, though that may be changing.[10]

On 'social messaging'[11]

Daniela Dimitrova and her colleagues (2011), analysing panel data for social messaging, have established that the use of social messaging has 'only weak effects [...] on political learning' even though some digital forms may have 'appreciable effects' on political participation. We can perhaps suppose from this that the determination of the PCC to engage with younger people through social messaging and blog sites may be doomed to frustrated failure if Twitter, Facebook, Whatsapp, Snapchat and other forms are not perceived by the target audience as appropriate for such 'official' communication. None of the PCCs we spoke to had considered surveying the impact of their social messaging, though some rather desultorily and occasionally added up their 'followership' and the number of comments and 'likes' that they obtained from their blog entries. It seems impossible to establish with any degree of accuracy what the age profiles are of such 'followership', and whether or not the PCCs' social messaging is reaching large numbers of young people (which is what it is primarily intended to do).

Some analysis of PCCs' social messaging

As an indicative exercise, we analysed the PCCs' use of social messaging systems over a three-day period in April 2015.[12] The three-day period constitutes about half of a typical PCC week, and therefore gave us a manageable window through which we could observe the PCC as blogger, social messenger, Tweeter, Facebooker, online news provider and furnisher of 'instant messaging' stories. Our data for each PCC is

---

[10] Matthew Davies has produced an interesting analysis in his 'Unravelling the Role of Police and Crime Commissioners', a paper he delivered at the British Criminology Conference in 2014, and from which we have quoted in this chapter (Davies, 2014b).

[11] The authors are grateful to Maddy Caless, Astrid Scott and Gareth Owens for occasional guidance through this often alien landscape, 'where they do things differently'.

[12] The data on the PCCs' sites fluctuates, but the time chosen for analysis was dictated by the available research period. It was before the May 2015 general election and just before the media were focused on likely outcomes.

in Table 3.[13] We based our data collection on the Twitter, Facebook, blog and other online sites (as appropriate) in each PCC's webpages, and we summarise the general data in Table 4.

Please note that these data are indicative, not definitive, and they are cumulative to the point at which we ceased the exercise. They will have increased many times since.

Every PCC uses Twitter in one form or another, though some are clearly more at ease with this deliberately brief messaging form than others. For example, the PCC for Northamptonshire (Adam Simmonds) has tweeted 15,600 times and has a 'followership' in excess of 33,000, which is impressive by most ordinary standards.[14] By contrast, the PCC for Gloucestershire (Martin Surl) has tweeted just 249 times and has only 361 followers. This is not to make an invidious comparison between the two PCCs, because usage here can be largely a matter of familiarity with the medium and the ease of the messaging. It is rather to point up the likelihood that the PCC Northamptonshire is reaching more people on social messaging sites than the PCC Gloucestershire, but there is no corresponding certainty that the Northamptonshire audience is predominantly young. There is also no objective way to establish the effects of such messaging on the 'followers' or a sound method to ascertain whether or not 'hearts and minds' are changed as a result of what a PCC says. Both PCCs use other means to communicate online, though PCC Northamptonshire uses Facebook extensively and PCC Gloucestershire apparently does not use it at all. Both have weblogs and online news pages, so both seem to exploit a range of technology to send and receive messages. What is not clarified is the qualitative effect of that messaging, or whether it has more impact than personal meetings with the public.

The Northamptonshire/Gloucestershire pair respectively constitutes the high and low of PCCs' social messaging, but we are in danger of skewing the overall data if we include either of them in analyses. In Table 5, therefore, we present the summary 'net' data, having excluded both, as giving a more accurate picture of the 'true average'

---

[13] It is important to note that the PCCs' own offices are responsible for the accuracy (and continued entry) of these data, which we had no independent means to validate. The data we used were the totals up to the day we ended the exercise (in other words, the data were cumulative), and we have assumed the data to be true.

[14] Some of those who figure largely in the gossip columns command huge followings: in May 2015, Katy Perry had more than 66 million while Britney Spears had 41 million, which may put even the most popular PCCs in a subordinate social messaging context (see www.statista.com/statistics/273172/twitter-accounts-with-the-most-followers-worldwide).

Table 3: PCC use of social media, by constabulary

PCC	Twitter		Facebook		Blog	Other
	tweets	followers	likes	visits	use of blog	
Avon & Somerset	6,561	3,984	387	-	Yes, 60 posts in three years	
Beds	1,509	1,651	ND	-	No	NOL only
Cambs	435	1,386	ND	-	ND	
Cheshire	2,708	2,991	228	-	No	NOL online
Cleveland	1,545	2,008	678	-	Yes	monthly newsletter
Cumbria	1,074	1,296	ND	-	No	webpages, Tumblr
Derbys	1,558	1,540	256	-	Yes (tends to be news-led)	
Devon & Cornwall	1,667	4,054	279	-	Yes	diary, newsletter, YouTube
Dorset	4,350	2,745	444	-	Yes	LinkedIn, YouTube
Durham	1,620	2,364	2,754	5	Yes	YouTube and Flickr
Essex	1,034	2,196	72	5	Yes	online diary and news feeds
Glos	249	361	ND	-	Yes	NOL
GMP	4,634	4,655	661	-	No	Flickr, webpage, NOL
Hants	2,245	2,913	263	-	No	weekly online diary
Herts	3,821	2,736	253	-	Yes	online diary, NOL
Humber	2,509	3,499	234	-	Yes	online diary
Kent	1,272	ND	ND	-	Yes	newsletter, daily diary
Lancs	3,869	3,500	2,194	-	No	webpages, NOL
Leics	4,011	2,765	ND	-	No	interactive webpage
Lincs	524	2,126	ND	-	No	NOL only
Merseyside	4,183	2,993	319	-	No	events pages, NOL

Table 3: continued

PCC	Twitter		Facebook		Blog	Other
	tweets	followers	likes	visits	use of blog	
Norfolk	1,176	2,103	502	-	Yes	NOL
Northants	15,600	33,000	48,721	-	Yes	YouTube
Northumb	3,716	4,279	ND	-	No	webcasts, online press releases
N Yorks	1,326	1,934	ND	-	No	online chat available
Notts	1,152	1,745	43	-	Yes, 28 posts in three years	
S Yorks	3,040	4,307	353	15	N	webpage, NOL
Staffs	4,102	3,005	1902	-	Yes	YouTube, LinkedIn, Thunderclap
Suffolk	694	1,337	ND	-	No	webpage
Surrey	3,318	3,382	ND	-	Yes	'decision log'
Sussex	2,317	2,779	286	-	No	newsletter, online diary
TVP	1,355	2,657	ND	-	No	Flickr, YouTube, NOL
Warwicks	1,506	1,762	ND	-	No	NOL, webpage
West Mercia	3,650	711	ND	-	No	NOL
West Mids	8,978	6,119	669	57	Yes, starting in 2014	
W Yorks	3,990	4,450	487	-	Yes	Flickr, YouTube
Wiltshire	968	1074	ND	-	Yes	webpages, NOL
Dyfed-Powys	4,963	2,211	46	-	Yes, blog use sparse	webpages
Gwent	2,589	2,191	ND	-	No	webpages
North Wales	877	1,126	ND	-	No	webpages
South Wales	853	1,983	ND	-	No	webpages, NOL

Notes: ND = No Data available or apparent;
NOL = News on line (usually as headlines and comment);
Avon & Somerset and Nottinghamshire PCCs are the only ones to show **blog usage** for every year since 2012

Table 4: PCC use of social media, by platform

Twitter	
	41 users
	100% usage
Total no of tweets	117,008
Average no of tweets	2,856
Highest no of tweets	15,600 (Northants)
Lowest no of tweets	249 (Glos)
Total no of 'followers'	133, 918
Average no of followers	3,266
Highest followership	33,000 (Northants)
Lowest followership	361 (Glos)
Facebook	
	23 users
	56% usage
Total Facebook 'likes'	62,031
Average no of 'likes'	2,697
Highest no of 'likes'	48,721 (Northants)
Lowest no of 'likes'	43 (Notts)
	Only 10% of PCCs log 'visits' to Facebook
Total no of 'visits' recorded	82
Highest no of 'visits' recorded	57
Lowest no of 'visits' recorded	5
Blogs and other online platforms	
	49% usage
	34% have a presence on other online platforms such as Flickr, YouTube, LinkedIn or news on their webpage

of use among the rest of the PCCs. Thus we can see in Table 5 that the total (cumulative) number of tweets by PCCs up to the end of our test analysis is about 100,000 with a broadly similar number of followers, giving a mean for the 'average' PCC of about 2,500 tweets and some 2,500 followers. This suggests a small but constant core of PCC 'watchers' who regularly use the websites, and a steady core of recipients for each 'tweet'.

A similar exercise with Facebook shows by contrast that only just over half of all PCCs use it (56%), and tracking its readership by 'likes'[15] across all items gives a total of about 62,000. However, once again we have to aim off for PCC Northamptonshire who on his own registers nearly 49,000 'likes'. Table 5 shows that, excluding PCC Northamptonshire from consideration, gives a total for the remainder (22 PCCs) of 13,267, giving a mean for the 'average' PCC of 603 'likes'.

Adjustment

As we noted earlier, these summary statistics are skewed somewhat by the very high use of social messaging media by the Northamptonshire PCC. If we remove the highest (Northants) and the lowest (Gloucestershire for *Twitter*, Nottinghamshire for *Facebook* 'likes') from the summary statistics, we obtain the following 'net' results:

Table 5: PCC median and total use of social media

	Median	Total
Net total of tweets	101,159	117,008
Net total followers	100,557	133,918
Net average 'tweets'	2,593	2,856
Net average followers	2,578	3,266
Net Facebook 'likes'	13,267	62,031
Net average Facebook 'likes'	603	2,819

As may be appreciated, the series of figures are snapshots rather than 'deep data analyses' and we do not propose them as in any way definitive. But they *are* indicative, and it is worth remarking that only five years ago there would have been even fewer means to estimate

---

[15] Users of the Facebook sites can (but do not always), register their approval or enjoyment of an article or entry by signalling that they 'like' it, operating a simple thumbs-up logo. What this does not do is register those who visited the site but did not signal approval, which in turn means that we have no way to ascertain a total readership. Nonetheless, the data are indicative, though not of the age range of users. Some analysts have suggested that younger people are turning away from Facebook in favour of Whatsapp, Snapchat and other messaging forms. Matthew Sparkes (2013) wrote: 'A study of how older teenagers use social media has found that Facebook is "not just on the slide, it is basically dead and buried" and is being replaced by simpler social networks such as Twitter and Snapchat. Young people now see the site as "uncool" and keep their profiles live purely to stay in touch with older relatives, among whom it remains popular.'

the police use of social messaging sites.[16] Many PCCs have come a long way in social messaging in a short time, but that does not mean that they are necessarily getting through to a younger age group, or indeed that their use is impacting on users to any measurable degree. What this situation calls for is *comprehensive analysis of all PCCs' use of all social messaging media*, together with precise qualitative analysis of impact and effect of such messaging on the PCCs' public audience; a massive undertaking which is considerably beyond the range of this book (and its authors).

Pressing the flesh: public encounters

We turn now to examine the nature of the relationship (outside social messaging) between the PCC and the 'public' at large, noting as we do so the extensive literature about opinion-forming through public consultation.[17] Most PCCs were in no doubt about the importance of their interface with the public:

---

[16] We have noted an article in *EModeration* which examines how the police began seriously to use social media from about 2009. The unnamed author of the apparently unedited article ('The UK police and social media. Partners in Crime?') asks: 'How is social media being used by the police?' and responds with his(?) own assessment:

Intelligence gathering – notably during situations like the London riots, but also for other real-time information from the public on emergencies like traffic accidents or floods.

Dissemination of local information – the police can use their social networks to put [out] messages and links to inform and safeguard the public

Engagement with local communities, supporting the police approach to neighbourhood policing towards the delivery of community policing, transparency, interaction etc which was designed to reassure and boost public confidence in the police.

Knowledge and best practice sharing within policing organizations, notably through POLKA, the Police Online Learning Knowledge Area, provided by the National Policing Improvement Agency.

Twitter is the most visible and easily measurable social medium, and arguably the most effective when it come[s] to broadcast and response'(See www.emoderation.com/uk-police-and-social-media/. More comprehensively, also see Bartlett et al (2013); and note Crump's piece on the police use of Twitter, 2011).

[17] Again though, there are no published analyses of the PCC/public interaction and we are not aware of any critical or statistical analyses of the effectiveness or quality of contacts between PCCs and the people whom the former claim to represent.

'It is a key feature of the role: the relationship between PCC and public has to be strong and visible, so I spend lots of time in surgeries and attending meetings. People representing all sorts of organisations, from the WI to self-help groups, were surprised that, when they rang up my office and invited me along to their meetings, I'd come. They couldn't get used at first to public figures who were accessible. And they liked the message I was giving too.' (Interviewee 54)

There is often a sense in the PCCs' description of how assiduously they work at their public interface, of a disproportionate amount of effort for not very tangible rewards. It is one thing to turn up to all and every meeting (one PCC was described by another as "prepared to turn up for the opening of an envelope"); it is another thing altogether to create an alchemy that turns the base metal of contact into the gold of direct support. As Niklas Luhmann observed, there can be an illusory aspect to contact with the public, whereby the effort of communication can be confused with the act, and he is right to remind us that

'The mere act of uttering something [...] does not, in and of itself, constitute communication' (Luhmann, 2000, p. 4)

Yet, again and again, PCCs reiterate the amount of time they devote to communication of all kinds as a means to getting across the message about responsive and responsible PCCs who will act to get things done that the public wants:

'[...] a very large part of my time, and the time of the small staff that serves me in this role, is devoted to finding out what people think and feel. There are public meetings, groups, walkabouts, blogs, Twitter, Facebook, social messaging of all kinds and 'stop-and-chat', daily contacts and weekly forums, where I put myself about right across the whole force area. It's time-consuming and hard work, but I'm good at it, people talk to me pretty readily on the whole and so I can speak for them with some authority.' (Interviewee 65)

However, assiduous the PCC's efforts are, the wider public seems to remain unmoved and disengaged from the messaging, unless or until some aspect of crime or policing impinges directly upon an individual. Then there is contact, impact and result (see below). For the PCC, there may be some hubris in believing that the message is important and the medium for that message is oneself. Compare PCC Interviewee 65's comments above with those of a chief officer observing the frenetic efforts of another PCC:

> 'Where he's not good — and it's a product of his age — is in handling social messaging sites. Some of the younger, more switched-on PCCs do this very well (one or two could tweet for England), but our PCC is not comfortable with blogs or Twitter, and prefers the more old-fashioned briefing or press conference. This spills over into his relations with the public, because people find him quite formal.' (CO12)

Some PCCs are quite convinced that their efforts are rewarded and that people recognise them, and respond to what is being done by the people's representative:

> 'I hold surgeries in supermarkets, encounters in village halls, and attend public meetings in the evenings all over the county. In a recent poll, conducted as a kind of 'vox pop',[18] 10 out of 13 people recognised me and what I did. The population feels that they own me and that's good, because I am their voice and their champion.' (Interviewee 57)

Another PCC, by contrast, seems almost overwhelmed by the scale of what he has undertaken in his pursuit of constant contact with the public, listening to what they have to say and communicating his messages about policing and community safety:

> 'The point about relations with the public is that there are so many of them. I could spend all my time just meeting people and it still wouldn't be more than a quarter of the electorate. [...] Thinly-attended meetings in cold village community centres don't do it for me. I'd rather be filmed talking to someone in a shopping centre or in a town square. Better visually and better in terms of media attention. That's the point: the media and the public are twin halves, often.

---

[18] A term to describe the media practice of stopping people at random as they go about their lives. It can be unconsciously biased, of course, because the media court controversial or antagonistic viewpoints.

> Appealing to one appeals to the other, and that's the basis
> of my strategy as PCC.' (Interviewee 59)

Being 'canny' may enable this PCC to husband his strength and communication resources, but every lost opportunity for contact may translate into a lack of votes for re-election. The PCC cannot forget that 'candidature' looms again in 2016 and 2020, and therefore he or she has to hustle to become familiar to the potential electorate.[19]

Diana Mutz found that 'individuals are exposed to far more dissimilar [...] views via news media than through interpersonal [...] discussants' (Mutz, 2001),[20] because people talk to those they know and with whom they share coincident, if not identical, points of view and interpretations. This could mean that PCCs may believe that they are communicating as equal to equal, but they may not come across, particularly on social media, like that.

> 'I use all the social media, especially Facebook and Twitter,
> to keep a dialogue going with the public, though privately I
> think these media are banal and no real insights ever come
> of them, Comments on my blog are a bit different, but still
> pretty weak. The best interactions I get are face-to-face with
> people in the street or in meetings – everything from the
> Soroptimists through the Round Table to Neighbourhood
> Watch – and I average 150 evening meetings every year.'
> (Interviewee 67)

This PCC is not alone in finding the contents of social messaging pages to be of a light, superficial and even trivial flavour, but that may be because of the use people make of social messaging rather than anything inherently "banal" or "weak" about using it. Indeed, some research by Anabel Quan-Haase and Alyson Young has suggested that most social messaging – in this case an analysis of Facebook – is actually concerned (for its users) with key dimensions that include leisure, fashion, the sharing of problems, the promoting of sociability within the 'group' and social information. (Quan-Haase and Young, 2010)

---

[19] One chief officer noted to us in early 2015 that his PCC "had already begun campaigning for re-election" (CO20), 15 months before the contest in May 2016.

[20] Mutz was discussing political views, but we have omitted the political considerations to reinforce the point that the PCCs talk to people about all kinds of community issues, not just political ones. Mutz's essential point holds, whether political or not.

Serious commentary about society, the fear of crime and personal unease hardly figure, because the purpose of the social messaging site is about having fun and unwinding (Quan-Haase and Young, 2010).[21] There may be a lesson here for PCCs that, although social messaging sites and blogs put them in touch, they suppose, with young people, the means of communication may not suit what PCCs are trying to say and as a result, the young people may turn off, or, as Cynthia Lewis and Bettina Fabos found, resist unwelcome messages (Lewis and Fabos, 2005). These researchers went on to note that this was a complex and sophisticated activity:

> '[...] participants manipulated the tone, voice, word choice, and subject matter of their messages to fit their communication needs, negotiating multiple narratives in the process.' (Lewis and Fabos, 2005, p. 489)[22]

This often entails 'screening out' messaging they do not want, from people they choose not to listen to, while they are engaged in 'multiple narratives' about who they are, what they are doing (often in tedious detail), and what they want to do or be (ditto). In other words, try as they might, PCCs may not be able to compete with the trivial and the superficial nature of social messaging, precisely because that is what its users want it to be:

> 'I use every means that I can to communicate to the public, from public meetings, forums for views, webcams of meetings, Twitter, Facebook, blogs, email, website, newsletters and leafletting. It's hard work putting yourself relentlessly about, but it has to be done.' (Interviewee 58)

---

[21] Quan-Haase and Young compiled their research data in 2009–10 by way of comments and views collected from undergraduate students based on 77 surveys and 21 interviews. It may be supposed that in some ways theirs is a rarefied sample, dealing as it does with a stratum of 98 literate and intelligent people, reliant on social messaging to sustain their contact networks; but actually such groups of young people are probably representative, in their use of messaging, of their whole generation.

[22] The sample used by Lewis and Fabos in 2005 was very small (just seven young men), but the detail of their analyses and the crisp conclusions to which they come about 'the hybrid nature of textuality' in the lives of young people, is both persuasive and innovative. It shows that people simply ignore or discard material they do not want to engage with. Thus, PCCs may text and text, but they do not even know if they are read (let alone believed and accepted).

This then is the pretty thankless treadmill that PCCs find themselves on: "putting [themselves] relentlessly about" in their force areas, addressing meetings, talking to groups, encountering people shopping or at leisure, accepting invitations, writing tweets and blogs, ensuring their constant presence on the various media, and exploiting other social messaging systems for all they are worth, merely to have more people recognise them and understand what they do, if they are lucky. Their conviction that this is worth it sometimes borders on the desperate:

> 'I use a wide range of social media to keep people informed: Twitter, Facebook, hashtags, webcasts and a monthly blog and I totally embrace all that because that is the way to reach a whole new generation, who just don't consume media through TV or newspapers. As a result, I think I get through to the youth in a way that others don't.' (Interviewee 56)

More hubris?

However, on occasions, PCCs can point convincingly to an intervention they have made that resonates with at least one member of the public, and which demonstrates that PCCs "add value" and "make a difference" (two key mantras that we heard from them time and again). This is an example that was provided to us by a laconic PCC, resigned to the degree to which he had to "put himself about":

> 'This role has high visibility and you have to be prepared to take people's views on board wherever and whenever you hear them. I had one person come up to me in a restaurant and make a complaint about the way she had been treated by the police. This was on a Friday evening. By Tuesday lunchtime, the matter had been resolved, she had had an apology and her problem put right and the media coverage was sympathetic to both sides, so it was a win/win. But it should never have happened in the first place.' (Interviewee 52)

The PCC used this example to explain to the interviewer that matters came to his attention through frustration on the part of members of the public with the responses they had received from the police. Making the effort in this example clearly paid dividends as there was one satisfied 'customer', but it is doubtful whether that could be translated or multiplied across the force area to make a cumulative sea change in people's attitudes. Another PCC agreed that "it is a big ask", because the public contact took time and effort, and she wished she could "split [her]self up" to cover the ground better:

> 'It is a big ask: I use social media, a blog, the press, the visual media, local councils, parish councils, focus groups and just going out and meeting people informally. It's a lot for one person and I sometimes wish I could split myself up a hundred ways to get around more, but you do what you can.' (Interviewee 51)

Quan-Haase and Young found that 'instant messaging' is not like the sociability of Facebook; it is more about 'relationship maintenance and development' (Quan-Haase and Young, 2010, p. 359). Neither factor applies particularly aptly to the PCC's communication with young people, and we continue to believe, in the absence of evidence to the contrary, that 'instant messaging' by PCCs may be falling on deaf or otherwise diverted ears, just as with Facebook. That said, Yongwhan Kim noted 'a positive and significant relationship' between social networking sites and exposure of their users to 'challenging viewpoints' which in turn supported the notion that such sites may 'contribute to individuals' exposure to cross-cutting political points of view' (Kim, 2011, p. 974). Provided that the social networking sites are those targeted and populated by PCCs, there may indeed be a chance that some users of a more thoughtful disposition may be stimulated by the content of the PCCs' messages. Firm evidence of this is lacking, however. Work by Florian Foos and Eline de Rooij on other aspects of political messaging (Foos and de Rooij, 2013) suggests that people accept or reject messaging with a political content entirely on the basis of their own party affiliations, which in turn suggests that messages can be blocked by voters who do not share the candidate's affiliations; therefore a PCC campaigning on a party platform may not get his or her message over to voters from other parties.

Jeremy Crump (2011), researching the police use of Twitter, found that the police were often over-cautious in using the messaging site, only reinforcing messages sent in other ways, and it may be a leap of faith for PCCs to be more proactive and absorptive of the new messaging systems than of the older, tried and trusted means of getting messages across. It depends what they target as their preferred audience. In absolute terms, their principal voters are likely to be older people.[23] Scale and intensity could pose problems, but they could also be the

---

[23] Much as they are likely to be in general elections too.

basis of a new kind of opinion-sampling. Brendan O'Connor and his colleagues (2010) analysed political and public opinion based largely on analyses of hundreds of Twitter accounts from 2008–09, and found that very large numbers of users broadcast their views and opinions on a wide variety of topics. The biggest problem that the academics found in attempting their analysis was 'signal to noise ratio'; but after screening out much of the 'noise' of the messaging, O'Connor et al, using 'a simple sentiment detector', were able to establish what people thought about a variety of topics. Essentially, what this provided was a tool for sampling public opinion that was cheaper, quicker, more detailed, spread more widely and more comprehensively than standard opinion-sampling techniques (O'Connor et al, 2010). This methodology could be germane to finding out whether the PCCs' messages get across to social messaging site users and if those messages generate discussion.[24]

The chief police officer view of PCCs as communicators

It is likely then that PCCs will try to be effective in personal contact with their electorate, either through face-to-face contact or through some form of public meeting; but they will also persist with social messaging in most cases, because it offers a third option. The 'semi-detached' views of their chief officers, who often accompany PCCs to venues, offer us a parallel insight into the effort that PCCs make to engage with people. Some meetings are more successful occasions than others:

> 'My PCC is happiest with people his own age and older, but I've also seen him absolutely wow a WI or Mumsnet type audience of youngish women. He came out of one session grinning like a cat and saying that if all his electorate were half as bright and clued-up as that female audience was, he'd get a 99% mandate.' (CO12)

---

[24] But, as we have noted earlier on PCCs' social messaging, such an analytical undertaking is beyond the scope of our research, or indeed our expertise, and will have to wait for future analysts. However, any outcome is unlikely to be as inaccurate as political opinion polls in 2015 (witness the predictions of voting in the general election that were so wildly astray).

On the other hand, some PCCs are clearly uncomfortable when they are challenged in public by persistent questioners, as this chief officer observed with rather gleeful malice:

> '[...] intelligent questions (and there are some, especially from Neighbourhood Watch people) throw him and he flannels about, which irritates the questioner. We had one real Jeremy Paxman[25] at a Parish Council meeting out in the sticks who just wouldn't let it go, and kept asking the PCC the same question again and again. The PCC got quite flustered, and of course, we, the police top team there, just sat on our hands and did not help him out. He was cross with us afterwards but I pointed out to him that the question had nothing to do with policing, so how could we have helped? "You just sat and watched me dig a hole!" he shouted. "Yes" I said, "you dug it very well," and that really has set our relationship on edge a bit ever since.' (CO2)

Such a hostile observation of a PCC's discomfiture is rather unusual and this was one of the few negative examples we encountered, and is probably the product of a deeper hostility and resentment. Another chief police officer was altogether indifferent to his PCC's courting of the public:

> 'I don't see that much of her at public events unless they're on telly or I'm frog-marched along as the token uniform. I just think that putting herself about to the public is time-consuming and mind-numbingly dull, but that's my take on it, not hers.' (CO5)

By contrast, a chief officer who watched the PCC for his force at public meetings, expressed admiration for the effort and for the message, as well as for the persistence of the PCC in communicating thoughts and opinions that would not always be welcome. We reproduce his long comment verbatim:

> 'He's always much less formal and stiff than a cop would be in a public gathering and he has a real knack for encouraging

---

[25] Jeremy Paxman is a familiar presenter of TV programmes in the UK and formerly a formidable questioner on topical news programmes on the BBC; he is also the question master on *University Challenge*.

people to speak. Of course, what each audience doesn't
see is that his message is the same each time (I could
certainly repeat it word for word): hold cops to account,
reduce crime, increase and support neighbourhood teams,
reassurance, cut anti-social behaviour, cope with budget
cuts, prevent crime, care for the environment and the rest.
Good stuff of course and usually goes down well with
audiences and his approval ratings are steady. It's not always
a political message though and he is not always reassuring.
I saw the mask slip once when he rounded on some
whingeing Neighbourhood Watch types and told them that
it was easy to be obsessive about crime when you never see
any. He told them to go and live on a 'sink estate' and see
what crime really is. Didn't go down at all well with NW,
but it did with the police who were there, and surprisingly
never made it to the media.' (CO6)

The PCC probably regrets that his views "never made it to the media"
on the basis that all publicity is good publicity if it raises the PCC's
profile, though there have been occasions, as we have noted earlier,
when that has been counter-productive.

All the same, the PCC spends considerable portions of his or her
working time with the media and with the public. Whether that is
time well spent and whether or not there is a measurable impact will
probably be determined in the 2016 and 2020 elections, by the number
returned after re-election if by no other yardstick. Let us now visit the
larger policing debate itself and examine what the PCC contributes.

SIX

The debate with no end: PCCs' remit and the problems of policing

'At the strategic end, the [police] had a one-dimensional view of the world and the possession of ideas, capability and the will to change was related too much to rank. You could only innovate if you had lots of silver braid: the problem was that once you got lots of silver braid, you didn't want to innovate.' (Interviewee 57)

'I think [the PCC] is the most switched-on 'outsider' I know. I like the clarity of his instructions, I like how well tapped-in he is to the communities and I like that he thinks all the time about how to make policing better.' (CO11)

When the concept of the Police and Crime Commissioner took firm hold in Conservative thinking,[1] the primary object, as we saw in Chapter One, was to ensure democratic accountability for the police, and to replace the 'invisible' police authorities. That original formulation appears to have grown; indeed, following the general election in May 2015,[2] it is probable that, by 2018–20, the 'PCC-as-oversight' will extend to the other emergency services and possibly to other parts of the criminal justice system (prospects which we shall look at in greater detail in Chapter 7). In this chapter, however, we want to examine what the PCC's remit is and how it works, while also considering the impact of the PCCs' involvement both in budget setting and in policing priorities and their sometimes fraught relations with Police and Crime Panels. We hope that this will give a picture

---

[1] It is worth noting that the idea was originally Labour's, with the then Home Secretary, David Blunkett, mooting in 2003 the notion of 'directly elected police authorities' to give democratic oversight of the police. 'In 2008, the Labour government dropped plans to introduce direct elections to police authorities following opposition from local government' (Cousins, 2012, p. 3), only to revive them momentarily in Lord Stevens' Independent Police Commission in 2013

[2] In which, it may be remembered, the Conservative Party was returned with a workable though small majority and the Labour Party, then under Ed Miliband, was decisively rejected as a potential government.

(perhaps more truly 'warts and all' than the Home Secretary's claim in 2013[3]) of the PCC's engagement with the problems of policing and the way in which the role has expanded from 'democratic oversight' into something much closer to strategising the (local) police and partners' responses to crime.

The government stated at the outset that it did not want 'to shackle Commissioners with reams of guidance and prescription on their role' (Home Office, 2010, para 2.14) but suggested that 'five key roles' would be common to all. These were: representing communities' policing needs, setting priorities to meet those needs, holding the chief constable to account, setting the police force budget, and hiring and firing the chief constable (Home Office, 2010, para 2.9). The government's description of what this might entail borders on the woolly when it asserts that the 'local focus' of PCCs 'will be largely determined by the public' (Home Office, 2010, para 2.14). In other words, how these tasks were to be accomplished was up to the individual PCC working in his or her own way, and influenced by what people told him or her.

In 2010, the Home Office wanted to consult a wider spectrum of opinion in its quest to 'reconnect police and people'[4] and sought views on a proposition for some 'key responsibilities' that all commissioners should have. The first of these was making sure that 'policing is available and responsive to communities', principally through neighbourhood policing teams, but also through 'the full service of response, investigation and problem-solving across all communities' so that they could protect 'the public from serious harms and threats' (Home Office, 2010, para 2.15). This meant, the document suggested, that commissioners 'will need to look beyond their own force borders' and be 'under a strong duty to collaborate [on] cross border, national and international crimes (such as fighting serious organised crime and terrorism)' (Home Office, 2010, paras 2.16 and 2.17). However, a public poll conducted in 2013 suggested that the public did not think that PCCs had made any tangible difference to crime: 64% of people surveyed thought that PCCs had made *no difference* to the police's effectiveness in combating crime and a similar percentage (63%)

---

[3] In a speech to the Policy Institute in November 2013, Theresa May discussed 'Police and Crime Commissioners One Year On; Warts and All' (Strickland, 2013). The reference is to Oliver Cromwell's alleged instruction to his portrait painter, Sir Peter Lely, not to seek to flatter him but include 'warts and all' (see Horace Walpole's *Anecdotes of Painting in England, with some account of the principal artists*, 1764, but the attribution may be fanciful).

[4] Part of the title of the 2010 Home Office paper is 'Reconnecting police and people'.

thought that the police had *not changed* in terms of being accountable.[5] Only 3% thought that PCCs had made the police more effective, which is scarcely a ringing endorsement, while 89% could not name the PCC for their force area. Perhaps these percentages have changed for the better in the interim,[6] but it is difficult to ascertain with objective evidence what the public thinks of its PCCs – indeed, whether it actually thinks of them at all. Meanwhile, public opinion surveys are in the doldrums.[7] In addition, as we have noted throughout, some chief police officers consider that PCCs are over-focused on neighbourhood policing and not focused enough on serious and organised crime in their force areas, let alone having any regional or national perspective on crime. One chief officer observed "My specialism is major, serious and organised crime and I do not think that more than a handful of PCCs understand what we do and why." (CO7)

Another chief officer commented that:

> "The downside is that the PCC doesn't show much interest in organised or major crime which is a pity." (CO11)

A third observed that:

> "She understands the bits she understands. She has no interest in serious and organised crime but is thoroughly engaged with restorative justice and victim-centred justice; she knows more about both than my officers do." (CO20)

Other PCCs, by contrast, do indeed grasp the larger picture and respond to chief officers' representations, though perhaps with no immediate intention of action:

---

[5] This was a YouGov/Times poll conducted in November 2013; its results may be viewed at http://d25d2506sfb94s.cloudfront.net/cumulus_uploads/document/jwnzb06i31/YG-Archive-131112-TimesPCCs.pdf; and were also quoted in Longstaff (2013), p. 2

[6] The Home Secretary thinks so: she claimed in 2014 that 70% of people now knew who their PCC was. We remain sceptical.

[7] Polls have suffered a fall in credibility somewhat since failing to indicate a Conservative victory in the May 2015 general election, which, until the BBC 'Exit Poll' broadcast at 2200 hours on 7 May, continued to predict a 'hung' parliament and did not foresee the disastrous showing by the Liberal Democrats, let alone so few Labour gains in key marginal seats. Electoral Calculus noted a 6% error in the poll forecasts: see www.electoralcalculus.co.uk/homepage.html;, but it seemed to lay observers to be larger than this. *Private Eye* (15 May 2015) carried a satirical headline a week *after* the election: 'New Poll Shows Miliband Ahead'.

> "[...] he listens to me when I discuss organised crime and he understands that there is a wider policing and crime picture to which all forces contribute." (CO12)

In fairness, the PCCs were elected in the first place to make a difference in local policing and accountability and that probably means that their focus is inevitably parochial in crime terms (Jones et al, 2012). This would be manifested in close attention to neighbourhood policing and what communities thought of the way they were being policed, as well as the nature of what disturbed them and their fear of crime, rather than determination to coordinate effort against a larger national or more serious threat of organised crime (Gilmore, 2012). It may be that serious and organised crime is something that PCCs will pay more attention to as their local concerns are allayed. The government merely notes it as 'a strong duty' for PCCs rather than a statutory obligation to fulfil; after all, the local electorate is hardly likely to register a PCC's strategic crime focus outside the immediate vicinity, unless the local news reports are heavily 'spun' to that effect.

A further 'key responsibility' for PCCs is in encouraging local partnerships, which we looked at in some detail in Chapter Four and merely wish to note it here as part of the context of the PCCs' remit. Another requirement noted by the Home Office is the need for close cooperation between the PCC and the rest of the criminal justice system (CJS). We shall consider this in greater detail in the next chapter, when we examine the PCCs' 'take' on the prospects of extending their oversight. Here it may be enough to observe that the government makes allowance for later expansion of the PCC's role because it:

> '[...] sees a potential future [sic] role for Commissioners in respect of the wider CJS as further reforms develop.' (Home Office, 2010, para 2.20)

This aspiration, however vague, was echoed by a PCC who remarked:

> 'The role needs a wider remit over time.' (Interviewee 54)

While PCC imaginations may know no bounds, the reality of restricted funding may concentrate their attentions on more mundane issues.

Money matters

Close attention to 'value for money' and insistence on police accountability for budgets are major responsibilities for PCCs and it is no surprise that the outline remit for the role makes much of the budget control that PCCs are expected to exercise. The government describes this *key responsibility* as a fourfold activity: reporting to the public on how funding is being used, holding forces to account for 'their local use of resources', paying attention to any economies of scale that might be obtained through 'national arrangements for buying goods and services' and holding police forces accountable for what they spend on 'collaboratively provided services' within their region. The incessant difficulty that PCCs encounter (and one that has aligned them tightly, often, with their chief officer teams) is that the government progressively reduces its central provision of funds for policing while telling PCCs that budgeting is their devolved responsibility. PCCs as a result have looked hard at what they can raise locally through the precept, but this too is capped by government. Many PCCs find it frustrating that they do not have autonomous control of police finances; instead they have to account for what they are allowed to have, which is quite a different matter. One PCC observed morosely that "The financial 'flex' is very limited and a real improvement would be a new national funding model." (Interviewee 67)

Given the austerity that surrounds public finance and the 'ring-fencing' of major spenders of public money like the NHS and Education, the prospect of a "new national funding model" for policing is remote and PCCs have been bracing themselves for further large scale cuts in the next spending round to 2018/19.[8] Some have made decisions about force spending that have had impacts on costs: the most obvious was the general withdrawal of funding for ACPO (which had previously 'top-sliced' forces) but Abie Longstaff draws attention to cost-cutting activities such as the West Midlands PCC's abrupt ending of the 'Business Partnering for Policing Programme' on his first day in office, while other PCCs have halted sometimes well-advanced plans 'to outsource their forces' organisational support services' (Longstaff, 2013, p. 5, and see below). Several PCCs have rationalised their police estate, closed police stations, engaged with private finance initiatives (PFIs) for buildings and have considered options to relocate their force headquarters, while robustly bidding to increase their precepts

---

[8]   In the event, the Chancellor of the Exchequer left police budgets intact in his Autumn Statement of December 2015.

(Longstaff, 2013). It has been a source of considerable frustration for chief officer teams when PCCs have rejected careful plans for "comprehensive outsourcing" of "everything, from catering to estates and from statement-taking to transport" and the officers concerned believe that this is because of political pressures on some PCCs from their "national party headquarters". Here is a typical description of what was involved:

> 'I drew up plans for comprehensive outsourcing in consultation with my team and with the Police Crime Panel. We looked at everything, from catering to estates and from statement-taking to transport. We had good plans drawn up, and calculated that this would save something like £5 million–£8 million in annual costs. We put this to the PCC as a fully worked-out plan with all the financial calculations and he refused to do have anything to do with it. Someone had got to him, and we think it was his national party headquarters telling him to back off the notion of privatisation altogether. His masters were afraid that there would be too much political fallout.[9] So, instead of keeping my frontline intact and outsourcing most of the force's unwarranted functions,[10] I now have to look for deep cuts in my operational capability – and all because the PCC is too weak to stand up for us and is too much driven by Whitehall. Is it any wonder I'm sceptical of the PCC's "added value"?' (CO18)

Adam White, in a short study of the difficulties of 'privatising' the police, noted that PCCs and police leaders both 'enjoy considerable autonomy when weighing up [...] options' (White, 2014a, para 3, p. 2). According to him, the police are not well-versed in outsourcing because they have no 'mindset' or experience in considering the commerciality of devolving police functions elsewhere: 'police forces don't think in terms of business processes and unit costs. They think in terms of victims and criminals, evidence and arrest' (White, 2014a). This is generally true but we have noted an increasing emphasis on

---

[9]   This confirms Adam White's findings; see White (2014b).

[10]   The speaker means those functions which do not have to be undertaken by a police officer holding a warrant. This usually means non-confrontational and non-coercive activities, for which regular officers are not required (such as routine foot-patrol, statement-taking, crime-scene investigation and the like)

acquiring business skills at chief officer level,[11] and careful planning of the kind that CO18 evidences in his narrative above, can be frustrated by PCCs with different ideas.[12]

By contrast, some PCCs registered frustration with the invariability with which chief officer teams supposed that budgetary restraint meant losing people from posts, whereas it could mean "doing things smarter and better". This PCC succinctly describes the differences of approach to "cuts in budgets" between him and his chief police officer team:

> '[...] the leaders in the force didn't understand money, budgeting, accounts or financial principles. They always assumed that cuts in budgets meant cuts in people, and it took me months to show them that actually you didn't need to cull staff; you could make savings, substantial ones, by doing things smarter and better. I saved £5 million in the first year without losing a single frontline officer.' (Interviewee 57)

That may have held true quite widely in the first round of cuts from 2013–14, but a number of PCCs acknowledge that in the last year or so, additional and substantial reductions in funding have them verging on the desperate:

> 'We have lost more than a fifth of our budget since 2010, and when I tell you that 80% of our costs are people and pensions, you'll see that there isn't much slack. So we've had to look really hard at whether functions are 'nice to do' or 'need to do', and cut our cloth accordingly.'

> [*Interviewer:* let me pursue this for a moment. How sustainable are your cuts in the light of more to come? Where will you be in a year's time?][13]

> 'The cuts are currently sustainable, but I'd be a fool (and I'm not) if I thought that we could take another 15%–20% and it not affect the service the police give the public. If there

---

[11] See Caless (2011), pp. 184–5, where he discusses the Strategic Command Course's business learning modules.

[12] White (2014a) goes on to note the example of Lincolnshire Police, which has embarked on a £229 million outsourcing project with G4S.

[13] The interview took place in mid-2014.

are further really deep cuts, then some things we do will
have to go. Some kinds of policing will not be deliverable.
We may have to take a really radical look at whether or
how we investigate some kinds of crime, for example. Or
equip our officers. Or buy new IT systems.' (Interviewee 62)

Jeffrey Ross noted that 'underfunding' was a key complaint of police
officers in the United States (Ross, 2011), and it would not be
surprising if the same argument was made here about the inability of
the police to match public expectations because of a chronic shortage
of money. PCCs are alert to the danger:

'I and the chief constable are absolutely at one on this; but
he is hobbled by the budget reductions that mean he loses
officers and staff all the time, thanks to the national cuts.
He runs an efficient force, but you simply cannot keep
doing the things you must and address all the problems of
organised crime, gang crime, the criminalisation of young
people, hate crime and repeat offending, if you are having
your budget slashed, year on year.' (Interviewee 60)

It is not yet clear whether or not this message is being received
sympathetically by the media and the public, but in the general context
of fiscal austerity, it is certainly a familiar complaint in public service. All
the same, some PCCs are impatient of the police (and of their fellow
PCCs) for using financial stringency as an excuse not to do things.
One commissioner argues that such a budgetary "cliff edge" can often
be the result of police incompetence or inadvertence as much as, or
more than, the result of cuts in funding:

'Finance is a real nightmare and I can see the edge of a cliff
approaching in the force's budgets and finance management
generally, which we'll fall over like lemmings unless
something is done and done quickly. The successive cuts on
police budgets imposed nationally are only the beginning
of what needs to be done.' (Interviewee 52)

Such a bleak assessment of police abilities to handle strategic finance
is fairly rare among PCCs, many of whom continue to seek common
ground with their chief officer teams in facing, and trying to mitigate,
the effects of more funding cuts. One PCC tried to put the prospect of

future reductions in the context of "the frontline delivery of policing" and the even larger context of "the country's debts":

'This time round[14] we have found it much harder because all the slack had been taken, and of course present cuts will affect the delivery of policing to some degree. What worries me greatly is if we have another drastic budget cut for 2016–18. If that happens, it really will impact [on] the frontline delivery of policing and we will simply have to stop doing some things. I hope that it won't come to that, but the signs are ominous and this all takes place in the context of generally trying to come out of this recession and to reduce the country's debts. Policing, though important, is contextualised by the need to save money and to live, nationally, within our means. But it's not easy, even right now, to get the balance right.' (Interviewee 69)

Currently, there seems to be little sign of "slack" in the future funding of policing and "get[ting] the balance right" will continue to be a major preoccupation of PCCs for the foreseeable future, and of course, for their chief police officer teams. Some PCCs think that there will be a reaction against continued austerity and that the government will quietly drop plans to cut more from policing:

'On reduced police budgets, they [the government] have us over a barrel, because they call the tune in the context of the greater national need. I'd be more convinced if that need to economise extended also to health and to education.[15] But reducing the policing budget may well come back and bite the government, because local people will get fed up with local cuts and start to make noises about the consequent loss of services and police presence. If that is taken up by the media, there may be a U-turn or a quiet leaving-alone of the harsher cuts. We'll see.' (Interviewee 68; our footnote)

Alternatively, this could be wishful thinking. The *key responsibility* of handling force finances may be much larger and broader than first envisaged, and to a degree, it overshadows some of the other remits

---

[14] The interview was in autumn 2014.
[15] As we noted earlier, the budgets for both the NHS and the Department for Education are ring-fenced and thereby inviolable.

in the PCC list. Only a couple of the key responsibilities remain to be noted: in addition to abjuring the PCCs to encourage diversity within the police workforce 'to reflect the diversity of the population it serves' (Home Office, 2010, para 2.22), the outline consultative remit for the PCC concludes with commentary on the Police and Crime Panels, which we shall examine in more detail shortly. Let us first consider the possible implications and impacts of the entire remit.

Considering the PCC remit

Abie Longstaff reminds us that introducing PCCs in the first place 'was a major reform and incoming PCCs had no blueprint to work from as there is no equivalent post elsewhere in the world or in any other public service in the UK' (Longstaff, 2013, p. 8).

That said, the newness of the role should perhaps not excuse the vagueness with which its 'job description' has been couched. Such vagueness is not normally characteristic of government legislation, but the weight of the Home Office lies heavily over the description of what PCCs are expected to do, and the (often contradictory) insistence that the role is devolved away from central government may explain why there is little circumscription of, or tight boundaries for, a role that is still effectively in its infancy. The PCCs themselves occasionally feel uncomfortable with the shadowy outline of their purpose:

> "The PCC has no job description; only a list of statutory duties and obligations" (Interviewee 51)

and:

> 'Interpreting the role went through a series of phases, I suppose. I came in with a blank slate and had no particular expectations; I was new to local government and new to the police.' (Interviewee 54)

Another PCC saw the role only in terms of impact and outcome. He thought the "effectiveness" of the PCC role would determine its purpose:

> 'I see this role almost entirely in terms of *effectiveness*: what can I do to make the relationship between public and police more effective? What are the major effects that I must identify to make people feel safer? How, by holding

the police to account, do I make the justification of police actions more effective?' (Interviewee 65, speaker's own emphasis)

but some merely thought that the job was simply to be a massive improvement on the police authority:

'The role of PCC is straightforward, even if it is poorly-defined by the Home Office in functional terms. I do what the police authority used to do or was set up to do, but I do it directly, immediately, professionally, full time and on behalf of all of the people of this county.' (Interviewee 62)

while a chief officer, with slightly more detachment, observed that the PCC role "allows of enormous latitude in interpretation" but actually needed to be "carefully defined and given rigour" perhaps through some sort of "statute and legality" if there is to be consistency of function and process across England and Wales:

'[...] the vagueness of the role – utterly undefined by the Home Office – allows of enormous latitude in interpretation. This is pernicious because it means that a PCC in one part of the country can do things that a PCC in another part of the country does not or will not. Where is the consistency? The role should be carefully defined and given rigour, as well as having its own effective checks and balances to make sure that the office is not abused. What the PCC role needs is statute and legality.' (CO12)

James Cousins observes that 'it would be remarkable if no [PCCs] used their democratic mandate to justify a more activist approach than police authorities ever did' (Cousins, 2012, p. 12), adding that 'ultimately, it will be down to a matter of personality'. In other words, while some might deplore the vague and generalist outline of the PCC role, others will relish the opportunity to push that outline into shapes that had never been conceived or anticipated. As Cousins observes of PCCs, using a sheriff analogy, 'They may be unarmed but can recruit a formidable posse' (Cousins, 2012, p. 14).

The first four-year term of office for PCCs is characterised by the way they have tested the limitations of what they do: making decisions alone that were previously collective and corporate (if slow); determining policing priorities that previously had been the unchallenged province of the police themselves; engaging with communities all over their force areas in ways that the former police authorities had never thought of; while challenging the police robustly and continuously to justify what *they* do. In pushing at the boundaries in this way, PCCs will not achieve consistency of the kind admired or required by the chief officer (CO12) cited earlier, since it is doubtful that the remit enjoyed by a PCC in one part of the country will be exactly replicated in another: inevitably, circumstances will alter cases. But it would not be uniform if the incumbents were elected mayors either; it is perhaps a chimera to suppose that 'one size fits all' in respect of the commissioner role. If each PCC tailors his or her approach to local policing problems, and develops a singular way of working to galvanise police, partners and public, the only complainants may be those who look for national consistency at the expense of local needs.

Let us turn our attention now to the impacts, measurable or otherwise, of the PCC on policing itself before concluding with an examination of the Police and Crime Panels.

"They and I and the public want the same things" (Interviewee 66), or how the PCC and the police have begun to align

What did PCCs encounter from the police when they first took up office? One reflected that "I found a static, unregarding, unselfcritical senior team here and I have changed the way they work" (Interviewee 62), which is one way of registering the impact that PCCs have had on the work of the police. Another was provocative about his " 'can do' attitude", which of course satirises the identical responsiveness on which police officers generally pride themselves: "Occasionally my 'can do' attitude stimulates a kind of blocking mechanism by the police and I have to wait for them to catch up" (Interviewee 66).

A third PCC was openly derisive of the chief officer team:

'Do you know the difference between God and a chief constable?'

[*Interviewer*: OK, tell me]

'God doesn't think she's a chief constable.' (Interviewee 51)

There is a sense in these remarks that PCCs found the police both arrogant and inept when they arrived in post and we have already seen (in Chapter Three) how at first PCCs and chief police officer teams circled around each other with wary hostility. We have since charted a decline in confrontation and a steady rise in cooperative alignment, well expressed on the 'commissioner side' by this PCC:

> 'I have to say that I have excellent relations with the long-serving and very eminent chief constable here, who was very sceptical at first about what was intended by the PCC. Over time, he has come to realise that I really want the same things as him: we want to tackle crime and disorder, we want people to feel and be safer and we want to hit organised criminals very hard indeed. I think that we have grown to respect each other and each other's boundaries. I don't tell the chief constable how to run his force and he doesn't try to dispute who is in charge of policing responsiveness and strategy.' (Interviewee 65)

The fact that they "have grown to respect each other and each other's boundaries" may signal a significant softening of attitudes on both sides, which had at first been characterised across England and Wales by antipathy and a kind of mutual incomprehension. Some of that improvement in relations may be because the police officers have a better idea now of what the PCC wants, but also the PCC may have a more realistic expectation of what the police can achieve within increasingly harsh budget constraints and the "horribly difficult" job that they have to do:

> 'The job that the police do is horribly difficult, often heart-breaking and the people who do it are exceptional human beings. I admire them very much. But they can get so wrapped up in the means of doing something that they forget that there are real people in the process suffering hurt and loss. The police need to be reminded about victims quite often. It's probably because the police take refuge in procedure and the mechanisms of the law to conceal or suppress their feelings. [...] And here am I telling them what they should do it better! Of course they resent it sometimes, but mostly they can see that they and I and the public all want the same things.' (Interviewee 66)

'Victim-centred justice' has become a staple of academic and criminological fare in recent years, and the PCC's comment above about victims resonates with research done by Mark Clark (2005) on a 'new philosophy' of policing which is victim-centred and which he argues will enhance 'police legitimacy' as well as with work done by Francesca Gains and Vivien Lowndes (2014) on 'gendered processes' in victim-centred justice that may affect policy outcomes on, for example, violence directed against women and girls, or female genital mutilation. Gains and Lowndes claim in their paper that 'Female PCCs are more likely to prioritize violence against women and girls in their annual Police and Crime Plan' (Gains and Lowndes, 2014), but we have seen little substantial evidence to suggest that the PCCs' policy planning is directly reflective of such concerns. And it does not always follow that a female leader will champion other females: Margaret Thatcher did singularly little to advance either female politicians or break the 'glass ceiling' during her incumbency as prime minister. It may not be the case that PCCs as a 'gendered organisation of political life' have a feminist agenda either.

At the same time, chief officers have acknowledged their own shortcomings and with some magnanimity have accepted that much of what the PCCs wanted was right:

> 'A hell of a lot of what he said made sense: we *had* lost touch with communities, we *did* impose what we thought policing ought to be, we *did* rush around the place in closed cars not talking to people, and we *did* ignore anything that wasn't crime. The reorienting [sic] of resources and police presence to better Community Policing was the PCC's idea and it is a good one.' (CO10; speaker's own emphasis)

We may suggest then, with some tentativeness, that relations between the PCC and his or her chief officer team have bedded in, have matured and are now significantly more cooperative. There will of course be exceptions to this and some of the dislike between the two sides in some forces has intensified, but our general impression is of a whole-hearted mutuality, which bodes well for the second term. Matthew Davies has noted that at first, PCCs seemed to see themselves in one of two modes, either as 'Police Managers' or as 'Crime Reduction Coordinators' (Davies, 2014b, p. 19), but it seems to us that, in the last 18 months or so, those two roles have fused and have become indistinguishable as PCCs have aligned the police to their communitarian aims, and as the police have reciprocally aligned PCCs towards what is practicable and achievable within available funding.

The strategic impact that the PCC has had on the business of policing itself is harder to quantify, especially as there is no template for "being responsive to what customers need" and "being always ready to adapt and evolve" in a context of profound and long-term change:

> 'I have run my own business, and I understand what is involved in making the business profitable and viable. Policing is a public service but there are elements that are the same as running a business: being responsive to what customers need, being the best that you can be in your field, being always ready to adapt and evolve, knowing your subject or products inside out and listening carefully and open-mindedly to feedback and comment. Now if I am able to persuade the police to do all of these things, policing in this county will be transformed in the space of a couple of years.' (Interviewee 68)

It is of interest that this PCC notes that any strategic success in transforming policing is conditional upon his being "able to persuade the police to do [...] these things" in a businesslike and professional manner. Many chief officers would argue that that is already the prevailing mode for the police in their approach to crime and disorder, but what this PCC intends is something altogether more radical and possibly empowering. A fellow PCC observed ironically that the urge for change seemed to dissipate the further up the police ranks you progressed, and that therefore the likelihood of radical strategic transformation being embraced willingly at the top of policing was remote:

> 'At the strategic end, the [police] had a one-dimensional view of the world and the possession of ideas, capability and the will to change was related too much to rank. You could only innovate if you had lots of silver braid: the problem was that once you got lots of silver braid, you didn't want to innovate.' (Interviewee 57)

This is by no means only a perception of policing; the same complaint may be heard in many boardrooms and senior common rooms, in the

Armed Forces[16] and even in parliament. Another PCC, perhaps with less subtlety, noted that his strategic purpose had been to delegate decision-making further down the line precisely to empower those managing the police/public interface:

> 'I insisted that power went back into community policing and I wanted the ability to decide registered at that local level. Paradoxically, with that increase in local responsibility at Inspector and Sergeant and even below has come a greater relish for the role. Things are really humming along in the communities now.' (Interviewee 54)

The delegation of decision-making and responsibility to the operational level within a broadly-agreed strategic approach characterises much of contemporary military leadership doctrine, but is not often seen in frontline policing. This PCC has managed a form of empowerment that clearly has had a positive effect on morale, yet, in common with most other forces, the change continues to be threatened by a scarcity of resources. The answer, another PCC suggests, lies in careful planning:

> '[...] we have a four and eight year plan for everything we do. I was suggesting two years ago that we drew up scenarios to deal with a 30% cut in budgets and that we needed to build in capacity to deal with more widespread Islamic fundamentalist extremism, and this force thought I was mad. Who's mad now? Me for looking ahead, or them as typical coppers, not lifting their heads from the sand to look at the horizon?' (Interviewee 69)

The timeframes noted here refer to the PCC's projected terms of office as much as to the accuracy of his forecasting, but it is to be hoped that both the police and the PCC are able to work in parallel as they face an uncertain future. From the police side, there are, more often than before, expressions of goodwill and some admiration for the PCC's 'vision' and how it complements what the chief officers also want to achieve:

---

[16] General Sir Nick Parker noted that army officers at and above Brigadier rank (roughly ACC and above) subscribed to 'a culture of risk aversion, conformity and addiction to bureaucratic process [...] fostered by an increasingly politicised MOD', *The Times*, 24 January 2015, and cited by Caless (2015).

> 'I want to make a difference in engaging communities, I want to recreate trust between people and police and I want to proactively prevent crime rather than charge about clearing it up afterwards. Surprise, surprise; so does the PCC.' (CO11)

And:

> 'I like that he thinks all the time about how to make policing better.' (CO9)

It is not always a mutual admiration society, however, and occasionally resentment can bubble up to the surface, as the following cautionary tale shows. One chief officer had observed to her PCC about the irritating habit people in her force had of sending emails on Friday afternoons which required action from the recipient but which were not urgent.[17] They could easily have been sent at another, more convenient, time. The officer argued that Friday afternoons should be 'email free', but the PCC was unsympathetic:

> ' "Come in on Saturdays," he said. "You get paid enough." I was Gold[18] that weekend as it happens and we had an incident in the small hours of Saturday morning. I very much enjoyed ringing him to "put him in the picture" as he had once insisted he should be. I even gave him an update at midnight on Sunday. I thought "Bugger you: I'm up and active; you bloody well should be too. You're paid enough." '(CO1; our footnote)

A perennial reservation expressed by the police is about the lack of depth in a PCC's knowledge about policing, even though the strategic vision he or she articulates about re-engagement with communities

---

[17] There are good academic analyses of the 'tyranny of emails'. While not specifically about the police, they make a strong case all the same for having a more disciplined approach to using emails which directly impinge on 'work–life balance' (a discussion of which in relation to PCCs is in Chapter 7); see Waller, A. D. and Ragsdell, G. (2012) The impact of e-mail on work-life balance, *Aslib Proceedings*, 64(2): 154–77.

[18] Strategic direction of policing operations out of hours, or in major emergencies: 'Gold' (usually a chief officer, or a Chief Superintendent in a smaller force) gives authorisation to the deployment of armed officers, for example, or high profile arrests. 'Silver' commands at the tactical level and 'Bronze' is coordination of the active front-line level. All three terms were borrowed from the military.

may chime with the aspirations of the police. Nonetheless, one chief officer observed of his PCC that:

> 'I'm not sure how bright he really is. He takes a long time to grasp the essentials of a police problem; for example, last week I tried to explain to him the concept of the squishy balloon[19]– you know what I mean – but he was still saying at the end that displacement was obviously very helpful to the police and stopped criminal planning. I think he was confusing it with disruption.' (CO4; our footnote)

This tends to be a 'damned if you do; damned if you don't' philosophy in which the PCC is either castigated for not knowing enough about policing or criticised for trying to apply what he has learned. It is of a piece with the views of specialists in many other spheres who look with (often good-humoured) contempt on those lay people who aspire to understand the esoteric aspects of the specialism. It will come as no consolation to the PCC but such disapprobation applies equally to all non-police officers in a force,[20] and was extended to PCSOs in the early years of their deployment.[21] On the same or reciprocal basis, PCCs are often disparaging about the police grasp of strategy and their alleged inability to formulate plans that look more than five years into the future – as we noted above. There will probably always be such mutual incomprehension at the shortcomings of the 'amateur'. To marvel at how little others know is the favourite activity of the self-appointed expert,[22] and neither the police nor the PCC is exempt from such petty human triumphs. One chief officer offered qualified

---

[19] The 'squishy balloon' refers to the *displacement* of crime. For example, if prostitution is suppressed in one area, and kerb crawlers made an example of, the offenders will locate elsewhere and the problem starts over again in a different area. Police find this frustrating because all they are doing is giving the problem to someone else, or collecting a problem from another district. *Disruption*, by contrast, is a well-practised means of upsetting criminals' plans or targets and can often have the effect of moving a planned crime elsewhere or having it called off entirely. It is often favoured by detectives and senior officers because it seldom makes headlines, is effective as crime prevention and deflects those with criminal intent (and there is little paperwork).

[20] As one of the authors experienced as a 'civilian' during the course of eight years in a police force

[21] See Caless (2007) and Caless et al (2014).

[22] Not least the split infinitive or the apostrophe ... see for example David Crystal's (2006) delightful debunking of experts in *The Fight for English: how language pundits ate, shot, and left*, OUP.

praise of his PCC, noting too that it has been "really hard to engage him in the 'higher end' work of serious crime":

> 'I hope I've not given the impression that my admiration of the PCC is unqualified, because it's not. Sometimes it has been really hard to engage him in the 'higher end' work of serious crime – especially when it is against some generic villains who may not live in the county but simply transit it. [...] I will say that he listens to reason, but sometimes his agreement is either very hedged about with conditions or it's quite reluctant, and I have to work hard to persuade him.' (CO10)

In all events, it is probably still too early to judge the impacts that PCCs have had upon local crime and disorder, on police/community relations, on budgeting for large scale police operations and on people's fear of crime. We may have to wait for a public judgment on the role and function of the PCC until the May 2016 and 2020 elections. Even then we may not be able definitively to measure the PCCs' impact, as the sometimes gloomy James Cousins observed:

> [...] arguably, the Police and Crime Commissioners will never be the masters of their own destiny; whatever their powers, factors like the economy, education and housing will always play as much a part in crime (and electoral success) as the police on the street or the punishments meted out by the courts. (Cousins, 2012, p. 17)

In such a broad societal (and arguably meaningless) context, "transforming the police" (Interviewee 68) will always seem minor or incidental.

Police and Crime Panels: "the old police authority all over again, but without purpose or point" (Interviewee 51)

Abie Longstaff pulled even fewer punches than this most acerbic of PCCs: 'No proper assessment has been published on the effectiveness of Police and Crime Panels (PCPs)', she said, in December 2013, going on to note that:

> There are concerns about their efficacy [...]. For example, a former member of Hertfordshire PCP described it as "a

toothless, worthless, ineffectual waste of time, money and space", while another former member of the same PCP described it as "a crocodile with rubber teeth". (Longstaff, 2013, p. 3)

A toothless crocodile with rubber teeth may give us pause (if only for the apocalyptic 'Peter Pan Meets the Zombie Dentist' image it conjures up), but the original conception of the PCP was meant to be dynamic and positive. The Home Office declared in 2012 that the PCP:

> [...] will ensure there is a robust overview at force level and that decisions of the Police and Crime Commissioners are tested on behalf of the public on a regular basis. (Home Office, 2012, para 2.26)

This sounds fairly toothy, and academic commentators at the time broadly welcomed a mechanism for 'robust overview' of PCCs, but presciently expressed doubts about how it might be done and with what success. Peter Joyce in 2011 commented that there was a danger of politicising the police through the PCC and went on to note that 'it is open to debate as to whether the powers possessed by [the Police and Crime] Panels constitute an effective check on the powers of the PCC' (Joyce, 2011, p. 9). Fraser Sampson (2012) agreed with Joyce that politicisation of the police would happen with the introduction of PCCs, and he too considered that the PCP was an inadequate hedge against those dangers. Stuart Lister and Michael Rowe noted dispassionately that PCPs have internal contradictions: they are supposed to act as 'checks and balances' on the authority of the PCC yet also are expected to offer the PCC support; in practice it is sometimes hard to do both (Lister and Rowe, 2013). In a piece published a year later, Stuart Lister drew timely attention to how limited the powers of the Police and Crime Panel were, in which the inherent contradictions of the 'critical/friend' model of scrutiny were exposed, either when there was friction between the scrutinisers and the person being scrutinised (the PCC), or worse, when there was political alignment and consensus between them, which rendered the panel's scrutiny ineffective and unchallenging (Lister, 2014). Barry Loveday shares the general unease about glib assumptions that panels will constrain PCCs when the former's powers seems deliberately confined to an advisory category. Such advice could be ignored by the PCCs because there is no sanction on them to act on what panels advise (Loveday, 2013). Sophie Chambers argues that central government has been required to take a more prominent role in scrutiny of PCCs in certain regions than first envisaged, because of the ambiguity and uncertainty in the original legislation and a consequent failure of PCPs to be able to challenge PCCs effectively.

Against this nearly universal academic barrage of caution and reservation, the PCC practitioners have largely treated their Police and Crime Panels (PCPs) with indifference, leading the Police Foundation to note 'concerns about [the panels'] efficacy' (Longstaff, 2013, p. 3) and to comment that 'PCPs also appear to have been largely unsuccessful in persuading PCCs to overturn decisions' (Longstaff, 2013). In three cases, Humberside, Sussex and West Mercia, the panel did not support the appointment of the Deputy PCC, but in all three, the PCC went ahead with the appointments anyway. In 2014, when calls were growing in volume for the PCC of South Yorkshire, Shaun Wright, to resign because of the Rotherham sex scandals, the local Police and Crime Panel could do nothing to force him to go, perhaps reinforcing the criticism noted earlier that Panels are "toothless" and "worthless". Interviewee 65 remarked that PCCs needed to be held to firm account, but this would involve "a more powerful oversight group than the feeble Police and Crime Panel, which is just the old police authority allowed to meet in the warm."

Another PCC is in no doubt that his Panel is wanting in effort and application, and notes too how frustrating that can be:

> 'I'd like to see more effective challenge from my Police Crime Panel. The PCC has all this power and the panel needs to hold him or her to account. Too many of the panels are the old police authority renamed, and that's simply not good enough [...]. Too few of the current panel understand strategic planning [...] and of course there is a role for a body acting on behalf of the people to make sure that not too many megalomaniacs make it to PCC in the first place and that none get to become megalomaniacs while in the job. But that requires credibility and strong independence, which the panels generally don't have.' (Interviewee 52)

There are a number of points in this long comment that are worth considering in greater detail. The notion that the panel is simply "the old police authority renamed" is a common one among PCCs and engenders some contempt for the composition of the panels' membership. Another PCC agreed:

"I could look to the Police and Crime Panel but they're just the police authority by another name and are even less effective than the PA was" (Interviewee 69).Since the original composition of the PCPs contained elected county councillors, there may be some truth in what the PCCs say, but we have not been able to ascertain whether the majority of panel members are formerly part of their old police authority or not.[23] We suspect not, but proof is elusive. Interviewee 52 went on to note that members of his Panel did not "understand strategic planning" and implied that the quality of those appointed to the panel (there are no direct elections) was lacking in major respects. Again, Interviewee 69 agrees:

'I know other PCCs consult their panels on a more regular and respectful basis – both sides. All I can say is that they must have a better calibre of panel than the deadbeats and time-expired councillors that I'm stuck with. I have no say in their composition of course, otherwise the panel would be full of local business people, academics and [Armed Forces] leaders, who would do a proper job in supporting, yes and in modifying and sometimes challenging, what I do.' (Interviewee 69)

What has happened to the original government intention that the Police and Crime Panel would offer a robust and effective challenge to PCCs? The intention was plainly stated:

We will create Police and Crime Panels in each force area drawn from locally elected councillors from constituent wards and independent and lay members who will bring additional skills, experience and diversity to the discussions. We are clear that these relate to the Commissioner and not to the force itself. (Home Office, 2012, para 2.26)

Perhaps the fault lies in the 'locally elected councillors' aspect, since it was probably thought likely that those best placed to challenge the Police and Crime Commissioner were councillors who had had some experience of dealing with the police and criminal justice in the past,

---

[23] Largely because few PCPs publish their members' biographies and because some who were members of the old Police Authorities do not now say that they were. Greater transparency about the composition of PCPs *and their antecedents* would help.

and this inevitably would entail some re-designation of former police authority members. That said, the government makes it evident in the final sentence of the citation given above that the purpose of the panel is to challenge the commissioner not the police force, so it might be argued that prior experience of oversight of or work alongside the police is not a requirement. Nonetheless, human nature being what it is, the time-poor leader of a Council might be excused for shoehorning former police authority members into the Panel as an expedient. In some instances undoubtedly, this was also intended to act as a political brake on the PCC who might be of a different political persuasion. There is no evidence that that has worked either.[24] The addition of 'independent and lay members' to the panel also smacks of the police authority practice of old, particularly that following the Crime and Disorder Act of 1998 in which 'lay' appointments (to include Justices of the Peace) became statutory.

The PCCs themselves vary in whether they want to be challenged or not. One (most of whose comment we have cited before) was in no doubt that the panel was an irrelevance:

> 'I will say that I think the Police Crime Panel is a waste of time. It's really the old police authority all over again, but without purpose or point. The PCC cannot be held to account by people who are not elected. Only the people can do that. So I don't take any notice of the Police Crime Panel at all and they are too wishy-washy to do anything about it, even if they could. Which they can't.' (Interviewee 51)

The constitutional point made here is an important one and although we examined it when we considered 'democratic oversight' in Chapter One, it bears repetition: "The PCC cannot be held to account by people who are not elected." This is an absolutist position, taken by a PCC who enjoys controversy and who is often deliberately provocative, but the comment is nonetheless resonant. The Independent Police Complaints Commission has the remit to examine PCCs suspected of a criminal offence, but not for any other reason. The courts cannot intervene on a generalised basis (although one or two civil challenges mounted by police officers for judicial review were successful), because there is, quite properly, a separation of the judiciary and the executive

---

[24] Kent is a case in point: the county council has created a largely Conservative PCP which cannot constrain the 'independent' incumbent, Ann Barnes. The same applies (in 2015 anyway) to North Wales, Surrey and others.

in the conduct of public affairs. That lends point to this plaintive comment by a clearly frustrated PCC:

> 'I think that an independent process is needed to call into question the judgment of a PCC.[25] I don't want it to be easy to unseat a PCC, because s/he is an elected official, but there ought to be a mechanism to set in train if the PCC loses the confidence of the people between formal elections. What I think we need is some sort of Ombudsman, possibly a High Court Judge, who can look into processes and ascertain if there is a case for the PCC to answer. Sounds like suicide saying this, but [...] the process to hold a PCC to account is flawed and that Police Crime Panels are worse than useless.' (Interviewee 70; our footnote)

It is not clear what an "Ombudsman" could do constitutionally to challenge a PCC, except over matters such as misuse of expenses or corrupt or venal conduct in a public office. The PCC could not legally be challenged over matters of judgment or disbursements of funding, for example. This dilemma is exacerbated by the rather complacent assumption by the government in 2012 that its mechanism of panel challenges to the PCC sufficed: no one seemed to consider what the position would be were the PCC to ignore the panel's comments, challenges and concerns. In response to this, one PCC wondered if a challenge could be mounted by a process similar to that which 'de-selected' an MP:

> 'I think there has to be some mechanism to unseat the entirely inadequate or mad PCC without waiting four years. But I frankly don't know what that might be, that doesn't override the democratic mandate. Perhaps it would be a mechanism like that in parliament where the equivalent of a by-election is called and the people are given a chance to comment [...] there are lots of possibilities, none of them perfect.' (Interviewee 68)

---

[25] The Home Secretary described this as a 'recall' process. She said in a speech in November 2014 to PCCs: 'I have asked officials to examine ways to allow communities to recall police and crime commissioners should they fail in their duties.' (May, 2014a). It is not yet clear what will be involved in 'recall' and whether or not judicial challenge to it could be mounted by recalcitrant PCCs.

How to ascertain the inadequacy or madness of a PCC is fraught with challenge and counter-challenge. Interviewee 52's comment about curbing the actions of "megalomaniac PCCs" would take even longer to substantiate, we believe. The details of 'recall' are awaited, but in the interim we can perhaps see a precedent of what that might entail in the controversy about the powers of a PCC to dismiss a chief constable and the number of judicial reviews and media criticisms that such early departures occasioned in 2013. This moved the House of Commons' Home Affairs Select Committee to note that the PCCs had close to absolute power (because they were mostly unchallengeable) to dismiss and appoint chief constables. The opening paragraph of the HASC 2013–14 Report noted the following:

> Within a few days of the [November 2012] election, Avon and Somerset Chief Constable Colin Port declined to re-apply for his job after the incoming Commissioner, Sue Mountstevens, indicated that she wanted to recruit a new chief constable whose tenure would cover her entire term of office. In Lincolnshire, Chief Constable Neil Rhodes was suspended by Police and Crime Commissioner Alan Hardwick—who also referred him to the IPCC—but was reinstated following a High Court judgement. In Gwent, Commissioner Ian Johnston invited Chief Constable Carmel Napier to retire, indicating that he was prepared to initiate the statutory process for her removal if she did not do so. (HASC, 2013b, para 1, p. 3; footnotes removed)

In a subsequent paragraph, the HASC noted the formal role of the Police and Crime Panel in acting as a brake on any precipitate action by a PCC to dismiss a chief constable. The actual process as described is rather convoluted:

> If, having considered [...] representations, the commissioner still intends to remove the chief constable, the police and crime panel must make a recommendation to the commissioner within six weeks as to whether or not he should do so. Before making a recommendation, the Panel may hold a scrutiny hearing at which the commissioner and chief constable are both entitled to be heard, and may consult HM Chief Inspector of Constabulary. (HASC, 2013b, para 3, p. 3)

Simply because the Police and Crime Panel possesses the function of scrutiny does not mean that the PCC is obliged to take notice of anything it says, or that any delay by the panel can inhibit the PCC's ultimate intention, so the PCP's function in this, one of its most important consultative remits, seems either emasculated or nugatory. Undeterred by the evident failure of the PCP to curb individual commissioners, the HASC went on calmly to observe that:

> It will be noted that the role of the panel is purely advisory. The final decision to dismiss a chief constable rests with the commissioner alone, though clearly it could in certain circumstances be very difficult for him to do so in the face of firm objection from the panel, particularly if the panel's view were supported by HMIC. (HASC, 2013b)

None of those 'circumstances' was actually sufficient to deflect any PCC from parting with a chief constable, and the idea of this being 'very difficult [...] to do' was simply ignored. The HASC was finally moved to comment adversely on this state of affairs, because as matters stand there is simply no check to the PCC's powers:

> The statutory process provides little safeguard, since there is nobody—not the police and crime panel, not the Inspectorate of Constabulary, not even the Home Secretary herself—who can over-rule a commissioner who has set his face to dismissing a chief constable. And even the limited scrutiny process can easily be sidestepped with the threat of a potentially embarrassing public scrutiny process in which there is clearly scope for a commissioner to cause serious damage to a chief constable's reputation and, by extension, the reputation and morale of the force. (HASC, 2013a, para 8, pp. 4–5; our italics)

Despite this robust analysis, the only outcome from the HASC's ponderous deliberation was that:

> [...] we recommend that police and crime panels should fully exercise their powers of scrutiny in examining and deciding whether the proposed removal of a chief constable is justified. (HASC, 2012, para 10, p. 5)

It is not clear from this whether the HASC thinks panels have not 'fully exercise[d] their powers', or whether it thinks that the full exercise of the panel's 'powers' is not enough to give the PCC pause. Either way, it seems there will be, literally as well as metaphorically, a cop out.[26]

The reason for examining this power of the PCC and the supposed capability of challenge by the panel in such detail, is that it highlights the dilemma of the inadequacy of the 'checks and balances' role the panel was intended to perform. There should perhaps be an amendment to the existing legislation that obliges the PCC to note *and act on* any reservations expressed by the panel on, say, three separate occasions, but this clearly needs a lawyer's attention to the fine detail. All we can do here is to observe that there is a tangible shortfall between what the panel was intended to do and what it can actually do to check the actions of a PCC. There seems self-evidently a need to replace the PCP's 'rubber teeth' with a denture that can, at least temporarily, offer a bite.

At the same time, perhaps, we might take note of some commissioners' reservations about the composition of their PCPs. This is a characteristic observation:

> 'They're generally supportive but they need more 'oomph'. The wrong sort of people are on the panel, I think. We need independent, clever, business-minded, perhaps elected, people who can exercise limited restraint over the PCC, perhaps by referring or delaying proposals. You know, like the House of Lords does to the Commons – not a veto but an invitation to re-think. That would be especially helpful to some of my more outré colleagues.' (Interviewee 66)

This "delaying proposals" mechanism proposition would only work if the PCC were obliged to take notice of what the panel said, which is emphatically not the case with many of the "more outré" of them at the moment. Even an "invitation to re-think" would be a step too far for some PCCs who have evidently excised the PCPs from their consideration entirely.

Other PCCs have an entirely different opinion of and working arrangement with, their PCPs:

---

[26] To date there is no sign that the Conservative majority government which came to power in May 2015 wants to amend the existing legislation, 'recall' or no. In this respect, the PCC is many times more powerful than the Police Authority ever was and looks dangerously untouchable.

'I get on with, and value, my Police Crime Panel very much indeed. You sound surprised. No really, I do. Well I don't know what other PCCs feel (though I can guess) but my panel is certainly not the police authority by another name. There are businessmen, entrepreneurs, barristers, lecturers and managers in the panel all bringing their different specialisms to bear and I really enjoy seeking their help to see my way round a problem. I genuinely do consult them often. Take the current budget round for example: [...] the panel is hugely helpful and supportive and what's more they suggest things to do that I'd never thought of. I test ideas against them and value their sane and experienced advice. They really are a bunch worth listening to, and I know of other PCCs who think the same [of theirs].' (Interviewee 67)

This is a healthy counterpoint to the prevailing mode which is for commissioners to bypass, sidestep or ignore their panels and disdain what they stand for. It says much for the cultivation of relationships between Interviewee 67 and his panel, that the outcomes he details can be so positive. On the other hand, it should be noted that he appears to be using his PCP as a consultative body, a sounding board against which he can "test ideas". There is no knowing what his response might be if the panel obstructed or opposed him in some fundamental respect.

Summary

The picture that emerges from this detailed look at what the PCC actually does may reinforce the idea that the PCC has outgrown, or never fitted, the original remit for the job. The remit itself remains vague and unfocused, allowing considerable latitude of interpretation and lacking the rigour of a normal 'job description', after which some PCCs evidently hanker. At the same time, progressive and confident PCCs relish the untrammelled scope they find in the role. Concurrently with this, we have found that there are progressive alignments between PCCs and the police: they seem pretty much to agree on some things, such as community policing, while in other areas, notably serious and organised crime, there is some concern on the part of chief officers that PCCs are insufficiently engaged. Nonetheless, the early hostility, caution and mutual incomprehension have largely been replaced by cooperative working and general agreement on local targets. This may have been a forcible bracketing, or tacit mutual protection, as the result of cuts in the policing budget and the sense in which the chief police officer team and the PCC faced together a common threat from the Home Office as austerity measures were imposed centrally. There is no suggestion yet that this pressure will ease, though some PCCs rather wistfully believe that pressures to deliver more with less will diminish or go away entirely.

We must conclude that the role of the Police and Crime Panel was ill-defined at the outset (of a piece with the vagueness of the PCCs' remit) and it is likely that at some point to come there will be tinkering with the legislation and some imposition of mechanisms to hold the PCC more firmly to account, outside the four-yearly process of election. It seems to us probable that major change will wait until after the May 2016 elections, when the government can ascertain the composition of the new PCC body and, most interesting of all, its political complexion. For all that the public seems to prefer 'independents' as PCCs, the party machinery will still play a prominent part. Curbing the "inadequate or mad PCC" is something still to be accomplished, it would seem.

In our final chapter, we turn attention to what the PCCs think their remit and jobs should become, and whether their re-election (should they stand again) will bring an expansion in the range and nature of their local democratic oversight.

SEVEN

"I wonder if the game is worth the candle": PCCs, their 'work–life balance' and their future

'And I'll tell you another thing: the hours we work are ludicrous. Sometimes when I'm driving myself home late at night after yet another meeting in the back of beyond, and knowing I've still got to be up early next day, I wonder if the game is worth the candle. This is an accident waiting to happen. [...]'

Interviewer: Does the PCC role have a long-term future?

'Dunno. Ask me when I grow up! Seriously, it might be too early to think about this, though some sort of role in the wider criminal justice system seems to beckon, once we've sorted out policing.' (Interviewee 74)

Many PCCs and their chief officers have drawn our attention to the commissioners' very heavy workloads, and we should consider, in the context of the literature on the subject, what the implications are of such workloads for the PCCs' current and future effectiveness, health and wellbeing. At the same time, PCCs responded to our standard question about the future of the role,[1] by speculating where they might expand or develop their remit. There is no doubt that most PCCs are energised by their role, engrossed in what they consider to be their duty and assiduous in their responses to invitations to meet 'their'

---

[1] The question 'Does the PCC role have a long-term future?' was asked of PCCs both before and after the general election of 2015, the outcome of which assured the existence of PCCs until 2020, if not the longer future. It may appear seamless now, but a constant theme throughout 2014–15, when we undertook the majority of our interviews, was whether the PCC role would survive the May 2015 general election. The Labour Party had pledged in 2013 to discard the PCC post and it seemed, according to the polls, that Labour might form a government, so many PCCs prepared themselves for the abolition of their elected role before 2016. This explains some of the tentativeness in their views of what lay ahead.

public. That does not mean that they are blind to the drawbacks, as Interviewee 74 indicates above, which include late night travelling and very long working days. It may appear perverse, then, that they seek additional work and an expansion of what they do, if they are already stretched. As will become clear, many see additions or extensions to the role as logical next steps, predicated on the assumption that they will have "sorted out policing" beforehand. This final chapter explores the PCCs' current work–life balance (or lack of it) and their often rueful commentary on their work, together with their views of where the role might go in the future. We seek to contextualise both elements in wider academic research and analysis.[2]

'Work–life balance'

What might those who ensure that their work and their non-working lives are held in careful balance, expect as benefits? Bryn Caless noted in 2011 that:

> Those who do have a work–life balance are adjusted individuals who have their working lives in perspective and who also can make time for families, children, partners, social skills, additional learning, fitness and relaxation. They are less likely to be ill, less likely to die 'in harness', less likely to make errors of judgment [...] less likely to be divorced or estranged and less likely to suffer long-term health problems [...] (Caless, 2011, p. 69)

He went on to note that the police generally, and chief officers in particular, worked overtime as a matter of course (unpaid above sergeant), they considered a long week (55 hours minimum) to be the operational norm and actively cultivated a 'presenteeist' culture in which only those who were visibly at work were considered to be working (Caless, 2011, pp. 68–78). Additionally, chief police officers have fixed term contracts which allow them to derogate from the European Working Time Directive's limit to the working week of

---

[2] We note that there is little in the literature specifically on PCCs, but there is plenty on work–life balance in the police and in other occupations, as well as a constant stream of research and comment on the future of policing. We extrapolate from these in addition to analysing the PCC's own comments.

48 hours.[3] Chief police officers work 65–75 hour weeks as standard, whether or not their role is operational. Caless' study, drawing on medical as well as human resource evidence, concluded that 'increased competitiveness, growing resource pressures and a workload that never diminishes will continue to hold chief officer policing in thrall' (Caless, 2011, pp. 79–80).

If Caless' study held good for chief police officers in 2011, how should we regard the work–life balance of Police and Crime Commissioners a few years later? One PCC was in no doubt:

> 'I drive myself everywhere, but some days can be very long, and I have to go all over the county to speak and listen, and there are times when I am really, really tired. To have yet another abstemious night followed by a late drive home is a pain. And what if I'm not well? I can't ask my family to drive me and there is no provision for a PCC driver – but there should be.' (Interviewee 52)

This was a constant complaint by PCCs, many of whom thought that a tired commissioner driving home at the end of a fatiguing week, to the other side of his or her force area, was "an accident waiting to happen" (Interviewee 74). Such tiring travel and constant attendance at meetings seem to be part of the price PCCs have to pay to "put themselves about", because many of them will never pass up an opportunity to be seen in public fora and most have a very strong sense of commitment to the public that voted them into power in the first place. In such a context of commitment, there was a strong trend of opinion that PCCs should have a permanent driver. Another PCC commented that:

> 'Not allowing the PCC to have a paid driver is just daft; do you know I can't even order a taxi? That'll have to change: I have enough to do without being my own chauffeur as well.' (Interviewee 51)

One PCC was at pains to point out that the chief constable of his force had a permanent driver, but did not work as long or travel as much as the PCC did, while another PCC commented that:

---

[3] The European Working Time Directive is subject of much commentary and criticism, particularly in the provision of hours worked by young doctors in British healthcare, but for a general treatment see Barnard et al (2004).

'I can only be in one place at a time, in spite of quantum physics,[4] and I have to say that being a PCC is far, far harder than I ever thought it would be. It takes a long time to travel across my county and at the end of a long day, the drive home can be fraught, especially as I know that I shall be up early again the next day.' (Interviewee 64; our footnote)

The impact of this is that, because PCCs spend a lot of time behind the wheel, traversing their force areas, often at unsocial hours, they are frustrated at what they see as 'lost time' and their impotence to do anything constructive about it. The need to be seen, to attend meetings, to address groups and to 'put yourself about', means that:

'[...] you never get a moment's peace: I'm in meetings 6 days out of 7, including lots and lots of evenings to fit in with people's work patterns, so this job is very demanding. [...] There are some very long days.' (Interviewee 53)

It is not simply the travelling that PCCs find difficult. The 'statutory' hours they work at the job itself takes its toll:

'The time I am expected to put in, and which I feel I have to put in, is insane. I hardly ever see my family and have no time whatever for hobbies, leisure or socialising. It's not something I can keep up for long, before I get sick and fall off my perch.' (Interviewee 74)

Despite recognising the potential for ill health and familial strain that result from the long hours culture in the police, PCCs seem unable to get off their own treadmills. Some of this reluctance to cut down on the hours they work is of their own making:

'I love the job and I thrive on it; I enjoy getting out of bed at 5.30[am] and coming to work. I can see the changes I have made starting to take effect.' (Interviewee 56)

---

[4] Apparently, particles at the 'quantum' level can simultaneously occupy the same space, or simultaneously occupy separate spaces, possibly both at the same time, at least until they are observed.

No one denies that there can be immense job satisfaction in a public-facing role like that of a police and crime commissioner; on the other hand, post-holders are not infinitely elastic:

> '[...] all this is the responsibility of one person on their own. I'm already stretched pretty thin to be honest, and if I got ill there would be no one to take the role forward in a significant way. I am the only elected representative of the people and I don't get much help outside my own support team. I have no one to unload to.' (Interviewee 69)

There are a number of elements in this rather defensive statement that are characteristic of the complaints that PCCs made to us about their workloads, and what Interviewee 69 says bears closer analysis. The first element is that indeed the role of PCC *is* the responsibility of one person: that is the price of being elected as the public representative of the public and of holding the chief constable to account, especially as 'policing' happens all the time, every day and night of every week. As a result it is not surprising that PCCs should be caught up in the long hours culture of ubiquity, of 'being seen to be at work' in the police.[5] The second element is the nature of the job itself and the fact that many PCCs feel "stretched pretty thin" by both the mental and physical demands of the job. One instance of the mental 'stretch' is the sheer amount of correspondence of all kinds that the PCC is expected to respond to. Some have counted how much they receive:

> 'The biggest drawback is the size of the job: nearly 10,000 pieces of correspondence in my first year in office, and every PCC needs a really strong team for support and sharing the administration.' (Interviewee 51)

The experience of Interviewee 51 in dealing with a very large correspondence[6] is shared by nearly all the PCCs we spoke to, and the continual task of many of the staff in the PCC Office is in formulating

---

[5] This is not to downplay the role of the Deputy PCC. The appointment by some PCCs of a deputy often relieves some of the administrative burden and increases a PCC 'presence' at meetings and ceremonial occasions, often as well as linking directly with the deputy chief constable in the chief officer team, but such roles are not universal and in any case do not possess the same executive power and mandate as the elected representative.

[6] Of all kinds: from physical letters to emails, tweets, social messaging, Facebook posts and comments on blogs, as we noted in Chapter Five.

replies on the PCC's behalf to correspondents and enquirers. Yet PCCs also see the volume of their correspondence as a measure of their contact with the public, so while on the one hand they complain about the sheer size of what they have to deal with, on the other, they see it as an indicative statistic of their public interface.[7] There can be something of bravado in the PCCs' complaint that they are inundated by correspondence while at the same time they use the volume of material as a measure of how hard they are working.

A third element in the comments by Interviewee 69 is that he does not "get much help" outside his own staff. This rather ambiguous comment may mean that there is no additional assistance available from the police themselves to the commissioner (unsurprisingly in the circumstances of reduced budgets and loss of 'non-essential' staff), but also it may signify a continuing hostility and 'withdrawal of goodwill' which characterises the police/PCC relationship in some forces. The line between offering support for the PCC and maintaining police operational independence is probably a fine one to draw,[8] and it is not clear whether Interviewee 69 is complaining about the police alone or whether he includes other Community Safety partners when saying "I don't get much help outside my own support team". Either way, the comment reinforces the loneliness that goes with the PCC job, and that brings us to the final element in Interviewee 69's observations that we can tease out a little further. He remarks that he has "no one to unload to" so an additional stressor for this PCC seems to be the absence of colleagues or fellow workers to whom he can unburden about what bothers him.

It was significant that most of the PCCs interviewed spent some part of the time talking to us about how the job affects them and the strain that they experience in doing it, which they would never have admitted openly, they said, to chief officers, their own staff or to professional contacts. Doing so would betray a weakness which has no place in the PCC's public profile.[9] In this, PCCs replicate the same

---

[7]   For example, Katy Bourne, PCC for Sussex, noted publicly that 'Combined with ongoing online and hard-copy consultations, a huge increase in public correspondence, pop-up feedback events and extensive use of social media, I have kept my finger on the pulse of public opinion' (Bourne, 2014b, p. 6).

[8]   See Caless and Tong (2013), and a stimulating article by Lister (2013) on the 'operational independence' of the police.

[9]   Talking to interviewers is different: they have no locus, no daily involvement in the work, no desire to profit from 'insider knowledge'; at the same time the PCCs' unburdening and talking about the stresses and drawbacks to the job was, for them, comfortingly anonymous and confidential.

'confessional' process that Bryn Caless noted in his dealings with chief officers (Caless, 2011, p. 231): command is a lonely place and too often there is no one to whom PCCs can unburden themselves of their fears and frustrations. The isolation of PCCs was noted by some perceptive chief police officers, one of whom commented:

'he works really hard at [the job of PCC] – far longer than I would – and I guess that his work balance [sic] is shot to pieces, as he's out 5–6 nights a week.' (CO13)

This reflects what PCCs themselves have told us about their workloads, and it is interesting that the chief officer notes his PCC works "far longer than [he] would" – and yet the police officer concerned has an operational portfolio. Another chief officer noted that the PCC was "almost as obsessive as chief officers" in his work ethic and 'presenteeism', but cynically observed that this was because the PCC has the ulterior motive of re-election and correspondingly is "careful to cultivate people":

'the PCC always has one eye on re-election so is careful to cultivate people wherever he goes. He works bloody hard at it: long days and long weeks – almost as obsessive as chief officers in the amount of time spent doing the job!' (CO6)

Another chief officer, observing her PCC with some sympathy, noted "the strain and tension" of doing such "a lonely job":

'[...] if you use cognitive behaviour therapy (CBT)[10] techniques on the PCC you'll detect the strain and tension fairly easily. Quite understandable: it must be a lonely job. I wonder who he unloads to?' (CO13, our footnote)

This isolation, a kind of 'self-containedness', evidently resonates with some chief police officers, because another commented that the PCC's work pressures were caused because "one individual" tried to do everything; the eventual outcome of which might be ill health or accident:

---

[10] Broadly, CBT is a 'talking therapy' based on psychologists' belief that how we perceive affects how we feel. It is used to help people understand how their thinking may be distorted by their emotions, and leads them through discussion to formulate problem-solving strategies and change 'destructive' behaviours.

'[...] he is overwhelmed [by the work] – the consequence of being one individual. Sometimes he can't see the wood for the trees. He works really long hours, inordinately long hours. Who is responsible for his health and safety? I don't know. There should be someone.' (CO17)

Matthew Davies,[11] remarks that, in his interviews with PCCs in 2012–13, their complaint to him about their excessive workloads was constant:

I found that there were a number of PCCs who were facing significant pressures related to the fact that they [...] had decided to take on a large proportion of the workload alone. As a result, almost half of all PCCs I interviewed made reference to the intensive workload they were facing [...]. (Davies, 2014b, p. 29)

Davies ascribes a personal responsibility to those PCCs concerned about 'significant pressures', since they 'had decided to take on a large proportion of the workload alone'. In effect, Davies suggests that PCCs are victims of their own cussed independence, and the time they put into the job is, partly at least, a product of self-inflicted pressure because they do not delegate. However, in the course of our research, conducted over two to three years, we found no diminution in the 'confessional' aspects of the interviews, whether the PCCs concerned had designated deputies and large entourages, or no deputies and a small 'private office'. This rather suggests that, whether the PCC soldiered alone or functioned at the head of a larger group, the feeling of isolation was a constant. Devolving some duties to a deputy or to staff did not necessarily relieve the PCC of the burden of office. In any case, the responsibility of being a titular PCC is not something than can be delegated, since it is the single individual who was elected, not a collective, and it probably goes with the territory that occupying such a position will entail solitude, however much one consigns or delegates to others. Nonetheless, in other professions, individuals usually 'unload' to a mentor or confidant; certainly many police officers do.[12] The PCCs

---

[11] Davies is an Oxford doctoral student and one of the first to undertake interviews with PCCs and research their roles.

[12] Mentoring is established business practice and it has been shown that those who have a mentor (sometimes described as *guide, philosopher and friend*) received more promotions and had higher incomes than those who did not. See Dreher and Ash (1990) for example.

who bottle up all the frustrations, stresses and tensions of high public office may be doing themselves a dangerous disservice. Gail Kinman and her colleagues conducted research into the work–life balance of police officers in 2012, and found that officers who experienced high levels of stress at work were at risk, over time, of exhaustion, distress, 'burnout' and post-traumatic stress disorder (PTSD); added to which were familial difficulties perhaps leading to marital breakdown and divorce (Kinman et al, 2012). In the same year, a Department for Business, Innovation and Skills' survey of work–life balance, led by Sarah Tipping, noted that:

> On average, employees worked 34 hours in a usual working week. Seventy-four percent of employees usually worked 30 hours or more per week, with six per cent working over 48 hours. (Tipping et al, 2012, p. 17)

while:

> Working more than 48 hours per week[13] was more common among men (ten per cent), those with higher qualifications (15 per cent among those with a postgraduate degree), those with higher incomes (24 per cent of those with an income of £40k or higher), those working in the private sector (seven per cent) and those in male dominated workplaces (ten per cent). (Tipping et al, 2012, p. 17; our footnote)

We can extrapolate what is said by Kinman and her colleagues about police officers, and by Sarah Tipping et al at the Department for Business, Innovation and Skills about working hours in other occupations, to Police and Crime Commissioners,[14] since they too appear to be part of a generally stressful public service pattern in which a long hours culture predominates, in which 'presenteeism' is a constant and where there is no, or little, relief from the constant pressures of work despite limited delegation. The need for all PCCs to "put themselves about" and the determined pursuit by many of a 're-electable profile', brings them inexorably into a cycle where work dominates life.

---

[13] That is, in excess of the hours recommended in the European Working Time Directive.

[14] With 'higher qualifications' in many cases, receiving 'higher incomes' and located in 'male dominated workplaces'.

Diane Houston, who has written extensively and expertly on work–life balance in the professions, observes that:

> A great deal of research has shown that working long hours has wide ranging negative effects on family life [...]. More generally, there are established physical and psychological costs of work-related stress [...]. Psychological research has also investigated the causes of errors in a wide variety of jobs and demonstrated that error-proneness is increased by continuous long periods of task performance, as well as by time pressure. (Houston, 2005, pp. 8–9)

It may be too early to describe any 'error-proneness' in PCCs or ascertain whether there have been 'negative effects on family life' as a result of the role, but there is no reason for us to suppose that PCCs are in any way exempt from or protected against the kinds of 'physical and psychological costs' which accompany the stress of 'continuous long periods of task performance'. The sad thing about working so hard and long is that there are actually no measurable benefits in work outcomes. Houston concludes that 'there is no good business case' for sustaining a long hours culture:

> [...] the evidence reviewed gives absolutely no indication that long hours are beneficial in terms of productivity [which], combined with the very substantial evidence of the impact of long hours on individual's health, wellbeing and performance, indicates that there can be no good business case for the perpetuation of a long hours culture. (Houston, 2005, p. 9)

However, other commentators have dismissed or modified the notion that a work–life *imbalance* is necessarily a bad thing. Doris Eikhof and her colleagues, for example, have challenged the 'overwork' aspect of work–life imbalance and suggest instead that attention is paid to 'reconceptualising' the nature of work (Eikhof et al, 2007). Richenda Gambles and her fellow researchers, by contrast, argue that putting policies in place that make work more flexible is only part of the answer, because those who seek flexible working are often seen by their orthodox and 'presenteeist' colleagues to be less committed to

the job in hand, and are not to be relied upon (Gambles et al, 2006).[15]
A negative attitude to flexible working is very probably still true of
the police,[16] and there is no provision whatever in the PCC role for
any structure other than "full on, tough and constantly demanding"
(Interviewee 67[17]). What may be needed instead is some kind of
cultural shift that recognises the need to keep work in perspective, and
perhaps different ways of doing the job ('smarter not harder'), however
unwelcome that may be in a time of financial austerity and shrinkage
(Barton and Barton, 2011).

Carrie Bulger and her colleagues (2007) take this 'cultural shift'
even further and suggest that, by applying what is called 'boundary
theory' to employment and home life, there can be a re-definition
of what 'work' is, and re-drawn 'boundaries' around the differences
between 'work' and 'leisure'.[18] Bulger et al analysed the 'boundary
management profiles' of more than 300 people at work and concluded
that greater flexibility and elasticity in approaches to how managers
defined work activities (the 'boundaries') produced a better work–life
balance for the individual worker (Bulger et al, 2007). That may be,
but it sounds very much as though 'work' is being redefined at the
expense of leisure. Kinman et al (2012) noted in relation to the police
(and other emergency workers), that structured leisure and relaxation
time were the most effective counters to work-related stress. The
problem for the police, and by extension, for PCCs, lies in the notion
of structuring leisure and 'downtime' in stressful jobs where very long
hours are worked, especially when there is such a powerful 'work ethic'

---

[15] There is often a gender aspect to this, where women seek more flexible employment
terms so that they can juggle childcare with work commitments; very little provision
is made for this in the policing world; see Smithson and Stokoe (2005).

[16] One of the authors encountered such police-entrenched attitudes directly in
2003–05 when attempting to implement human resource policies for 'annualized
hours' and '9 day fortnights' even though they are familiar and accepted HR
practices in other occupations. Yet many police forces have embraced willingly a
weekly shift pattern of four days at ten hours each day, followed by three days off.
Self-interest may be the dominant influence behind such attitudes. There is no
operational reason to eschew flexible working.

[17] What Interviewee 67 said in full was: "I didn't really know what I was taking on
with the job, none of us did really. It was not, as some expected, a part-time, non-
executive role. Instead it is a full-on, tough and constantly demanding job, and I
work 0600–2200 at least four days a week, with no time off for good behaviour at
weekends." This parallels the way that Interviewee 69 described his role as "full-
time, full-on and fully-committed".

[18] 'Leisure', or the period not spent at the workplace, is often described as 'downtime'
because such respite may not actually involve activities.

operating within policing.[19] PCCs do not have managers, of course, and this in turn may exacerbate their long hours culture, because there is, in effect, no one with the authority to tell them to go home. Commitment and responsibility are acute among nearly all the PCCs we spoke to; the corollary is that they nearly all work far too hard and have too little leisure.[20]

For the very few PCCs prepared to admit it, the workload and stresses of the role have proven too much:

> 'The major drawback of the job is the long hours and the poor pay. In fact, the long hours and poor reward for the work has convinced me that I should not stand again.' (Interviewee 55)

But others, while agreeing that the time spent at work and the isolation of command are "drawbacks", nonetheless are determined to carry on, supported by their families and office staff:

> 'The drawbacks are the long hours and the loneliness. This job is easy to get caught up in and you can become immersed in things [...]. I have a really good team here and a supportive family, so I don't resent the effort I put in, but there are times when I can't unload and I don't sleep very well.' (Interviewee 66)

One optimistic PCC, looking ahead to his re-election, commented on his need for "better transport systems" and let his imagination fly:

> 'I need better transport systems to get me round this large county and a helicopter would not come amiss, frankly, as being the best way to cover long distances. I haven't been able to interest the Crime Panel in that yet, but re-election

---

[19] It is not just a British problem either; it has been studied extensively in Europe, for example Collatz and Gudat (2011) critically examine a number of models of work-life balance including *Das Zeit-Balance Modell* (the time-strain model), and *Das Wellness Modell* (the model of personal wellbeing). Unfortunately, we can find no English translation of this perceptive paper. See also Kinman, McDowall and Cropley (2012). The 'can do' approach of the police, which evidently rubs off on PCCs too, exacerbates an already excessive commitment to the job (Caless, 2011, p. 232).

[20] As their PAs and staff in the OPCCs invariably told us when we spoke to them.

will open up more prospects of success in creating an integrated transport system for this office.' (Interviewee 59)

It would indeed be a robust return on the electoral investment in a PCC to provide him with a helicopter (presumably also with a pilot?) to cover the 'long distances' in his county; but an airborne PCC with "an integrated transport system" is likely to remain a speculative dream.

"Some sort of role in the wider criminal justice system seems to beckon" (Interviewee 74)

As we noted at the outset of this chapter, we asked all those commissioners whom we interviewed what they saw as the PCCs' future and what sort of changes they envisaged for the role. This was designed to encourage PCCs to talk about what they would like to do, particularly if their role continued beyond 2016.[21] From the very first interviews, it was clear that PCCs had robust views about local governance beyond the police, and it became evident that many were already thinking how their role might expand and what other aspects of local public service accountability could or should come under their purview. The remainder of this chapter will be an analysis of and commentary on what they told us.

Ian Loader argues that 'Police and Crime Commissioners are best interpreted not as a crime reduction measure but as a piece of constitutional reform, a radical recalibration of the relationship between citizens and [...] the police' (Loader, 2014, p. 48).

But, Loader continues, we must remain alive to the possibility that 'Police and Crime Commissioners are not the only, and may not be the best, way of giving institutional effect to what should rightly remain a left–liberal cause: democratizing policing' (Loader, 2014, p. 49).

Loader wrote this before the general election of 2015, and his caution about PCCs is in line with that of many other commentators in 2013–14 (ranging from Tim Newburn to Fraser Sampson), who wondered whether the 'radical recalibration' of PCCs was destined to be fleeting and experimental rather than fully or comprehensively the 'democratizing [of] policing'. Some commissioners agreed, wondering openly if their role would mutate, disappear or be subsumed into some

---

[21] We observed earlier that there was much uncertainty whether PCCs would survive the 2015 general election. Our question about the future of the role was designed to hurdle this uncertainty and at least afford the opportunity for PCCs to muse on the nature of the role and how, under positive conditions, it might develop.

other form of governance. Several took this uncertainty a stage further and wondered what the 'governance' role itself might become. Here is one PCC whose comment is worth quoting in full:

> 'When I began in 2012, I thought that the job of PCC began with the people and ended with the police. But since then, I have come to look longer and harder at the bigger picture. It isn't enough just to deal with the police aspects of crime: detection, investigation, patrol and so on. The need is for a more holistic approach to criminal justice, and that means engaging with the public aspects of the legal process [...]. I believe that there could be a coherent role for the PCC in time to come, where he or she is the public voice of criminal justice, representing the victims, the witnesses and the people much more solidly and coherently than at present.' (Interviewee 60)

The suggestion that PCCs might have a greater role as a sort of local champion of the people in the administration of criminal justice sounds innocuous enough and is sufficiently widespread among commissioners to have appeared publicly in print without provoking much in the way of adverse criticism. In his contribution to a collection of short essays titled *Think Blue Line* that appeared in 2014,[22] Christopher Salmon, PCC for Dyfed-Powys, wrote this:

> We should look at granting PCCs powers over court administration and probation. Local decision-making would allow us to smooth the progress of cases. We could make more use of magistrates in monitoring sentences. Courts could share other public buildings. *We could also look at powers to commission prosecutorial advice from alternatives to the CPS*, to reduce delays and increase capacity. (Salmon, 2014, p. 27; our italics)

---

[22] The collection, as we noted earlier, has to be treated with some caution since most of the essays (other than one by Mark Reckless, a former Conservative MP who defected very publicly to UKiP in 2014, but lost his seat a year later) were written by PCCs elected on a Conservative platform. There is a foreword by the Home Secretary, and the whole publication therefore promotes the concept of the PCC on a deliberately politicised basis.

This is also, on the surface, a fairly modest proposal, suggesting that PCCs should bring efficiency and a drive for greater celerity to bear on the processing of cases at court, together with some role in processing outcomes such as probation, while working in partnership with the magistracy. Yet there are some iconoclastic suggestions tucked within the statement that bear closer consideration. The "powers to commission prosecutorial advice" from lawyers or organisations other than the Crown Prosecution Service would actually be a radical departure from the normal provisions of criminal justice and would certainly provoke, if debated more extensively, an adverse response from the CPS and others in criminal justice, not to mention from the media and members of parliament. Co-locating courts with other parts of the criminal justice system, such as probation or police stations, might make a pleasing symmetry for those who see the courts as a continuum in a seamless 'brought to justice' process, but magistrates, police and probation officers might make strange bedfellows.[23] There is also an assumption in what Christopher Salmon says that speed in obtaining court outcomes and 'smooth[ing] the progress of cases' are good things in themselves. Those who have been victims of rough justice or hasty court judgments may beg to differ (Reichel, 2002).

Any potential critical commentary from the media, politicians or other parts of the criminal justice system does not seem to inhibit PCCs from thinking about possible extensions to their role, particularly because they could rely, as some put it, on the fact that they were elected to justify any speculation about what they might do. This is of a piece with the way that the role itself appears to have grown beyond what was originally intended, as we discussed in Chapter Six. Interviewee 62 typifies the way that PCCs have pushed at the outer edges of their rather vague remit, when he observed that it was not enough for him to deal with the police, but, as "an elected representative of the people", he should seek to influence "the rest of the criminal justice system in terms of its local responsiveness". His whole answer was:

'You can't just change the wheels on an aircraft and expect it to fly better. It may land a bit more gently but that's a different story (all landings are controlled crashes anyway).

---

[23] That said, co-locating the CPS with the police, which began seriously in 2005–6, has been successful after some initial headaches, and this 'convergence' has apparently produced a better standard of investigation and case preparation, see www.cps.gov.uk/publications/prosecution/justicegap.html. What works in penny packets though, may not work at all if greatly enlarged, as proposed above.

At the moment, dealing with the police, although it is vitally important to get policing right, is dealing with only one aspect of the criminal justice system. It seems to me logical that an elected representative of the people should also be influencing (even directing) the rest of the criminal justice system in terms of its local responsiveness.

'I don't say this because I have a massive ego and I want to have all the reins of power in my megalomaniac hands (though I know some who would), but because the public is not well served by the current criminal justice processes. As I don't interfere with operational policing, I would not interfere with the course of justice, the outcome in court or the punishment determined under the law: that is for the judges to exercise independently of the executive, and it is right that they should.' (Interviewee 62)

It may be disingenuous to suppose that such a departure from the norm would not be deemed by some to be concentrating too much power in a local representative's hands (whether or not "megalomaniac"). The "current criminal justice processes", argues Interviewee 62, are out of date and drastically in need of overhaul.[24] That did not mean that the PCCs wanted to take power from others, particularly Crown-appointed judges, but rather legitimately to secure his and his fellow PCCs' oversight of "current criminal justice processes". He went on:

'It would not be too difficult, or too onerous a challenge, to do the same with the courts, the processes, the costs, the long deliberateness and the outdated eighteenth century dogma of it all. To go back to the aircraft analogy: it's fun to fly a biplane, but you wouldn't go to war in one. Criminal justice need [sic] the equivalent of the EuroFighter, bang up-to-date kit and bang up-to-date pilots.' (Interviewee 62)

It would seem that this PCC envisages the Crown Court system coming under the PCC's purview as well as the magistrates' courts, when he refers to the "eighteenth century dogma of it all". The implication behind oversight by "bang up-to-date" PCCs is made clearer in the response of Interviewee 69, who commented more dogmatically, that:

---

[24] A perception that was examined extensively by Mike Hough and Julian Roberts in 2004.

'I don't think that the current government has thought through all the implications of local governance, because more and more I am seeing – along with my other PCC colleagues – that it is the whole of the criminal justice system that should be held accountable on a local basis. You can't just govern the police and ignore the courts, the CPS, probation and prisons. Come to that, judges and lawyers are pretty unaccountable too. I should like to see, if the PCC continues in post, a written job description which extends to and encompasses much of the criminal justice system and emergency services.' (Interviewee 69)

We have moved then, from helping magistrates' courts and probation to deliver more efficient and speedy outcomes, to reform of "the whole of the criminal justice system" which, it is proposed, "should be held accountable on a local basis". If seriously intended, this would entail a revision of constitutional practices, of the justice system itself and might well be interpreted as an attempt to subordinate the judiciary to the oversight of the legislature.[25] This in turn might provoke a considerable debate about the separation of powers which would not be the less impassioned because it was predicated on local accountability (as forensically discussed by Terrill, 2014, Chapter 1). The proposition that "judges and lawyers" should be included in the PCC's remit may be regarded by some as mere hubris, but we should remember that the PCCs' comments were made privately and in confidence, and were not formulated with the idea of provoking public debate. Nonetheless, it does suggest a direction which PCCs believe that the future may take, and it is a view shared by many of those we spoke to:

'I'd like to see the rest of the criminal justice system under my remit. The police are only the gateway to this process and if we speed up our end there is never a corresponding sense of urgency in the rest of the [criminal justice system] – even in the Prosecution Service. Cases grind to a halt and the process is not victim-friendly in the slightest.' (Interviewee 72)

and, with more sweeping inclusiveness, this comment:

---

[25] Time-honoured in their separation, at least formally.

'I'd like the Home Office to mandate PCCs to be able to do more. [...] The CPS, Court Service and the police should be working much more closely together and the only likely way for that to be done is to give oversight to the PCC. I think the exercise by PCCs of the power of direction to the criminal justice system is the only way ahead really.' (Interviewee 67)

while another PCC believed strongly that:

'[...] the PCC job could expand. I should like to see the PCC take responsibility for the whole of the local delivery of criminal justice: holding the Prosecution Service, the magistracy and the prisons and probation to account; possibly even the administration of criminal law as well. Unlike a judge, I'm elected!' (Interviewee 51)

This revisits the debate about the power of the elected over the power of the appointed that we considered when discussing Police and Crime Panels, but it would require extensive and careful consideration if PCCs were ever to be considered as having any kind of controlling remit over judges and the administering of criminal law.[26] The topic of judicial checks and balances and the inviolability of the legal process generally, is familiar in legal and parliamentary debates.[27] What is not yet widely debated is the role that might be played in the future by a locally elected "Criminal Justice Commissioner" (Interviewee 70, below). The idea clearly has appeal for the PCCs internally, but has yet to emerge in a public forum. A "more robust and more joined-up" approach to "the delivery of justice" is required, argues one PCC and this point of view anticipates exactly the kind of discussion that extending the PCC remit might entail:

'At the moment, the courts system is riddled with contradiction and ineptitude; judges are a law to themselves

---

[26] The desirability of the formal 'separation of powers' was discussed by Robert Stevens as long ago as 1999, and is something of a perennial topic in parliament, where the familiar and fallacious argument that the legal system should be subject to the will of the people (that is to the Commons) is aired especially when the independent judiciary opposes some government measure or proposal. How long someone may be detained in police custody was a celebrated example. The essential difference seems to be one of application: *Parliament formulates a law, but judges apply it.* It is into the gap between these processes that some PCCs seem to want to step.

[27] And is comprehensively discussed by, among others, LaPorta et al (2003).

and the CPS is pretty low powered. The defence teams have it all their own way with procedural emphases, not emphases on guilt or innocence. Therefore, the prosecution of offenders needs to be more robust and more joined-up and we need to make certain that the delivery of justice in this country is victim-centred, or it will never be credible. The reform of criminal justice could be through an expensive Royal Commission, or there could be a destructive media campaign, or the remit of the PCC could be extended with the agreement of both main parties, and the revolution will happen quietly and without fanfares. But it will be a revolution, believe me. The PCCs would love to bring democratic accountability to the rest of the [criminal justice service].' (Interviewee 68)

Envisaging a "revolution" in the criminal justice system would have to be preceded by an equal revolution in the constitutional separation of powers, and this would involve the Justice Ministry as well as the Home Office in deliberations about any extension to the PCCs' remit. It does not seem to us to be a proposition that would be embraced with any enthusiasm by national politicians; it also seems unlikely that "both main parties" could agree on extending the PCC's remit in the way described. The other options noted by Interviewee 68, such as a Royal Commission (probably presided over by a senior judge) or some kind of media campaign, perhaps akin to that of the MPs' expenses scandal or the phone-hacking investigation under Lord Leveson, present equally remote possibilities. All the same, one 'opposition' PCC thought that profound change (not perhaps as extreme as that envisaged above), could evolve over time:

'I'm Labour through and through and I did not like the PCC concept at all in the beginning. As I said, I only stood originally to spite the Tories. The whole notion then seemed like some alien American import and next we would be electing sheriffs, but I now think that most PCCs are doing a good job. We cooperate well across a spectrum of political views and we are slowly winning over the police, I think. [...]

'I want to secure and improve the PCC role as a Criminal Justice Commissioner, and even my party may come to that in time.' (Interviewee 70)

Fifteen of the twenty-three PCCs interviewed (65%) considered that some extension of the PCC role into local criminal justice was a logical step forward. This in turn suggests that the idea has taken firm root among many of the commissioners, however divergent individuals are in how it might be accomplished.[28] One PCC, however, was flatly against anything of the kind and denied that the issue had been openly debated at all. He had begun by saying that the PCC should look at taking on oversight of the other emergency services:

> 'I think it would be good to have a commissioner in charge of police, fire and ambulance.'
>
> [*Interviewer:* would that also include the rest of criminal justice?]
>
> 'No, no, not at all – the judiciary MUST remain independent. Why do you ask that?'
>
> [*Interviewer:* some of your colleagues have suggested it.]
>
> 'Really? That is news to me. It is ridiculous to suggest it.' (Interviewee 73)

Maybe it is, but the notion shows no signs yet of going away.

Other futures, other roles

A chief officer, whose view of his PCC had slowly changed from wariness to admiration, had no doubt about her achievements to date:

> 'I never thought I'd say it two years ago, but actually this PCC is good for policing and I support what she is doing. What's more, I know that supporting her is the right thing to do, because she represents the people. Peel would be proud wouldn't he?'[29] (CO5; our footnote)

---

[28] The general notion of a role for the PCC in local criminal justice, and specifically in oversight of the CPS, was aired in a presentation at the APCC's Conference at Harrogate in November 2014, and provoked some lively discussion, but the senior CPS speaker present was adamant that it could not happen.

[29] 'Peel's Principles' are commonly invoked when PCCs wish to appear demotic or traditional. The Principle referred to here is the familiar 'the public are the police and the police are the public', which we noted earlier.

Such a change of tone is by no means universal among police chiefs, some of whom remain as resolutely antagonistic to PCCs and 'democratic oversight' as they were at the beginning. Among the disenchanted, one noted that, during the first term in office, the PCC consistently failed to win over the public and that he, the chief officer, was being approached by rival candidates in advance of the 2016 election:

> 'Longer term, I don't think he has a future, even if the concept of the PCC survives, which is itself dubious.[30] I can't see the public returning him at an election and the other candidates have already started talking to me, so his days are probably numbered.' (CO8)

Another chief officer was even more damning of his PCC's achievements, and considered "his credit [...] about used up":

> 'I've tried to tell him about more complex forms of policing and so has the CC, but he seems to find it hard to step outside his restatement of the clichés that got him returned to office in the first place. [...] Now the PCC definitely has neighbourhood policing at the centre of his agenda; there is no doubt about that at all. But what he hasn't got across to the public is what he has actually achieved in any of his platforms. Meanwhile, their cars are getting nicked, kids are getting beaten up, there's a gang culture in some of our schools, drug taking is on the increase and everyone is aware of the swingeing budget cuts the police have had to take. To be honest, I think his credit is about used up.' (CO9)

But, for every critical or hostile chief police officer, there are others who regard 'their' PCC's achievements with respect and some admiration, anticipating a future in which the PCC might well cast about for a continuing "challenge":

> 'I have watched the PCC over the last 20 months or so and have seen him grow in knowledge and in understanding (not always the same things). He remembers too and has a real ability to link things together to find patterns. I'm not as analytical as that and just admire it as a skill. Long term,

---

[30] The speaker was interviewed in 2014.

he will get where he wants to be and I frankly wonder what the challenge will be for him then.' (CO10)

One PCC was equally sanguine about evaluating the role and developing it further, and observed that:

'[...] it may be five or six more years before we can say with any certainty that a PCC demonstrably adds value. That doesn't mean that in the interim there is not a really important job to be done.' (Interviewee 52)

Another PCC substantially agreed that the role needed to be evaluated "over a longish period of time", because only then would there be accumulated "a substantial body of evidence that the PCC makes a difference". This was in some ways an uncharacteristically downbeat assessment of PCCs' achievements, acknowledging that genuine reform "takes time" and, echoing the headpiece to this chapter, that formal assessment of the PCC is perhaps premature. All the same, the speaker could not resist a suggestion that, once the police are reformed into "a lean, mean fighting machine", the PCC will inevitably turn attention to reforming the rest of the criminal justice system:

'You see, this is the sort of role that recommends itself over a longish period of time, and when there is a substantial body of evidence that the PCC makes a difference. I can point to police reforms, the drop in crime and the responsiveness of the police to the community right now and I'm proud of that. But permanent reform, reform that goes to the heart of the police function, takes time. I'll need at least two terms to move this police force to a lean, mean fighting machine, and to carry out the initial reforms to the rest of the criminal justice system.' (Interviewee 59)

The prospect of future reform, whether embracing the other emergency services or embarking on a wholesale reform of local criminal justice, was something that most PCCs commented on when asked what they thought would happen to the role after the elections of 2016. It was this prospect of catalysis that gave Adam Crawford pause when he contemplated what might happen with a robust PCC and a shrinking budget:

> The contemporary confluence of 'electoral answerability' in the form of the new governance structure of Police and Crime Commissioners [...] and 'fiscal austerity' could prove to be a volatile mix. (Crawford, 2014, p. 173)

One PCC wondered if the ambitions of commissioners to reform the local "governance structure" would expand the job so much that one person could not cope with the remit, and that consequently, there might be a need for "two or three elected sub-PCCs":

> 'I can see the role growing and therefore the PCC will need more support. It may be that we'll need two or three elected sub-PCCs in the force area, one for policing itself, one for the emergency services and one for the CJS, all overseen by a 'head' PCC.' (Interviewee 69)

This idea takes us slightly closer to the Labour Party's plan for the future of local democratic accountability as outlined in Lord Stevens' Report of 2013, where an 'elected board' would run local policing. Perhaps a 'board' consisting of elected PCCs is not beyond the bounds of future possibility, though we, and many others, remain sceptical. By suggesting the notion of a "'head' PCC", which is not part of the Labour Party plan for local oversight, the speaker might instead be anticipating a role for an elected mayor of a conurbation such as Greater Manchester, with elected staff serving under him, as is envisaged by the current government (Sandford, 2015). It has worked, more or less, as a system in London with MOPAC, and there is no structural reason why local governance could not extend to criminal justice in general. It is rather that the constitutional obstacles are likely to be insurmountable, or requiring of a disproportionate effort to dismantle. Interviewee 69 goes on to suggest that we may have to be patient and "see what [the PCC role] turns into" over time. The stay of execution that PCCs achieved with the unexpected election result in May 2015 may yet enable the role to grow into areas we cannot anticipate, and for Crawford's 'volatile mix' to produce some unforeseen compounds.

Standing room only

As a final exercise in prospecting into the future, we asked our PCC interviewees if they would stand again for election in 2016. Their responses, shown in Table 6, were somewhat equivocal.

Table 6: Analysis of PCCs' replies to question 10a: *Will you stand for a second term?*

Yes	Maybe yes	Maybe no	No	Total
12	6	2	3	23 (100%)

The preponderance suggests that four times as many will stand again than will stand down, at which point those seeking re-election know that they will be judged on what they have achieved (or claim to have achieved). Most will hope for re-election on a larger mandate, however robust they have been about the size of their electoral turnout in 2012. From their comments, it seems that most consider the job is only half done. It could therefore be at least 2020 "before we can say with any certainty that a PCC demonstrably adds value" (Interviewee 52).

Summary

The effort that PCCs put into their working lives is unremitting, stressful and exacting, and, in common with others who work too hard and too long, cannot be sustained indefinitely without adverse effects. The literature is adamant that there are measurable negative consequences to excessive working, and PCCs are no exception to this rule, especially because they match, mirror and sometimes exceed, the 'long hours' and 'presenteeist' culture of chief police officers. The commissioners seem to want the best of both worlds; they complain freely about the amount of time and presence the job requires, the amount of travelling they have to do, and the number of meetings they must attend, and yet (often simultaneously) extol the virtues of 'putting themselves about', raising their profiles with the public, engaging as often as they can with communities, groups and organisations, and being seen to be doing the job for which they were elected. It is notable that chief officers, themselves no strangers to the macho competitiveness of being seen to be at work, sometimes marvel at the effort PCCs put in.

There is a corollary: plenty of PCCs admit privately to being stressed, over-worked, unable to sleep well and too often having no one to whom they can confide the burdens of their office. Some have discovered to their surprise that working as "the people's representative" can be very isolated; others expected it to be solitary because of previous experiences of command in the police or the military, a few take the loneliness in their stride, but bemoan the incessant effort to remain on top of the role. There seem to be some crumpled petals even in commissioners' beds of roses.

There is a preponderance of PCCs who anticipate an expansion of their role over the course of time. For some, it will embrace the "local democratic oversight" of the other emergency ('blue light') services, but for most it will entail a deliberate extension of the PCCs' remit into the local criminal justice system. To be fair, the interviewees were asked what the future might mean for their role and they responded by speculating freely, and in some cases, extravagantly. Nonetheless, the prospect of becoming, or morphing into, the local "Criminal Justice Commissioner" was a prospect that energised and enthused many of our interlocutors. Many agreed that reforms to the criminal justice system, and specifically to the Prosecution Service, case progression, the courts' administration, the magistracy and probation, were long overdue and considered that, once they had "sorted the police", this was a logical next move. What were privately expressed views may be aired more publicly in time, and a wide ranging debate may be held, not just with the various components of criminal justice, but with the public, the media and members of parliament about the advisability of extending the PCCs' role and responsibilities. Only when the issues have been dealt with in the open and consensus reached, could PCCs legitimately take on the mantle of Criminal Justice Commissioner. In any event, it is likely that extensions to the PCCs remit will take place slowly, over a long period, and will very probably be punctuated by recoil and controversy – not least on the part of those analytical commentators who hold the commissioners in their unwavering gaze. What such change must *not* be, it seems to us, is stealthy and disguised. For the moment anyway, PCCs are intent on their work with the police, their contacts with the public, the implementation of their Policing Plans and the prospects of being elected for a second term. It seems enough to be going on with.

General summary

One of the general questions posed in considering the role of Police and Crime Commissioners is the nature of governance itself, and oversight of the police in particular. The reason for a mechanism which holds the police to account is that the police have proven spectacularly unable to govern themselves (not just in the UK of course, but wherever the police wield force on behalf of the state). There is a defined and time-honoured need for checks and balances to police actions. That the creation of the PCC was a political act does not, of itself, detract from the requirement to oversee the police. Commentators are more or less agreed that establishing the PCC may usher in some politicisation of the police, but we have argued in this book that much of policing is already distinctly politicised, and the advent of stringent budgetary controls and consequent reductions in local staff and resources merely enhances that politicisation. Although much central control has been deputed or ceded to the PCC, there is no devolved autonomy over funding. The Home Office and therefore the government retains some control and some say over police finances. This is not inherently a bad thing, though consciousness of our civil liberties means that we, as citizens, must engage in continuous monitoring to guard against abuses from the centre, just as much as there needs to be alert governance of the police. We must persist in challenging those who 'guard the guards' however honourable their intentions.

What is different now from the situation in 2012 is that an 'elected individual' has replaced the old police authority and that individual is full time, salaried and can monitor the police on a daily basis, whereas the authority was part time, lay and occasional. The government condemned police authorities as 'invisible' and claim that nearly three quarters of the populace now know their PCC. We remain sceptical of such claims and believe that the next rounds of PCC election, in 2016 and 2020, will conclusively show whether the 'visible PCC' claim is justified or not. We have examined what the police thought of their authorities and what PCCs think are the changes they themselves have brought to bear, and we have placed that in the context of the governance debate. The important point for us in England and Wales is that the police themselves accept oversight of what they do, and that demands of them to justify their actions are integral to the job. A final point about the politics of the PCC is research by Ipsos Mori that showed, in a qualitative sample, that people wanted a politically neutral 'figurehead', not an overt politician, as PCC. We consider that fears of political bias have thus far been exaggerated and there is plenty of evidence that PCCs cooperate across the political spectrum. It remains to be seen whether that will persist.

The election of PCCs in November 2012 was a flawed business and the shortfalls in organisation, publicity, legislation, candidature and timings may all have contributed to a low turnout in the polls. PCCs are fluent and robust at defending their meagre mandate but there seems to be a whiff of siege mentality about their repetition of the mantra that 'one vote is enough if it is a majority'. They would have liked more. What is also clear is that the police were slow to catch on to the fact that power had been transferred very tangibly from them to the PCCs after the election. An inability to cope with this new regime may have been the primary cause for the abrupt departure of serving chief constables, but some of the commissioners' claims that they have reduced crime in their first years of office need to be interpreted in the context of a general fall in crime levels over a much longer period.

There has been a tangible and positive movement in the opinions of chief police officers, and to a lesser extent in the ranks below them, about the Police and Crime Commissioner. This does not seem to be born entirely of expedience or manipulation, and approbation is still individual rather than generic (which is probably par for most innovations). Some police officers continue to regard the mass of PCCs with some disfavour (no doubt influenced by their own 'grapevines' and by some instances of critical or negative publicity surrounding PCCs). Often, by contrast, they see 'their own' PCC in a favourable light, and in some cases, prefer their PCC's scrutiny and challenge of them to their own superior officers' querulousness. Acceptance of independent oversight now comes with the territory and much of the manoeuvring and jostling that characterised the first two or three years of PCC incumbency may well have been merely adjusting to the new forms of democratic oversight and seeing what differences PCCs made to the old, often rather too comfortable, relationships that the police had enjoyed with their local watchdog. What the police are in no doubt about now is that their new watchdogs have teeth (and not rubber ones), and most have accepted that the power centres in policing correspondingly have been relocated. For their part, some PCCs believe that the apparent accommodation of their challenge to the police is window-dressing, and one or two suspect that that the police may be going back to their old ways. There will continue to be some adjustment while the PCC and the police get used to each other and try to find ways not just to understand each other, but also to work together for the good of those who pay them.

There may continue to be private spats and 'confessional' comments about each side to researchers, but in general terms and judging by the preponderance of responses we had from chief officers, the police can now live with their PCCs.

Some of the significant partnerships of Police and Crime Commissioners with the Home Office, the Home Secretary and HMIC are worth exploring if only to point up differences in perceptions of usefulness or relevance. When PCCs commented on HMIC, it was often with a sense of frustration that HMIC duplicated in many ways what the PCC did: ascertaining how efficient and effective its police force was. Where HMIC 'scored' is in thematic inspection, which a handful of PCCs have used to highlight internal shortcomings. Paradoxically, there seemed to be no real consensus among PCCs that HMIC performs a function of value in the national determination of standards. Relations with the Home Office was less antagonistic, although some PCCs speculated whether the Home Office had been the right ministerial department to run the elections of November 2012, and indeed whether the role of the PCC has significantly exceeded its original conception. Many seemed content with the avowal of 'hands off' direction from central government; others – usually those practised in the ways of parliament and Whitehall – were entirely comfortable in quietly influencing policing matters behind the scenes.

Opportunities for partnership at a local and parochial level exist, and some PCCs argue that these are the really important ones, since they impact more immediately on the day-to-day community work which is the PCCs' primary focus, rather than the vaguer and broader picture represented by national level cooperation. Without the continued support and guidance of partners of all kinds, PCCs would be much less informed and supported in their roles of being responsible for the 'totality of policing'. At the same time, there is an undercurrent of frustration that formal partnerships do not do more and some PCCs feel that much of the partnership aspect of the role is involved in catalysing others, rather than 'steering' a situation already under propulsion. PCCs focus most on their communities: not only is this where their legitimacy as elected representatives comes from, it is also where the PCC has focused the Police and Crime Plans for his or her force. The 'local levers of power' are clearly where the PCCs see most potential impact and where partnerships can have immediate outcomes. It is by no means clear that Community Safety Partnerships will survive the PCC in terms of coordinating local effort, but if the former can sustain a strong and supportive input to the PCC's Police and Crime Plan, there may yet be another mutation in local partnerships to counter crime and disorder.

The PCC spends considerable portions of his or her working time with both the media and the public. It should not surprise us that PCCs think continuously about their relationship with the media, particularly when their persistent and prominent 'profile' is important not only to the job of engaging the public and promulgating a 'crime commissioner' message, but also in terms of the PCC being recognised by the electorate. Many PCCs spend time and considerable care in passing information to the media and are sometimes rewarded with a positive 'spin' on police stories, while a few continue to have an antagonistic relationship where each side struggles for either dominance or control. It is evident even so that PCCs are both more practised in and more effective with the media than are the police. Getting out to the public, meeting, greeting, listening and engaging are all parts of the active relationships with people which PCCs consider among the most important things that they do. There is a corresponding sense of commitment to seeing and being seen in public spaces. There is less precision in the PCCs' use of social media and digital messaging: although they make considerable effort to tweet, blog and populate sites such as Facebook, it cannot be ascertained whether such determined messaging is taken notice of by that audience, or that the audience itself is either as young or as big as PCCs hope. Some PCCs are prolific users, others much less so; but it seems clear from the data that each PCC has a core of followers on social media. Whether that 'core' constitutes part of the PCC's target audience is less clear-cut. Many PCCs believe that their blogs and tweets are important opportunities to "put themselves about" and such use will continue and may even grow, whether or not the audience has the demographic profile hoped for.

When we focus on what PCCs actually do, there is evidence that commissioners have outgrown, or never fitted, the original remit for the job. The remit itself remains vague and unfocused (despite subsequent opportunities for the government to consult, re-define or re-model it), and this allows PCCs considerable latitude of interpretation in what they do. Many relish the scope they find in the role and have set about extending their remit locally with an eye to the other partnerships they have with public service bodies and with the criminal justice system. Concurrently with this, we have found that there are progressive alignments between PCCs and the police: they seem pretty much to agree on some things, such as community policing, while in other areas, notably serious and organised crime, there is some concern on the part of chief officers that PCCs are insufficiently engaged. Nonetheless, the early hostility, caution and mutual incomprehension have largely been replaced by cooperative working and general agreement on local targets. This may have been a forcible bracketing, or a kind of tacit mutual protection as the result of cuts in the policing budget and the sense in which the chief police officer team and the PCC faced together a common threat from the Home Office as austerity measures were imposed centrally.

We have concluded that the role of the Police and Crime Panel was ill-defined at the outset (and is of a piece with the vagueness of the PCCs' remit) and it is likely that at some point in the near future there will be additional legislation to restrict or modify the scope of a PCC's powers. There may also be an attempt to impose or gain concurrence for mechanisms to hold the PCC more closely to account between elections. It seems probable that such changes will wait until after the May 2016 elections, when the government can ascertain the composition of the new PCC body and its political complexion. For all that the public seems to prefer 'independents', that is, non-partisan postholders, as PCCs, the party machinery will continue to dominate selection and play some part in political control. Most PCCs, academic commentators and politicians seem to agree that something has to be done to inhibit the "mad or maverick PCC", but agreement has not yet emerged on what that 'something' might be. Any checks on PCCs must take cognisance of the democratic process which put them in place, and any major inhibitions of the role should be subject to (judicial?) review.

The effort that PCCs put into their working lives is unremitting, stressful and exacting, and, in common with others who work too hard and too long, such effort cannot be sustained indefinitely. The literature is adamant that there are measurable negative consequences to excessive working, and PCCs are no exception to this rule, even though they match, mirror and sometimes exceed, the 'long hours' and 'presenteeist' culture of chief police officers. PCCs seem to want the best of both worlds: they complain about the amount of time and presence the job requires, the amount of travelling they have to do, and the number of meetings they must attend, and yet (often simultaneously) extol the virtues of 'putting themselves about', raising their profiles with the public, engaging as often as they can with communities, groups and organisations, and being seen to be doing the job for which they were elected. It is notable that chief officers themselves, no strangers to the macho competitiveness of being seen to be at work, sometimes marvel at the effort PCCs put in.

There is a corollary: plenty of PCCs have told us privately that they are stressed, over-worked, unable to sleep well and often have no one to whom they can unload the burdens of their office. Some have discovered to their surprise that working as "the people's representative" can be very isolated. As time goes on, PCCs will become accustomed to the loneliness of command, but, in common with others in similar positions, may not relish it.

There is a preponderance of PCCs who anticipate an expansion of their role over the course of time. For some, it will embrace the "local democratic oversight" of the other emergency services, but for most it will somehow entail an extension of the PCCs' remit into the local criminal justice system. Becoming the local "Criminal Justice Commissioner" was a prospect that energised and enthused many of our interlocutors. Many also thought that reforms to the criminal justice system (specifically to the Prosecution Service, case progression, the courts' administration, the magistracy and probation), were long overdue and considered that, once they had "sorted the police", this was a logical next move for them to take. What were privately-expressed views may be aired in public fora in time, and a wide ranging debate may be held, not just with the various components of criminal justice, but with the public, the media and members of parliament about the advisability of extending in this way the PCCs' role and responsibilities. Only when the issues have been dealt with in the open and consensus reached could PCCs legitimately take on the mantle of Criminal Justice Commissioner. In any event, it is likely that extensions to the PCCs remit will take place slowly, over a long period, and will very probably be punctuated by recoil and controversy.

The caution expressed about our research in 2014, and the counselling that we should wait until a decade has passed before embarking on it, seemed then, and still seems now, a prescription for unconscionable delay. The public in England and Wales elected the first PCCs in November 2012; they seem entitled at the least to an assessment of what the PCCs have done and where they might be going. The PCCs can point to core relationships that they have built (with the media, with their chief police officer teams, with partners in local public service and with elements in the criminal justice system, as well as – more guardedly – with national organisations like HMIC and the Home Office), to continuous contact with members of the public (with whom they now have a higher profile) and to less tangible things like reductions in local crime and anti-social behaviour, as well as closer engagement between public and police and a greater emphasis within policing on neighbourhoods and community. These are, in

Rob Adlam's words, 'big concepts' (Adlam, 2003) and we should not underplay how important they are, for us as citizens.

So as authors of this study of PCCs, we are unabashed: we believe, now more than ever, that our research was timely, justifiable, comprehensive and wide ranging. We engaged enthusiastically with the new 'cuckoos' in the police nest (though sometimes to the PCCs' discomfiture), and mostly enjoyed meeting these exceptional people for whom each day was a challenge and each problem was something to be taken on with relish. Their energy is astonishing, their commitment undoubted and their task daunting. What is more, we hope that we have opened the way for future research into and a more comprehensive assessment of the role and value of a 'directly-elected person' who holds the police to account on our behalf.

A final word

Our interviews with PCCs and chief police officers were very occasionally fraught, sometimes testy, a couple were cold and formal – but most were enormous fun. Our interviewees from both sides were painfully honest and interesting people, who shared a deep commitment to public service. We enjoyed meeting them and challenging them, but most of all we liked discussing their work with them. They were (nearly) all patient and (mostly) discreet people whom it was a genuine pleasure to talk to.

To finish, we thought you might enjoy the parting comment to one of us from a PCC:

> 'I must say that I've enjoyed our talk, but you are a lot more difficult to satisfy than the journalists I normally deal with. Being an academic in your university must be fun. Are you sure that you weren't an interrogator in a previous life?'

That really is another story.

Bibliography

Adlam, R. (2003) Nice people, big questions, heritage concepts, in R. Adlam and P. Villiers (eds) *Police leadership in the 21st century: Philosophy, doctrine and developments*, Winchester: Waterside Press, pp. 34–52

APCC (2012) Transitional Board of the Association of Police and Crime Commissioners, Press release, 22 November, www.wired-gov.net/wg/wg-news-1.nsf/0/A4F9627306C52F0680257ABE0048E902?OpenDocument

APCC (2013) *The independent review of ACPO*, http://apccs.police.uk/wp-content/uploads/2013/08/Independent-review-of-ACPO.pdf

APCC (2014) Press release – statement on the resignation of Shaun Wright, http://apccs.police.uk/press_release/apcc-statement-resignation-shaun-wright/

APCC (2015a) Police Chiefs given a new national voice http://apccs.police.uk/press_release/police-chiefs-given-new-national-voice

APCC (2015b) Role of the PCC, http://apccs.police.uk/role-of-the-pcc/

Baldi, G. and La France, C. (2013) Lessons from the United States Sheriff on the Electoral Selection of Police Commissioners in England and Wales, *Policing*, 7(2): 148–57

Barnard, C., Deakin, S. and Hobbs, R. (2004) *Reflexive law, corporate social responsibility and the evolution of labour standards: The case of working time*. ESRC Centre for Business Research, University of Cambridge.

Bartlett, J., Miller, C., Crump. J. and Middleton, L. (2013) *Policing in an information age*, London: Demos, www.demos.co.uk/files/DEMOS_Policing_in_an_Information_Age_v1.pdf?1364295365

Barton, L. and Barton, H. (2011) Challenges, issues and change: what's the future for UK policing in the twenty-first century? *International Journal of Public Sector Management*, 24(2): 146–56

BBC News (2001) Quitting police chief remains defiant, 26 June, http://news.bbc.co.uk/1/hi/uk/1409153.stm

BBC News (2013) Commentary on Police and Crime Commissioners, 12 November, www.bbc.co.uk/news/uk-politics-19504639

BBC News (2014a) West Midlands PCC election won by David Jamieson amid 10.4% turnout, 22 August, www.bbc.co.uk/news/uk-england-birmingham-28898347

BBC News (2014b) PCCs: Public should have power of recall suggests May, www.bbc.co.uk/news/uk-29130893

Beauregard, T. A. and Henry, L. C. (2009) Making the link between work–life balance practices and organizational performance, *Human Resource Management Review*, 19(1): 9–22

Beckford, M. (2009) MPs' expenses: 'Duck house' MP Sir Peter Viggers keeps up spending on garden, *Daily Telegraph*, 10 December, www.telegraph.co.uk/news/newstopics/mps-expenses/6781641/MPs-expenses-Duck-house-MP-Sir-Peter-Viggers-keeps-up-spending-on-garden.html

Berman, G., Coleman, C. and Taylor, M. (2012) Police and Crime Commissioner Elections, 2012, House of Commons Library Research Paper RP12/73

Bichard, M. (2005) Inquiry Into the Events Surrounding the murders of Holly Wells and Jessica Chapman in Soham, Cambridgeshire, in 2001, Home Office, HO Report No. 420, http://discovery.nationalarchives.gov.uk/details/r/C16566

Bourne, K. (2014a) APCC response to HMIC 'State of Policing' report, www.apccs.police.uk/press_release/apcc-response-hmic-state-policing-report/

Bourne. K. (2014b) You Said, I Listened, This Happened, in *Think Blue Line*, http://thinkblueline.uk/

Bowling, B. (1999) The rise and fall of New York murder: zero tolerance or crack's decline? *British Journal of Criminology*, 39(4): 531–54

Bradford, B., Stanko, E. A. and Jackson, J. (2009) Using research to inform policy: The role of public attitude surveys in understanding public confidence and police contact, *Policing*, 3(2): 139–48

Brain, T. (2010) *A history of policing in England and Wales from 1974: A turbulent journey*. Oxford: Oxford University Press

Brain, T. (2014) Police and crime commissioners: the first twelve months, *Safer Communities*, 13(1): 40–50

Brain, T. (2015) Officer Class, *Policing Today*, www.policingtoday.co.uk/officer_class_23571.aspx

Bratton, W., and Knobler, P. (2009) *The turnaround: How America's top cop reversed the crime epidemic*. New York: Random House LLC

Brogden, M. (1977) A police authority—the denial of conflict, *The Sociological Review*, 25(2): 325–49

Brookes, S. (2012) Why I'm not standing as a police and crime commissioner, *Guardian*, 13 July, www.theguardian.com/public-leaders-network/blog/2012/jul/13/police-commissioner-elections-political

Brown, J. (ed) (2014) *The future of policing*. Abingdon, Oxon: Routledge

Brown, M. K. (1981) *Working the street: Police discretion and the dilemmas of reform*. New York: Russell Sage Foundation

Bulger, C. A., Matthews, R. A. and Hoffman, M. E. (2007) Work and personal life boundary management: boundary strength, work/personal life balance, and the segmentation-integration continuum, *Journal of Occupational Health Psychology*, 12(4): 365–75

Burrows, J., Hopkins, M., Hubbard, R., Robinson, A., Speed, M. and Tilley, N. (2005) Understanding the attrition process in volume crime investigations, Home Office Research Report 295, Development and Statistics Directorate

Cabral, S. and Lazzarini, S. (2014) The "guarding the guardians" problem: An analysis of the organizational performance of an internal affairs division, *Journal of Public Administration Research and Theory*, doi: 10.1093/jopart/muu001,:

Caless, B. (2011) *Policing at the top: The roles, values and attitudes of chief police officers*, Bristol: Policy Press

Caless, B. (2015) How can policing meet the leadership challenges ahead?, *Keynote Address to Police Foundation Roundtable*, 12 February

Caless, B. and Tong, S. (2013) 'An Appropriate Space', chief officers and police accountability, *Police Practice and Research: An International Journal*, 13(6): 4–16

Caless, B. and Tong, S. (2015) *Leading policing across Europe; an empirical study of police leadership*, Bristol: Policy Press

Caless, B. (ed) with Spruce, B., Underwood, R. and England S. (2014) *Blackstone's policing for the PCSO*, third edition, Oxford: Oxford University Press

Chambers, S. (2014) Who is policing the Police and Crime Commissioners?, *Safer Communities*, 13(1): 32–9

Clark, M. (2005) The importance of a new philosophy to the post modern policing environment, *Policing: An International Journal of Police Strategies & Management*, 28(4): 642–53

Collatz, A. and Gudat, K. (2011) '*Work-Life-Balance*': *Praxis der Personalpsychologie*, Göttingen: Hogrefe Verlag GmbH [NB: no English translation]

College of Policing (2014) Direct Entry (Superintendent) Programme, made available to the authors through the Police Foundation, London

College of Policing (2015) About Us, www.college.police.uk/About/Pages/default.aspx

Committee of Standards in Public Life (2013) Local Policing – accountability, leadership and ethics, Issues and Questions paper, www.gov.uk/government/uploads/system/uploads/attachment_data/file/360941/Police_Accountability_Structures_-_Issues_and_Questions_Paper.pdf

Committee on Standards in Public Life (2015) Home Office: "Improving Police Integrity", February, www.gov.uk/government/uploads/system/uploads/attachment_data/file/404278/Committee_on_Standards_in_Public_Life_final_response_to_Home_Office.pdf

Cordner, G. (2014) Community policing, in M. Reisig and R. Kane (eds) *The Oxford handbook of police and policing*, Oxford: Oxford University Press, pp. 148–71

Cousins, J. (2012) *Essential guide: An easy guide to police & crime commissioners*, London: Local Government Information Unit, www.lgiu.org.uk/essentialguide/an-easy-guide-to-police-and-crime-commissioners/

Cowley, R. (2011) *A history of the British Police from its earliest beginnings to the present day*, Stroud, Gloucestershire: The History Press

Crawford, A. (2006) Networked governance and the post-regulatory state? Steering, rowing and anchoring the provision of policing and security, *Theoretical criminology*, 10(4): 449–79

Crawford, A. (2008) Plural Policing in the UK: Policing beyond the police, in T. Newburn (ed) *Handbook of policing,* second edition, Cullompton, Devon: Willan Publishing

Crawford, A. (2012) Police and Crime Commissioners are not just for Christmas, Building Sustainable Societies, University of Leeds, available at www.bss.leeds.ac.uk/2012/12/20/police-and-crime-commissioners-are-not-just-for-christmas/

Crawford, A. (2014) The police, policing and the future of the extended policing family, in J. Brown (ed) *The future of policing,* Abingdon, Oxon: Routledge, pp. 173–92

Critchley, T. (1978) *A history of police in England and Wales 900–1966*, second edition, London: Constable

Crump, J. (2011) What are the police doing on Twitter? Social media, the police and the public, *Policy & Internet*, 3(4): 1–27

Cushion, S. (2012) The democratic value of news: Why public service media matter, *British Politics*, (2013) 8: 383–4

Daily Mail (2014) No action against PCC over 'leaks', 17 September, www.dailymail.co.uk/wires/pa/article-2759199/No-action-against-PCC-leaks.html

Daily Telegraph (2012) Theresa May defends Police Commissioner elections after low turnout, 17 November, www.telegraph.co.uk/news/uknews/law-and-order/9685097/Theresa-May-defends-Police-Commissioner-elections-after-low-turnout.html

Davies, M. (2014a) The path to Police and Crime Commissioners, *Safer Communities*, 13(1): 3–12

Davies, M. (2014b) Unravelling the role of Police and Crime Commissioners, *Papers from the British Criminology Conference*, 14: 17–30, http://britsoccrim.org/new/volume14/pbcc_2014_davies.pdf

Dimitrova, D. V., Shehata, A., Strömbäck, J. and Nord, L. W. (2011) The effects of digital media on political knowledge and participation in election campaigns: Evidence from panel data, *Communication Research*, available at http://crx.sagepub.com/content/early/2011/11/02/0093650211426004.abstract

Drake, L. and Simper, R. (2003) The measurement of English and Welsh police force efficiency: A comparison of distance function models, *European Journal of Operational Research*, 147(1): 165–86

Dreher, G. and Ash, R. (1990) A comparative study of mentoring among men and women in managerial, professional, and technical positions, *Journal of Applied Psychology*, 75(5): 539–46

Dromey, J. (2014) After two years of Police and Crime Commissioners, we must assess their democratic value, *New Statesman*, 24 November, www.newstatesman.com/politics/2014/11/after-two-years-police-and-crime-commissioners-we-must-assess-their-democratic

Duffy, M. (2014) Anonymous sources: A historical review of the norms surrounding their use, *American Journalism*, 31(2): 236–61

Eikhof, D., Warhurst, C. and Haunschild, A. (2007) Introduction: What work? What life? What balance? Critical reflections on the work–life balance debate, *Employee Relations*, 29(4): 325–33

Electoral Commission (2012) Police and Crime Commissioner elections in England and Wales, Report on the administration of the elections held on 15 November 2012, March 2013; available at www.electoralcommission.org.uk/__data/assets/pdf_file/0003/154353/PCC-Elections-Report.pdf; accessed 11 December 2015

Electoral Commission (2013) *Police and Crime Commissioner elections in England and Wales: Report on the administration of the elections held on 15 November 2012*, www.electoralcommission.org.uk/__data/assets/pdf_file/0003/154353/PCC-Elections-Report.pdf

Emsley, C. (1999) A typology of nineteenth-century police, *Crime, histoire & sociétés*, 3(1): 29–44

Emsley, C. (2009) *The Great British Bobby: A history of British policing from the 18th century to the present*. London: Quercus

Emsley, C. (2014) *The English police: A political and social history*, London: Routledge

Farrell, G. (2013) Five tests for a theory of the crime drop, *Crime Science*, 2(1): 1–8

Feilzer, M. and Hood, R. (2004). *Differences or discrimination?* Youth Justice Board for England and Wales, http://yjbpublications. justice.gov.uk/Resources/Downloads/Differences%20or%20 Discrimination%20-%20Summary.pdf

Fielding, N. (1984) Police socialization and police competence, *British Journal of Sociology*, 35(4): 568–90

Fijnaut, C. (ed) (2002) Special Issue on Police Accountability in Europe, *Policing and Society: An International Journal of Research and Policy*, 12(4)

Flanagan, R. (2008) *The review of policing: Final report*, London: Home Office

Flinders, M. (2004) Distributed public governance in Britain, *Public Administration*, 82(4): 883–909

Foos, F. and De Rooij, E. A. (2013) The heuristic function of party affiliation in voter mobilization campaigns: Informational short cut or source cue? 21 November, http://ssrn.com/abstract=2374542

Foster, J. and Jones, C. (2010) 'Nice to do' and essential: Improving neighbourhood policing in an English police force, *Policing*, 4(4): 395–402

Francis, P. (2014) Kent crime commissioner Ann Barnes accused after Kent Police press office takeover move, 14 April, *Kent Messenger Online*, www.kentonline.co.uk/kent/news/ann-barnes-kent-police-press-office-15820/

Freeman, S. and Webster, P. (2006) Cameron pledges to root out failing police officers, *The Times,* 16 January; and cited in B. Caless and S. Tong (2013) "An appropriate space": chief officers and police accountability, *Police Practice & Research*, 14(1), p. 5

Gains, F. and Lowndes, V. (2014) How does the gendered organisation of political life make a difference? Examining an institution in formation – Police and Crime Commissioners in England and Wales, APSA 2014 Annual Meeting Paper, http://ssrn.com/abstract=2451829

Gambles, R., Lewis, S. and Rapoport, R. (2006) *The myth of work-life balance: The challenge of our time for men, women and societies.* Chichester, UK: John Wiley and Sons

Garland, J. and Terry, C. (2012) *How not to run an election: The Police & Crime Commissioner Elections*, Electoral Reform Society, www. electoral-reform.org.uk/sites/default/files/How%20not%20to%20 run%20an%20election.pdf

Garnham, N. (2006) Riot acts, popular protest, and protestant mentalities in eighteenth-century Ireland, *The Historical Journal*, 49(02): 403–23

Gibbs, B. (2010) The welcome arrival of elected police and crime commissioners, *Spectator*, 1 December, http://blogs.new.spectator.co.uk/2010/12/the-welcome-arrival-of-elected-police-and-crime-commissioners/

Gilling, D. (2014) 'Reforming police governance in England and Wales: Managerialisation and the politics of organisational regime change', *Policing and Society*, 24(1): 81–101

Gilling, D., Hughes, G., Bowden, M., Edwards, A., Henry, A. and Topping, J. (2013) Powers, liabilities and expertise in community safety: Comparative lessons for 'urban security' from the United Kingdom and the Republic of Ireland, *European Journal of Criminology*, 10(3): 326–40

Gilmore, M. (2012) Electing police and crime commissioners: the challenges and opportunities of the new role, *The RUSI Journal*, 157(5): 6–11

Glynane, B. (2012), The ludicrous story of Northamptonshire's new Policy and Crime Commissioner, *Liberal Democrat Voice*, 21 December, www.libdemvoice.org/the-ludicrous-story-of-northamptonshires-new-police-and-crime-commissioner-32298.html

Goldsmith, A. J. and Lewis, C. (eds) (2000) *Civilian oversight of policing: Governance, democracy, and human rights*. Portland, Oregon: Hart Publishing

Gove, M. (2005) If crime's on the up, your chief constable must explain why or be sacked, *The Times*, 15 March

Gove, M. (2008) Police should remember that they are servants of the public, *Scotsman*, 13 December, www.scotsman.com/news/michael-gove-police-should-remember-they-are-servants-of-the-public-1-1302173

Gravelle, J. and Rogers, C. (2011) Commissioning accountability: change to governance and the police, *The Police Journal*, 84(4): 320–32

Greer, C. and McLaughlin, E. (2012) Trial by media: Riots, looting, gangs and mediatised police chief, in T. Newburn and J. Peay (eds) *Policing: Politics, culture and control*. Oxford: Hart

Hamilton, F. (2014) Over half of crime chiefs accused of misconduct, *The Times*, 1 December, www.thetimes.co.uk/tto/news/politics/article4283614.ece

Healey, G., Kirton, G. and Noon, M. (2011) Work-life balance, in *Equality, inequalities and diversity: Contemporary challenges and strategies*, New York: Palgrave Macmillan Inc.

HMIC (2010) Learning Lessons: An overview of the first ten joint inspections of police authorities by HMIC and the Audit Commission, March, www.justiceinspectorates.gov.uk/hmic/media/learning-lessons-20100314.pdf

HMIC (2012) Working with police and crime commissioners, www.justiceinspectorates.gov.uk/hmic/publications/working-with-police-and-crime-commissioners-122012/

HMIC (2013a) *Crime recording in Kent: a report commissioned by the PCC*, www.justiceinspectorates.gov.uk/hmic/publications/crime-recording-in-kent/

HMIC (2013b) *Policing in austerity: Rising to the challenge*, www.justiceinspectorates.gov.uk/hmic/publications/policing-in-austerity-rising-to-the-challenge/

HMIC (2013c) #021/2013 – HMCIC: "The operational integrity and independence of chief constables is sacrosanct.", Press release, 11 July, www.justiceinspectorates.gov.uk/hmic/news/releases/0212013-hmcic-john-harris-memorial-lecture/

HMIC (2014a) About Us, www.justiceinspectorates.gov.uk/hmic/about-us/

HMIC (2014b) HMIC inspection programme 2014/15, www.justiceinspectorates.gov.uk/hmic/publications/hmic-business-plan-201415/

HMIC (2015) Our work, www.justiceinspectorates.gov.uk/hmic/our-work/

Holtzhausen, S. (2001) Triangulation as a powerful tool to strengthen the qualitative research design, paper presented at the Lancaster University HE Close Up Conference, 16–18 July, www.leeds.ac.uk/educol/documents/00001759.htm

Home Affairs Select Committee (2013a) *Oral evidence – The work of HMCIC,* Tuesday 17 December 2013, www.publications.parliament.uk/pa/cm201314/cmselect/cmhaff/c895-i/c89501.htm

Home Affairs Select Committee (2013b) Police and Crime Commissioners: power to remove Chief Constables, www.publications.parliament.uk/pa/cm201314/cmselect/cmhaff/487/48703.htm

Home Affairs Select Committee (2013c) *Police and Crime Commissioners: Register of Interests*, 6 May, HC 69 2013–14, www.publications.parliament.uk/pa/cm201314/cmselect/cmhaff/487/487.pdf

Home Affairs Select Committee (2014) *Police and Crime Commissioners: progress to date*, www.parliament.uk/business/committees/committees-a-z/commons-select/home-affairs-committee/inquiries/parliament-2010/police-and-crime-commissioners1

Home Office (2004) Communications between the office of the former Home Secretary David Blunkett and/or the office of the chief constable of Humberside Police, David Westwood, and/or the office of the Humberside Police Authority (published 2006), www.gov.uk/government/publications/communications-between-the-office-of-the-former-home-secretary-david-blunkett-and-or-the-office-of-the-chief-constable-of-humberside-police-david-westwood-and-or-the-office-of-the-humberside-police-authority

Home Office (2010) *Policing in the 21st century: reconnecting police and the people.* London: Home Office, www.gov.uk/government/publications/policing-in-the-21st-century-reconnecting-police-and-the-people

Home Office (2012) Policing by consent, www.gov.uk/government/publications/policing-by-consent

Home Office (2013) *PCC Bulletin*, Issue 20, 13 August 2013, www.gov.uk/government/uploads/system/uploads/attachment_data/file/230245/PCC_bulletin_20.pdf

Home Office (2014a) Home Office rewards police innovation with £50 million, www.gov.uk/government/news/home-office-rewards-police-innovation-with-50-million

Home Office (2014b) Home secretary announces the reappointment of HMCIC Thomas Winsor, www.gov.uk/government/news/home-secretary-announces-the-reappointment-of-hmcic-thomas-winsor

Home Office (2015) Improving police integrity: reforming the police complaints and disciplinary systems, www.gov.uk/government/consultations/improving-police-integrity-reforming-the-police-complaints-and-disciplinary-systems

Hoogewoning, F., van Dijk, A. and Punch, M. (2015) *What Matters in Policing? Changed leadership and a comprehensive paradigm.* Bristol: Policy Press

Hough, J. M. and Roberts, J. V. (2004) *Youth crime and youth justice: Public opinion in England and Wales.* Bristol: Policy Press

Hough, M., Jackson, J. and Bradford, B. (2013) Legitimacy, trust and compliance: An Empirical test of procedural justice theory using the European Social Survey, in J. Tankebe, and A. Liebling (eds) *Legitimacy and criminal justice: An international exploration,* Oxford: Oxford University Press

Hough, M., Jackson, J., Bradford, B., Myhill, A. and Quinton, P. (2010) Procedural justice, trust, and institutional legitimacy, *Policing*, 4(3): 203–10, http://policing.oxfordjournals.org/content/4/3/203.abstract

Houston, D. (ed) (2005) *Work–life balance in the 21st century*. New York: Palgrave Macmillan

Hughes, G. and Rowe, M. (2007) Neighbourhood policing and community safety Researching the instabilities of the local governance of crime, disorder and security in contemporary UK, *Criminology and Criminal Justice*, 7(4): 317–46

Imbert, Lord (2011) House of Lords debate on the Police & Social Responsibility Bill 2011, *Hansard*, 27 April, Col. 169, www.publications.parliament.uk/pa/ld201011/ldhansrd/text/110427-0002.htm#11042793000134

Innes, M. (2004) Reinventing tradition? Reassurance, neighbourhood security and policing, *Criminal Justice*, 4(2), 151–171

Innes, M. (2014) *Signal crimes*, Oxford: Oxford University Press

Ipsos-Mori (2010) *Police accountability and governance structures: Public attitudes and perceptions*, survey commissioned by the Association of Police Authorities, www.ipsos-mori.com/researchpublications/publications/1387/Police-Accountability-and-Governance-Structures.aspx

Ipsos Mori (2013) Trust in Professions, www.ipsos-mori.com/researchpublications/researcharchive/15/Trust-in-Professions.aspx.

James, T. (2013) How could the PCC elections have been better run? *Huffington Post*, 15 January, www.huffingtonpost.co.uk/toby-james/pcc-elections-police_b_2137577.html

Jennings, T. (2013) I'm not fiddling expenses says police and crime commissioner, *Oxford Times*, 13 May, www.oxfordtimes.co.uk/news/10414718.I_m_not_fiddling_expenses_says_police_and_crime_commissioner

Johnson, W. (2012) MPs split as Tom Winsor is made HMIC chief, *Independent*, www.independent.co.uk/news/uk/home-news/mps-split-as-tom-winsor-is-made-hmic-chief-7908029.html

Johnston, L. and Shearing, C. (2003) *Governing security: Explorations in policing and justice*. Abingdon, Oxon: Routledge

Johnston, L. (2003) From 'pluralisation' to 'the police extended family': discourses on the governance of community policing in Britain, *International Journal of the Sociology of Law*, 31(3): 185–204

Johnston, P. (2001) Chief constable quits over fatal shooting, *Telegraph*, 27 June, www.telegraph.co.uk/news/uknews/1310465/Chief-constable-quits-over-fatal-shooting.html

Jones, T., Newburn, T. and Smith, D. J. (2012) Democracy and police and crime commissioners, in T. Newburn and J. Peay, *Policing: Politics, culture and control: Essays in honour of Robert Reiner*, Oxford: Hart Publishing, pp. 219–45

Joyce, P. (2011) Police reform: from police authorities to police and crime commissioners, *Safer communities*, 10(4): 5–13

Keeble, R. and Mair, J. (2012) *The Phone Hacking Scandal: Journalism on Trial*, Bury St Edmunds, Suffolk: Abramis Academic Publishing

Kelly, N. (2012) A boycott of the police commissioner elections could let in extremists; with low voter turnout expected on 15 November, we could see the quiet election of one of the many far-right candidates, *Guardian*, 22 October, www.theguardian.com/commentisfree/2012/oct/22/police-commissioner-election-extremists

Kinman, G., McDowall, A. and Cropley, M. (2012) Work-family conflict and job-related wellbeing in UK police officers – the role of recovery strategies, paper presented to the Work and Family Researchers' Network Conference, New York, 14–16 June, http://epubs.surrey.ac.uk/787222/

Kochel, T. R., Parks, R., and Mastrofski, S. D. (2013) Examining police effectiveness as a precursor to legitimacy and cooperation with police, *Justice Quarterly*, 30(5), 895–925

LaPorta, R., Lopez-de-Silane, F., Pop-Eleches, C. and Shleifer, A. (2003) Judicial checks and balances (Research Working Paper No. 9775), National Bureau of Economic Research, subsequently published in 2004 in the *Journal of Political Economy*, University of Chicago Press, 112(2): 445–70

Leishman, F., Loveday, B. and Savage, S. P. (eds) (2000) *Core issues in policing*. Harlow: Pearson Education

Lentz, S. and Chaires, R. (2007) The invention of Peel's principles: A study of policing 'textbook' history, *Journal of Criminal Justice*, 35(1): 69–79.

Lewis, C., and Fabos, B. (2005). Instant messaging, literacies, and social identities, *Reading research quarterly*, 40(4): 470–501

Lewis, S., Gambles, R. and Rapoport, R. (2007) The constraints of a work life balance approach: An international perspective, *International Journal of Human Resource Management*, 18(3): 360–73

Lister, S. (2013) The new politics of the police: police and crime commissioners and the 'operational independence' of the police, *Policing*, 7(3): 239–47

Lister, S. (2014) Scrutinising the role of the Police and Crime Panel in the new era of police governance in England and Wales, *Safer Communities*, 13(1): 22–31

Lister, S. and Rowe, M. (2013) Electing police and crime commissioners in England and Wales: prospecting for the democratisation of policing, *Policing and Society*, 25(4): 1–20, www.tandfonline.com/doi/full/10.1080/10439463.2013.868461

Loader, I. (1997) Policing and the social: Questions of symbolic power, *British Journal of Sociology*, (48)1: 1–18

Loader, I. (2006) Fall of the 'platonic guardians' liberalism, criminology and political responses to crime in England and Wales, *British Journal of Criminology*, 46(4): 561–86

Loader, I. (2014) Why do the police matter? Beyond the myth of crime-fighting, in J. Brown (ed) *The future of policing*. Abingdon, Oxon: Routledge, pp. 40–51

Longstaff, A. (2013) *The Home Affairs Committee's inquiry on Police and Crime Commissioners: The Police Foundation's response*, www.police-foundation.org.uk/uploads/holding/policy/pccs_resp.pdf

Loveday, B. (2013) Police and Crime Commissioners: the changing landscape of police governance in England and Wales: their potential impact on local accountability, police service delivery and community safety, *International Journal of Police Science & Management*, 15(1): 22–9

Loveday, B. and Reid, A. (2003) Going local: Who should run Britain's police? Policy Exchange, 2 January, www.policyexchange.org.uk/publications/category/item/going-local-who-should-run-britain-s-policeLuhmann, N. (2000) *The reality of the mass media*. Translated by Kathleen Cross. Stanford, CA: Stanford University Press

Macintyre, D. (2014) How the miners' strike of 1984–85 changed Britain for ever, *New Statesman*, 13 June, www.newstatesman.com/politics/2014/06/how-miners-strike-1984-85-changed-britain-ever

Mark, Sir R. (1977) *In the Office of Constable*, London: Collins

Martin, I. (2014) MPs' expenses: A scandal that will not die, *Telegraph*, 13 April, www.telegraph.co.uk/news/newstopics/mps-expenses/10761548/MPs-expenses-A-scandal-that-will-not-die.html

Mawby, R. and Wright, A. (2005). Police accountability in the United Kingdom, report for the Commonwealth Human Rights Initiative, www.humanrightsinitiative.org/programs/aj/police/res_mat/police_accountability_in_uk.pdf

Mawby, R. C. (1999) Visibility, transparency and police-media relations, *Policing and Society: An International Journal*, 9(3): 263–86

Mawby, R. C. (2003) Completing the "half-formed picture"? Media images of policing, in P. Mason (ed) *Criminal Visions*, Cullompton: Willan Publishing, pp. 214–37

Mawby, R. C. (2010) Police corporate communications, crime reporting and the shaping of policing news. *Policing & Society*, 20(1): 124–39

Mawby, R. C. and Wright, A. (2008) The police organisation, in T. Newburn (ed) *Handbook of policing*, second edition, London: Routledge, pp. 224–52

May, T. (2014a) Speech to APCC Summit, Harrogate, 18 November, www.gov.uk/government/speeches/home-secretary-at-apcc-partnership-summit

May, T (2014b) A model that works: A government's role in combating human trafficking, speech to the Vatican Conference, 9 April, www.gov.uk/government/speeches/a-model-that-works-a-governments-role-in-combating-human-trafficking

Mazerolle, L., Antrobus, E., Bennett, S. and Tyler, T. R. (2013) Shaping citizen perceptions of police legitimacy: A randomized field trial of procedural justice, *Criminology*, 51(1): 33–63

McCombs, M. (2013) *Setting the agenda: The mass media and public opinion*. John Wiley and Sons

McDermott, J. (2013a) PCCs 'slowing collaboration processes', *Police Oracle*, 22 July, www.policeoracle.com/news/Police+Staff/2013/Jul/19/PCCs-slowing-collaboration-processes_68352.html;

McDermott, J. (2013b) Government refuses calls for PCCs' Interests Register, *Police Oracle*, 8 August www.policeoracle.com/news/Police+Staff/2013/Aug/08/Government-refuses-calls-for-PCCs-interests-register_69069.html/news

McDowall, A and Lindsay, A. (2014) Work-Life Balance in the Police: The Development of a Self-Management Competency Framework, *Journal of Business Psychology*, 29: 397–411, http://link.springer.com/article/10.1007/s10869-013-9321-x

McKee, C. (2014) *Crime Outcomes in England and Wales 2013/14*, Home Office Statistical Bulletin, HOSB: 01/14, 17 July, www.gov.uk/government/uploads/system/uploads/attachment_data/file/331597/hosb0114.pdf.pdf

McLaughlin, E. (2005) Forcing the issue: new labour, new localism and the democratic renewal of police accountability, *The Howard Journal of Criminal Justice*, 44(5): 473–89

McLeod, J. M., Scheufele, D. A., and Moy, P. (1999) Community, communication, and participation: The role of mass media and interpersonal discussion in local political participation, *Political Communication*, 16(3): 315–36

Mcleod, S. A. (2014) The interview method, *Simply psychology*, www.simplypsychology.org/interviews.html

Meško, G. (2007) The Obstacles on the Path to Police Professionalism in Slovenia: a Review of Research, in G. Meško and B. Dobovšek (eds) *Policing in emerging democracies: Critical reflections*, Univerza v Mariboru, Fakulteta za varnostne vede, Slovenia, pp. 17–55

Metcalf, C., Harboe, G., Tullio, J., Massey, N., Romano, G., Huang, E. M. and Bentley, F. (2008) Examining presence and lightweight messaging in a social television experience. *ACM Transactions on Multimedia Computing, Communications, and Applications*, 4(4), Article 27

Metcalfe, B. and Dick, G. (2000) Is the force still with you? Measuring police commitment, *Journal of Managerial Psychology*, 15(8): 812–32

Millen, F. and Stephens, M. (2011) *Policing accountability and citizenship: The work of police authorities*, yesMinister (now archived), www.thecrimereport.org/system/storage/2/2d/a/827/police_reform_-_police_authorities_and_elected_commissioners.pdf;

Millie, A. and Bullock, K. (2013) Policing in a time of contraction and constraint: Re-imagining the role and function of contemporary policing, *Criminology and Criminal Justice*, 13(2): 133–42

Morris, S. (1981) British Chief Constables: the Americanisation of a role? *Political Studies*, 29(3): 352–64

Muir, R. and Loader, I. (2011) Progressive police and crime commissioners: An opportunity for the centre-left, IPPR, www.ippr.org/articles/56/7957/progressive-police-and-crime-commissioners-an-opportunity-for-the-centre-left

Mutz, D. C. (2001). Facilitating communication across lines of political difference: The role of mass media, *American Political Science Association*, 95(01): 97–114

Myhill, A. (2007) Police authorities' public accountability role: Learning from three community engagement demonstration projects, *Policing*, 1(2): 173–83

Myhill, A., Dalgleish, D., Docking, M. and Yarrow, S. (2003) *The role of police authorities in public engagement*, Home Office Report Online 37/03, London: Home Office Research Development and Statistics Directorate[1]

Myhill, A., Quinton, P., Bradford, B., Poole, A. and Sims, G. (2011) It depends what you mean by 'confident': Operationalizing measures of public confidence and the role of performance indicators, *Policing*, 5(2): 114–24

Newburn, T. (2003) Policing since 1945, in T. Newburn, *Handbook of policing,* second edition, Cullompton, Devon: Willan Publishing, pp. 84–105

---

[1]   No longer available in Home Office or National Archives under any search criterion, though the authors consulted HO37/03 as recently as 2012.

Newburn, T. (2012) Police and crime commissioners: the Americanization of policing or a very British reform? *International Journal of Law, Crime and Justice*, 40(1): 31–46

O'Neill, M. (2014) Playing nicely with others, in J. Brown (ed) *The future of policing*, Abingdon: Routledge, pp. 204–31

O'Neill, M. and McCarthy, D. J. (2014) (Re) negotiating police culture through partnership working: Trust, compromise and the 'new' pragmatism, *Criminology and Criminal Justice*, 14(2): 143–59

O'Connor, B., Balasubramanyan, R., Routledge, B. R. and Smith, N. A. (2010) From tweets to polls: Linking text sentiment to public opinion time series, *ICWSM*, 11: 122–9

Office for National Statistics (ONS) (2013) Statistical Bulletin: Crime in England and Wales, Year Ending March 2013, www.ons.gov.uk/ons/rel/crime-stats/crime-statistics/period-ending-march-2013/stb-crime--period-ending-march-2013.html

Osborne, S. P. (ed) (2010) *The new public governance? Emerging perspectives on the theory and practice of public governance.* Abingdon, Oxon: Routledge

Osse, A. and Dossett, G. (2011) *UN Handbook on police accountability, oversight and integrity*, New York: United Nations, www.unodc.org/documents/justice-and-prison-reform/crimeprevention/PoliceAccountability_Oversight_and_Integrity_10-57991_Ebook.pdf

Painter, C. (2013) The UK Coalition government: Constructing public service reform narratives, *Public Policy and Administration*, 28(1): 3–20

Peachey, P. and Lee, O. (2012) Who will police the police? *Independent*, 10 April, www.independent.co.uk/news/uk/crime/who-will-police-the-police-7628073.html

Peterson, R. A. (1992) Understanding audience segmentation: From elite and mass to omnivore and univore, *Poetics*, 21(4): 243–58

Pidd, H. (2013) Police panel questions commissioner's response to expenses leak, *Guardian*, 19 April, www.theguardian.com/uk/2013/apr/19/cumbria-police-inquiry-chauffeur-leak

Police Federation (2012) Letter to the Home Secretary, 22 March 2012, www.polfed.org/documents/HOME_SECRETARY_Winsor2.pdf

Poole, R. (2006) 'By the Law or the Sword': Peterloo Revisited, *History*, 91(302): 254–76

Prenzler, T., and Ronken, C. (2001) Models of police oversight: A critique, *Policing and Society: An International Journal*, 11(2): 151–80.

Punch, M. (2009) *Police corruption: deviance, accountability and reform in policing.* Abingdon, Oxon: Routledge

Quan-Haase, A. and Young, A. L. (2010) Uses and gratifications of social media: A comparison of Facebook and instant messaging, *Bulletin of Science, Technology & Society*, 30(5): 350–61

Raine, J. W. and Keasey, P. (2012) From police authorities to police and crime commissioners: Might policing become more publicly accountable? *International Journal of Emergency Services*, 1(2): 122–34

Rallings, C. and Thrasher, M. (2013) *The 2012 Police and Crime Commissioner elections in England and Wales: aspects of participation and administration*, Electoral Commission, www.electoralcommission. org.uk/__data/assets/pdf_file/0005/154472/PCC-2012-electoral-data-Report.pdf

Rawlings, P. (2002) *Policing: A short history*. Abingdon, Oxon: Routledge (first publishing by Willan Publishing)

Reichel, P. L. (2002) *Comparative criminal justice systems: A topical approach*. Upper Saddle River, NJ: Prentice Hall

Reid, K. (2005) The home secretary and improved accountability of the police? *Journal of Criminal Law*, 69(3): 232–55

Reid, L. (2014) Adding value through new public leadership, *International Journal of Leadership in Public Services*, 10(4): 233–42

Reiner, R. (1989) Dixon's decline: Why policing has become so controversial, *Contemporary British History*, 3(1): 2–6

Reiner, R. (1991) *Chief Constables*. Oxford: Oxford University Press

Reiner, R. (2003) Policing and the media, in T. Newburn (ed) *Handbook of policing,* second edition, Cullompton, Devon: Willan Publishing, pp. 259–81

Reiner, R. (2010) *The politics of the police*, fourth edition. Oxford: Oxford University Press

Reiner, R. (2013) Who governs? Democracy, plutocracy, science and prophecy in policing, *Criminology and Criminal Justice*. 13(2): 161–80

Reisig, M. and Kane, R. (eds) (2014) *The Oxford handbook of police and policing*. Oxford: Oxford University Press

Reisig, M., Tankebe, J. and Meško, G. (2014) Compliance with the law in Slovenia: The role of procedural justice and police legitimacy, *European Journal on Criminal Policy and Research*, 20(2): 259–27

Reynolds, E. (1998) *Before the bobbies: The night watch and police reform in metropolitan London, 1720–1830*, Stanford, CA: Stanford University Press and Macmillan

Rix, A., Joshua, F., Maguire, M. and Morton, S. (2009) *Improving public confidence in the police: a review of the evidence*. Home Office Research, Development and Statistics Directorate

Ross, J. (2011) *Policing issues: Challenges and controversies*, Burlington, MA: Jones and Bartlett Publishers

Rowe, M. (2012) *Introduction to policing*. London: Sage

Salmon. C. (2014) Public Sector Entrepreneurs: where next for PCCs? *Think Blue Line*, pp. 27–8, http://thinkblueline.uk/

Sampson, F. (2012) Hail to the Chief?—How far does the Introduction of Elected Police Commissioners Herald a US-Style Politicization of Policing for the UK? *Policing*, 6(1), 4–15

Sandford, M. (2015) *Directly-Elected Mayors*, House of Commons Briefing Paper No 05000, 12 May, http://researchbriefings. parliament.uk/ResearchBriefing/Summary/SN05000

Seneviratne, M. (2004) Policing the police in the United Kingdom, *Policing & Society*, 14(4): 329–47

Shao, G. (2009) Understanding the appeal of user-generated media: a uses and gratification perspective, *Internet Research*, 19(1): 7–25

Shearing, C. and Johnston, L. (2013) *Governing security: Explorations of policing and justice*. Abingdon, Oxon: Routledge

Sheptycki, J. (2002) Accountability across the policing field: towards a general cartography of accountability for post-modern policing, *Policing & Society*, 12(4): 323–38

Simmons, Kami. C. (2009) New governance and the new paradigm of police accountability: A democratic approach to police reform, *Cath. UL Rev.*, 59: 373.

Skolnick, J. H., and McCoy, C. (1984) Police accountability and the media, *Law & Social Inquiry*, 9(3): 521–57

Smith, G. (2009) Citizen oversight of independent police services: Bifurcated accountability, regulation creep, and lesson learning, *Regulation & Governance*, 3(4): 421–41

Smithson, J. and Stokoe, E. H. (2005) Discourses of work–life balance: negotiating 'genderblind' terms in organizations, *Gender, Work & Organization*, 12(2): 147–68

South Yorkshire Police and Crime Commissioner (2014) Shaun Wright resignation statement, 16 September, www.southyorkshire-pcc.gov.uk/News-and-Events/News-Archive/2014/Shaun-Wright-Resignation-Statement.aspx

Sparkes, M. (2013) Young users see Facebook as 'dead and buried', *Telegraph*, 27 December, www.telegraph.co.uk/technology/facebook/10539274/Young-users-see-Facebook-as-dead-and-buried.html

Statutory Instrument (SI) (2011a) *The Electoral Local Policing Bodies Order 2011*. London: HMSO

Statutory Instrument (SI) (2011b) *The Policing Protocol 2011*, No 2744. London: HMSO

Stenning, P. (2007) The idea of the political "independence" of the police: international interpretations and experiences, "Ipperwash" Inquiry research paper, www.attorneygeneral.jus.gov.on.ca/inquiries/ ipperwash/policy_part/meetings/pdf/

Stenning, P. (2009) Governance and accountability in a plural policing environment—The story so far, *Policing*, 3(1): 22–33

Stevens, J. (Lord) (2013) *Policing for a better Britain*, Report of the Independent Police Commission, http://independentpolicecommission.org.uk

Stevens, R. (1999) A loss of innocence?: judicial independence and the separation of powers, *Oxford Journal of Legal Studies*, 19(3): 365–402

Stone, C. (2007) Tracing police accountability in theory and practice from Philadelphia to Abuja and Sao Paulo, *Theoretical Criminology*, 11(2): 245–59

Stone, L. (1983) Interpersonal violence in English society 1300–1980, *Past and Present*, 101(1): 22–33

Stott, C., Adang, O., Livingstone, A. and Schreiber, M. (2007) Variability in the collective behaviour of England fans at Euro2004: 'Hooliganism', public order policing and social change, *European Journal of Social Psychology*, 37(1): 75–100

Strickland, P. (2013) *Police and Crime Commissioners*, Commons Briefing papers SN06104, House of Commons, http://researchbriefings. parliament.uk/ResearchBriefing/Summary/SN06104#fullreport

Swift, R. E. (2007) Policing Chartism, 1839–1848: The role of the 'Specials' reconsidered, *The English Historical Review*, 122(497): 669–99.

Tankebe, J. (2013) Viewing things differently: The dimensions of public perceptions of police legitimacy, *Criminology*, 51(1): 103–35

Tankebe, J. and Liebling, A. (eds) (2013) *Legitimacy and criminal justice: An international exploration*. Oxford: Oxford University Press

Tanner, W. (2012) If the government wants to introduce a real revolution in law and order, it should devolve powers and budgets for all criminal justice and emergency services to PCCs, *British Politics and Policy*, LSE (blog), 1 November, http://blogs.lse.ac.uk/ politicsandpolicy/crime-vru-tanner/

Taylor, D. (1997) *The new police in nineteenth-century England: Crime, conflict, and control*. Manchester University Press.

Terrill, R. J. (2014). *World criminal justice systems: A comparative survey*. Abingdon, Oxon: Routledge

Thwaites, C. (2013) Increasing the effectiveness and impact of Community Safety Partnerships in two London boroughs: Practitioners' Perspectives, unpublished doctoral dissertation, University of Portsmouth, http://eprints.port.ac.uk/12139/

Tipping, S., Chanfreau, J., Perry, J. and Tait, C. (2012) *The Fourth Work–Life Balance Employee Survey*, Department for Business Innovation & Skills, London: HM Stationery Office, www.gov.uk/government/uploads/system/uploads/attachment_data/file/32153/12-p151-fourth-work-life-balance-employee-survey.pdf

Travis, A. (2012a) Second police commissioner candidate withdraws over juvenile conviction, *Guardian*, 10 August, www.theguardian.com/uk/2012/aug/10/police-commissioner-candidate-withdraw-conviction

Travis, A. (2012b) Spoilt ballots point to protest in PCC elections, study suggests, *Guardian*, 19 November, www.theguardian.com/uk/2012/nov/19/spoilt-ballots-pcc-elections-analysis

Travis, A. (2014a) Tom Winsor defends police reform programme, *Guardian*, 12 June, www.theguardian.com/uk/2012/jun/12/tom-winsor-defends-police-reform

Travis, A. (2014b) Labour would replace 'fundamentally flawed' elected police commissioners, *Guardian*, 21 September, www.theguardian.com/uk-news/2014/sep/21/labour-would-replace-fundamentally-flawed-elected-commissioners

Walker, N. (1993) The Accountability of European Policing Institutions, *European Journal on Criminal Policy and Research*, 1(4): 34–52

Walker, S. (2003) New paradigm of police accountability: The US Justice Department pattern or practice suits in context, *Louis U. Pub. L. Rev.*, 22(3).

Walker, S. E. and Archbold, C. A. (2014) *The new world of police accountability*. Thousand Oaks, CA: Sage Publications

Walsh, D. and Conway, V. (2011) Police governance and accountability: overview of current issues, *Crime, Law and Social Change*, 55(2–3): 61–86

Walsh, W. F. (2001) COMPSTAT: an analysis of an emerging police managerial paradigm, *Policing: An International Journal of Police Strategies & Management*, 24(3): 347–62

Waters, I. and Brown, K. (2000) Police complaints and the complainants' experience, *British Journal of Criminology*, 40(4): 617–38

Watson, T. and Hickman, M. (2012) *Dial M for Murdoch*. London: Penguin

Weaver, M. (2014) Rotherham child abuse: Shaun Wright clings on as calls for him to resign grow, *Guardian*, 28 August, www.theguardian.com/uk-news/2014/aug/28/rotherham-child-abuse-shaun-wright-calls-grow-resign

Webster, J. (2015) Effective third-party policing partnerships or missed opportunities? *Policing and Society*, 25(1): 97–114

Welch, M., Fenwick, M. and Roberts, M. (1997) Primary definitions of crime and moral panic: A content analysis of experts' quotes in feature newspaper articles on crime, *Journal of Research in Crime and Delinquency*, 34(4): 474–94

White, A. (2014a) 5 reasons why it's difficult to privatise the police, *British Politics and Policy*, LSE (blog), 29 October, http://blogs.lse.ac.uk/politicsandpolicy/five-reasons-why-its-difficult-to-privatise-the-police/

White, A. (2014b) The politics of police 'privatization': A multiple streams approach, *Criminology and Criminal Justice*, 1748895814549643

White, M., Hill, S., McGovern, P., Mills, C. and Smeaton, D. (2003) High-performance' Management Practices, Working Hours and Work–Life Balance, *British Journal of Industrial Relations*, 41(2): 175–95

Whitehead, T. (2014) Embattled PCC Shaun Wright serves on Home Office child abuse task force, *Telegraph*, 9 September, www.telegraph.co.uk/news/uknews/crime/11085813/Embattled-PCC-Shaun-Wright-serves-on-Home-Office-child-abuse-task-force.html

Williams, M. (2013) Lincolnshire Police and Crime Commissioner Alan Hardwick: "I will not quit", *Lincolnshire Echo*, 31 March, www.lincolnshireecho.co.uk/POLL-Lincolnshire-Police-Crime-Commissioner-Alan/story-18555685-detail/story.html

Willis, J. J., Mastrofski, S. D. and Weisburd, D. (2007) Making sense of COMPSTAT: A theory-based analysis of organizational change in three police departments, *Law & Society Review*, 41(1): 147–88

Winsor, T. (2013) Operational independence and the new accountability of policing, John Harris Memorial Lecture, 11 July, www.justiceinspectorates.gov.uk/hmic/publications/john-harris-memorial-lecture-2013/

Zedner, L. (2006) Policing before and after the police: The historical antecedents of contemporary crime control, *British Journal of Criminology*, 46(1): 78–96

APPENDIX

Interview questionnaires

The basic questions for PCCs and separately for chief police officers were as follows:

Confidential questionnaire: police and crime commissioner

1. Why did you become a PCC? How do you interpret your role?
2. What qualities/experience do you think you bring to the role? What aren't you good at?
3. What are your relations with your chief officer team? Do you agree with Michael Gove that 'chief constables ... need the fear of God put into them'?[1] Is that what you do?
4. Do you prefer to conduct negotiations in public or behind closed doors? Why?
5. What are your relations with the media?
6. Describe your experience of relations with the public.
7. Describe your relations with ACPO. This question was subsequently replaced with 'Describe the process whereby you hold the chief constable to account'
8. Describe your relations with HMIC and the Home Office. What changes would you like to see in the role? What drawbacks are there to the role?
9a. Will you stand for a second term? (if not, why not?)
9b. Does the PCC role have a long-term future?

Please note:
Your replies will <u>not</u> be attributable to you by name and <u>all information relating to your identity will be removed</u>. Your replies to questions, if used in subsequent publications, are guaranteed anonymity and will be assigned a random 'interviewee number'.

---

[1] In a *Times* article (Gove, 2005).

Confidential questionnaire: chief police officers

1. What is your view of the role of Police and Crime Commissioner?
2. How does it compare with the Police Authorities which preceded PCCs?
3. How do you assess the job that the PCC does? What does s/he do well? What does s/he do badly?
4. How precisely does the PCC hold you to account?
5. Have there been any areas of disagreement or emphasis between you and a) the PCC and/or b) the PCC's team? If so, how were such problems resolved?
6. How well does the PCC handle the media?
7. How well does the PCC handle the public?
8. How well does the PCC understand policing?
9. What are your tactics/methods for dealing with the PCC on a daily/ weekly basis and on a longer-term basis?
10. How will you advise your successor to deal with the PCC?

Please note:
Your replies will <u>not</u> be attributable to you by name and <u>all information relating to your identity will be removed</u>. Your replies to questions, if used in subsequent publications, are guaranteed anonymity and will be assigned a random 'police interviewee number'.

Index